# Investor's Guide to the Stock Market

## FIFTH EDITION

**Gordon Cummings**

First published     October 1979
Reprinted     February 1981
Second Reprint     May 1981

Second Edition     November 1981
Reprinted     January 1983

Third Edition     September 1984
Reprinted with amendments     June 1985

Fourth Edition     November 1986

Fifth Edition     1988

**FSA 1986:** Companies mentioned in this book are in no way intended as investment recommendations. If in any doubt, a professional investment adviser should be consulted.

Published by
Financial Times Business Information
7th Floor, 50-64 Broadway
London SW1H 0DB
Registered Number 980896

Typeset by York House Typographic Ltd.
Printed by Camelot Press, Southampton

ISBN 1 85334 016 2

# Contents

# Preface

The long-running bull market had to come to a halt or go into reverse sometime. And it was Wall Street which in a one-day session, plunged it into a raging bear market by falling a record 22.5 per cent on Black Monday, 19 October 1987. Inexorably, the rest of the world's stock markets slumped in more or less degree, with London down on its Black Tuesday by 20 per cent from the previous Thursday, the day before Autumn gales brought power supply cuts to hit trading on the electronic screens. 'Shattering', 'cataclysmic', and 'traumatic' were only a few of the emotive reactions to the Crash of '87.

Gloom and despondency were not confined to the future of stock markets: there were immediate comparisons with the Wall Street Crash of 1929. Without pause to look at hard facts, the merchants of doom — and there were many of them round the globe — wailed that the US was in a recession that would repercuss on all the free world's economies. Bearish predictions of a further slide were not dissipated by the reluctance of the 'Big Money' investors (the institutions with their trillions of dollars, pounds and yen of funds) to start picking up stocks which soon proved to be bargains. It was the little man, the private investor, who had the guts to seize on a cheap opportunity, justified by subsequent recovery in all markets and with Tokyo eventually hitting all-time record highs.

It was not all on the minus side, however. Some positive features came from what might alternatively be termed the 'Purge of '87'. Those of major importance were:

- Speculative booms based on pie-in-the-sky hopes of a never-ending upsurge in prices have been halted, at least for the time being.
- A timely reversion from an almost total emphasis on takeover prospects and profit projections to the well-tried basics of asset values, management ability, trade prospects, financial soundness and other meaningful criteria which make for successful and profitable investment has taken place.
- Unhealthy practices such as insider trading have been curtailed, if only temporarily.
- The weaknesses and human frailties of professional investors and advisors have been brought to light, as has the fact that some of the young apprentices have a lot to learn before being let loose on the public.
- The dangers of concentrating billions of dollars and pounds worth of funds into the control of small groups of 'wholesale' investment managers motivated by computer programmes at the expense of the good old non-scientific guide of instinct have become obvious.

- Lessons have been learnt from the shock reaction to the massive selling concentrated into a few hours, or even minutes, which took place. Wall Street choked to the extent that late movers found the exit shut and couldn't deal, although this, as it turned out, was to their eventual advantage – chickening out at the bottom would have brought them no advantage.
- The advantages of being small enough to get out before the stampede starts, and of being in a position to take contrary action by buying into weakness in the subsequent 'bargain basements' have been proved.

All this is now history. Let us turn to the future, starting with potential trouble areas and other key factors to keep well in mind.

*America* will continue to be a bad and a good pace-setter. Though most of the indicators are set fair to good, uncertainties over the enormous budget deficits, adverse overseas trade shortages and the nervous dollar could hold back sustained recovery in stock markets. Equally vital is the impact on the economies and stock markets of other nations which, one way or another, depend on the US progress or regress for their own good. Until American politicians put their country's economic well-being before the retention of the title 'senator' or 'representative' before their names, doubts about them taking tough remedial action quickly will prevail. Perhaps commonsense will come to the fore after the Presidential election.

*Balancing national budgets* by borrowing and sales of assets is, at the least, an economic running sore, whatever the economists may claim. Rife in the UK for too many years, it is, as already mentioned, a much bigger and more urgent headache in the US due to reluctance to achieve a true balance either by increased taxation or spending cuts. A simple analogy of this vote-soothing policy would be to the corner shopkeeper whose takings start falling behind his expenditure. Bank and other borrowing is the first stop-gap. Then he has to sell his assets, with the best going first. Finally comes bankruptcy, with the receiver moving in. This is what the budget-deficit nations are in effect doing. They, however, leave it to posterity to pick up the loan tab, without thought that posterity may one day say 'we may have benefited from this mountain of debt but we've had enough of the interest bill — we'll cut the face value of the national debt in half or cancel the lot'. Exaggerated? Perhaps — but worth a thought by government stockholders.

*Privatisation* of electricity, water and other national assets will in the meantime continue to pour more capital into the Exchequer – and tempt the politicians to sweeten voters with over-generous tax cuts. All these capital receipts should be applied to debt reduction and, with it, interest costs. This would help to restore government stocks to their former glory, and would see a start on buying in War Loan and other undated stocks. It would also be helpful to collect more revenue from increased taxes for the purposes of restarting regular sinking funds for redemption of the entire debt over, say, 25 to 30 years. Write-downs by future generations could thus be averted.

*Banks,* with masochistic proneness to crises, will continue to be danger spots. Struggling already with third world and banana republic debt headaches, two more loss-makers are looming: a plastic card and home loans crisis; and another property loan crisis which could far exceed the collapse of 1974/75. More dangers are global inter-relationships through banks' holdings of each others' loan paper and joint ventures. Already, medium and small US banks, mostly in Texas, California and other local trouble areas, have shut their doors or are being helped to cope with unwieldy soured loans. It goes without saying that if bank crashes really get out of hand, no country will be unaffected. This would put bank stocks on the same kind of risky foundations as oil and mining exploration shares.

*New issue activity,* as was to be expected, slowed down sharply after Black Monday but is currently on the upturn, with a minor flood of small placings in the USM and Third markets. To the good of both investors and the market, stagging has been dampened down. Heavy over-subscriptions have been relatively rare, and there have been a few flops and occasional hold-overs of issues until marketing conditions improve. It's the way of life. But it has taken a Black Monday crash to get home the message that stagging can be a time-consuming operation which can tie up lots of money only in the end to (*a*) get no allotment; (*b*) get so few shares that brokerage on a sale can wipe out a gain; or (*c*) if the offer flops, get landed with many more shares than can be paid for. Think well before risking damaging your antlers as a stag.

*Takeovers* are now for the most apart unsportsmanlike affairs: they have become tumultuous slanging matches with bankers, brokers, issuing houses, underwriters, lawyers, accountants and other professionals, whether on the winning side or not, skimming off plentiful cream. The relative newcomers to the action are the 'arbs', or arbitrageurs. They are big-time punters either out for a quick turn or hoping to 'greenmail' defenders into buying out their shares for (in the US) a fancy price or to get the bidders to up their price. It can be profitable to bet on the 'Arb Stakes'. But don't forget that if it becomes a no-contest scrap, the only winners may be those shareholders who sold in the market and the City backers whose fees and commissions can run into the tens of millions of pounds or dollars.

As the Rowntree/Nestle/Suchard tussle underlined, there are no geographic boundary lines to takeovers. The whole free world's an oyster. British companies have been beavering away at the busiest area, America. Some sky-high prices have been paid for US companies, some of them bigger than the UK bidder. A potential trouble spot in some US acquisitions is the saddling of the bidder with heavy and costly debt by way of high coupon 'junk' bonds which it could be a struggle to service out of cash flow.

*The Japanese* are rumoured every now and again to be about to make large scale moves into the UK market, perhaps as the only reason that can be dug up to explain a sharp rise in particular shares. Credence is added now that some of the mightiest Japanese banks and investment houses have become financial powers in the City. True, there is Japanese interest in portfolio investment, but so far nothing hinting at larger scale takeover gambits. The Japanese, what-ever goes on in their own markets, are canny, cautious businessmen not in any hurry to change their present ways of acquiring British interests. They choose to start from scratch on greenfield sites, to negotiate joint partnership operations or to mutually arrange buyouts of established businesses.

*Company accounts* do not always, do what they should, namely, show unequivocally the progress of the business and its financial state. Extraordinary and exceptional items such as profits or losses on asset sales which cloud the normal trading results now come into profit and loss accounts instead of being dealt with through reserves as they were in rational, conservative accounting days. Another cover-up is the netting out in balance sheets of group capitalisation. Long and short term borrowings are netted out 'above the line' with their total having to be winkled out from notes. All borrowings less cash assets should be below the line, to show just how they relate to the permanent capital. Adherence to accounting conventions and company law may force auditors to qualify accounts if directors choose to stick to unrealistic ways of presenting figures. A qualification due to using clarity and common-sense should be a plus, not a minus.

Company reports can, incidentally, reflect the ability and canniness of the management. Elaborate, glossy, and heavily illustrated effusions can cover up mistakes and declining business. Economically produced reports giving essential facts and figures in clear, succinct form come, on the other hand, from well-managed, prosperous and progressive companies. Judge the package by its content, not its wrapper. Moves to allow shortened versions which stick to down-to-earth basic facts (with the right to ask for the full version) have been stimulated by the large number of small privatisation shareholders now on company registers. Some of the 'glossies' of big companies cost millions of pounds to produce and mail!

*Investment analysts* are not the all-powerful figures they might appear to investors. Their passion for profit projections can, and frequently does, upset share prices without basic justification. Good or even excellent actual profits can be characterised as 'poor', or 'failing to meet expectations' simply because they are below the gurus' forecasts. This practice has become a very debatable area of investor service and is attracting increasing criticism. Projections can be based on outside observations and trade sources generally. But only a company management can attempt to make feasible profit and other key forecasts, all subject to caveats. If these are passed on to analysts without simultaneous notification to shareholders and the investment world at large, both management and the analysts could be guilty of witholding price-sensitive information and, perhaps, of insider trading. Not surprisingly companies are dropping analyst get-togethers, lunches and outings, their action being prompted by the tendency of callow novitiates to make wrong interpretations and assumptions. Analysts' reports may therefore have to be taken with a pinch of salt. After all, the wise investor has always paid plenty of attention to fundamentals such as net asset values and borrowing/liquidity ratios in appreciation of the fact that all kinds of unforeseen happenings can make a monkey out of the profit projections of even the most astute company accountants and chief executives.

*The Financial Services Act,* now in full force, is akin to the curate's egg. It is good in its massive attempt to eliminate bucket shop activities, and to increase the responsibilities of all financial advisors. It is bad in its imposition of niggling, time-consuming and costly 'small print' rules and restrictions on brokers' services, some of which rub off on investors – at added cost. It is realised, however, that all fraudulent activities will never be stamped out. There are loopholes in all legislation, and the wide boys are already winkling them out. Cold telephoning from UK bases is now barred – but not from offshore 'boiler rooms' in Spain and elsewhere. There is only one way to deal with such over-enthusiastic pushing of dubious mining, oil and hi-tech companies – put down the receiver. One risk which is difficult to guard against, however, is what might be termed 'honest ineptitude'. The entry of banks, building societies, estate agents, share shops and so on into the share dealing business has multiplied the demand for experienced and reliable experts to the extent that a limited pool of expertise is being spread thinner and thinner over a widening field. The result is that staff who are not properly trained may be giving off-the-cuff advice which is inadequately researched, or may be simply passing on standard computerised advice on a limited number of shares transmitted electronically from head office. Use member firms of the Stock Exchange for preference: they can be found in most cities and large towns as well as in London.

Now for the nitty-gritty of investment strategy post-Black Monday. Influences common in some degree to all stock markets will be inflation, interest rates, exchange rates, budget deficits/surpluses, overseas trade balances, and internal expansion/recession. Until the US sorts out its budget and trade headaches it will continue to be the major influence on world economic affairs.

Specifically in the UK market, factors which will at the time of writing move prices overall or in particular sectors are: inflation; overheating of the economy; overseas trade deficits; sterling rates as against the dollar and Deutschemark; unemployment trends; interest rates; and Wall Street gyrations. Ups and downs are inevitable, but another Black Monday is unlikely (although you can never be certain in these hectic days). However, looking on the positive side, the trend might be upwards, if only slightly.

The possibility of takeover is now an habitual consideration in the selection of most equity shares. But, as I have already advised, attention should above all be given to the basics of a good investment — net asset values; debt/equity ratios; liquidity; trading outlook; management; and, until the dollar rate settles down, the amount of overseas trade, particularly with America. Other datum lines should be average or minimum yields in the three to five per cent area at least twice covered; and price-earnings ratios of eight to ten or eleven. Generally, the safest selections will continue to be the top alpha companies: by sector this means food manufacturers and retailers, stores, leisure, and the big and proven conglomerates (but not the flashy newcomers). Banks, and media and other 'people' sectors are for danger money only. Otherwise, there are three sectors which in their varying way are worth consideration for part or all of a portfolio.

First, look at natural resources shares. Base metal miners are now returning to prosperity after a period of overproduction and under-consumption during which many operations were closed down for good or were mothballed, leaving the survivors in streamlined condition, more efficient and ready to benefit from the recovery in demand and prices. Even though new mines are coming on stream and mothballed ones are restarting operations, the only serious dampener to a bright future is a world recession, which, on the present reckoning, looks unlikely. Gold, on the other hand, has lost some of its glitter and will need a sharp and sustained rise in price to produce fireworks – but watch for a boomlet as an inflationary hedge. And, though a dirty word just now, coal could have a big comeback from current over-production as the anti-nuclear lobbies win a reversion to coal-produced electric power.

Second, to give a much wider and varied spread, are investment trusts. Backers of the UK will find several trusts having all or most of their holdings in the home-based companies while most of the others have various percentages up to one hundred in one or more countries such as Japan, or geographic mixes like North America or Europe. The titbit is the discount of up to 20 per cent or over on the net asset value at which shares can be bought. The possible handicap is that trusts may be only short-term investments as a result of takeovers, which are on the increase.

Third are the low risk with higher yield attractions of convertible loan stocks and preference shares. There is a wide and increasing selection; but because of poor marketability it can be good policy to stick to the bigger issues. It is also worth looking at the good range of euro-convertibles which offer some interesting options.

Big Bang has simplified direct investment in overseas stocks. Japan has long been a popular area, but one which should be left to the experts who claim, or hope, to understand a market which cannot be judged by normal rules. Canada and Australia have promise as long-term propositions. Both countries are rich in almost every natural resource, their economic prospects are amongst the best of the advanced countries, they are reasonably stable politically, and exchange rates have been moving in their favour. True, Australian markets are prone to sharp, sometimes violent, movement. In the end, however, the leaders bound back and go on to new highs.

Whatever the individual investment strategy, one age-old fact is that the City loves band wagons. Hi-tech, oil exploration, media services — with anything new and successful, the followers and imitators jump in, and quality usually falls away as the race quickens. Whether for a new idea or a run of the mill boomlet, the moral is clear: get on the wagon before the band strikes up and get off before it reaches crescendo — leave something, if only hope, for the buyer.

Understanding the working of stock markets and being a successful investor are the prime objectives of this book. Reactions to Black Monday have shown that because the very size of the funds they have under management hinders their manoeuvreability, the institutions can underperform the small investor, at least in the short term. This restriction is an argument in favour of the individual, DIY management of portfolios; in any market it is usually much easier to deal in a few thousand pounds worth of shares then in multi-million pound lumps. Anyhow, that has been my policy over the years: contrary action has produced net gains of more than twice those of some leading investment trusts and the indices.

Personal research and reading or listening to other people's views apart, my major tactics have been flexibility and patience. The first involves moving from sector to sector but with a strong bias for (*a*) natural resources shares and (*b*) sound companies without market friends but with prospects of weathering a bad patch. This calls for patience in waiting for the big kill and not being afraid to average down on a sliding market in shares with strong recovery chances.

Of course, there have been losses, even disasters, but these have been limited to a small percentage of the gains, and in some cases these losses were the result of untested tips. Many, many chances have been missed — but no one can buy the whole of the market! It is sometimes very hard to cut a loss; and it is all too easy to step in too soon to average shares on the slide before a recovery sets in. But it has always been a strength rather than a weakness to take profits the Rothschild way — before the buying rush looks like peaking.

Finally, here are four operational guide lines to bear in mind.

*Greed* What goes up can come down, very swiftly at times. The only sure top price is a cash takeover. Don't hang on for the last penny — leave something for the buyer to go for.

*Conceit* Not every venture is a winner. The more the winners, the greater the need for caution and restraint in going for new own-selection hopefuls. Examine why losers go wrong. Be humble in the sight of Midas.

*Secure profits* on the way up. There could be another Black Monday. When prices begin to wobble, it's easier to sleep at nights with only half a holding left in at next to nothing. Selling portions at rising prices averages down the net cost of the balance.

*Euphoria* is a great danger. Optimism over hand-picked or widely tipped shares is easy to build up. When the sky looks to be the limit, check on how much solid floor-boarding supports the castle in the air – and take at least some of the profits if there are signs of rot. Ponder the Greater Fool Theory — if you have bought shares too high, hope that a greater fool will take you out at an even higher price.

Note that none of the companies cited in later pages are intended as investment recommendations but are meant simply as illustrations.

Many City friends and acquaintances have helped me to a knowledge of stock markets and have saved me from gaffes and mistakes as a commentator and investor. For this edition I have been helped with facts and figures by Alexanders Laing & Cruikshank, whose Eastbourne staff cheerfully and efficiently do my often demanding business; Barclays de Zoete Wedd for their statistics; and Grant Thornton for their co-operation on Capital Gains Tax. Any errors of fact are my own responsibility, as are my views and comments.

In these rapidly changing times, it is inescapable that facts, figures and examples have to be those ruling at the time of going to press. It is hoped, however, that later changes will not affect the main objective of providing a practical and profitable DIY guide to the stock market and its workings.

GORDON CUMMINGS, FCA
October 1988

# 1

# No mystique about the Stock Exchange

Contrary to a widely-held view there is no mystique about stock exchange investment. The uninitiated may be daunted by professional terms and jargon, trading methods and mechanics, and the privacy of membership; but only until these things are understood. Take a few basic facts:

**Fact one:** The Stock Exchange is a market place like any other centralised market — vegetables, cattle, fish, base metals, produce or what have you — where buyers and sellers can do business in the most convenient and speediest ways at the fairest open prices. Prior to the October 1986 Big Bang membership was strictly divided into two classes — brokers dealing on behalf of the public and jobbers (now called market makers) dealing only with brokers or amongst themselves. Now firms can be both brokers *and* market makers, or one or both, with some carrying on solely as brokers.

**Fact two:** Stockbroking is not confined to London and a few big cities. Aberdeen, Dundee, Stirling, Dumfries ... Newcastle-upon-Tyne, Lancaster, Bradford, Norwich, Derby, Westcliff-on-Sea, Oxford, Cheltenham, Eastbourne, Bournemouth, Torquay, Truro ... Bangor, Cardiff, Swansea ... Isle of Man ... Belfast, Newry, and in Eire, Dublin, Cork ... Guernsey, Jersey ... every community of any size has one or more stockbrokers who are electronically linked by the sophisticated communications systems to the central market in London. And if there is no broker handy, banks, solicitors and accountants can provide agency facilities for dealing and obtaining expert advice.

**Fact three:** Stock exchange investment is not a sole and divine right of the rich and of the pension funds, life assurance offices and other so-called 'institutions' which are responsible for managing vast and increasing amounts of our mutual savings. A few hundreds or many hundreds of thousands of pounds, the market is open to anyone with money to invest or securities to sell. Flotation of nationalised industries such as British Telecom, British Gas, British Airways, Cable and Wireless and British Aerospace plus the conversion of the Trustee Savings Bank into a publicly owned company have brought — or tempted — millions of new investors into the share market, to raise the total of the share-owning democrats to about nine million; or one in five of the adult population.

**Fact four:** Prices, like those of so many other things, fluctuate with supply and demand which, as discussed later, are motivated by a variety of factors such as wars, political moves, strikes, booms and slumps, economic changes and so on.

This means that there is always some risk, the degree of which can, however, be minimised by knowledge, study, judgment, anticipation and getting reliable advice.

**Fact five:** Choice is wide and varied. There is something for all types of investment needs and situations. All told, over 7,000 widely different securities with a market value in the region of £1,600 billion are traded in three market sectors: Listed, Unlisted and Third. Together they make up broad groups which spread out like a huge oak tree into branches and sub-branches. Included are the stocks and shares of more than 3,000 British and overseas companies which range from household names with world-wide ramifications to relatively small, highly specialised and local businesses.

**Fact six:** A tremendous expansion in electronic dealing and communications plus the invasion of US, European and other overseas merchant bank/ investment houses coming into play with Big Bang has made London a market where it is also easy to deal in tens of thousands of varied stocks and shares whose home base is in New York, Toronto, Tokyo, Hong Kong, Sydney, Paris, Amsterdam, Brussels, Frankfurt and other bourses. London really lives up to its new title: The International Stock Exchange of the United Kingdom and the Republic of Ireland.

**Fact seven:** While the terms stocks, shares, debentures, preference shares, equities, and so on, may sound like technical mumbo-jumbo, their meaning — and investment functions — can easily be mastered and profited from after a little study.

# 2

# Stocks and shares

Two main types of securities are dealt in on the Stock Exchange — stocks and shares. Their nature and differences are a basic part of investment mechanics.

## STOCKS

For many generations, stock was the universal unit for all types of investment. It had a par, or nominal, value of £100 and was traded in such a unit. Today, with relatively few exceptions, it is the unit only for government and similar securities, foreign stocks, water undertakings; and, in the company sector, debenture and loan stocks, and a few investment trust and company preference issues.

The important point is that the price is quoted per £100 nominal of stock, which means that if the quotation is, say, £80 this is the cost of £100's worth. But, depending on the issue terms, purchases and sales may be (a) in units of a round £100 of stock; (b) in units of £1; or (c) as with government securities, in fractions as small as one pence, such as £746.31 of stock.

Some few years ago, there was a move amongst companies to rename their shares 'stock', the idea being to do away with the long-standing practice of numbering all shares by making them anonymous 'units' of stock. Dealings were, however, still in units of the original par value such as £1,5s. (25p) or 2s. (10p). There has since been a reversion to the nomenclature 'shares', though some companies which made the changes still use the 'stock' description. For all practical purposes there is no difference between the two terms.

## SHARES

Shares have a fixed par, or nominal, value which is the unit in which they are traded. Par may be any amount from as little as 1p up to £5 or £10. Though the figure for many shares is £1, a large proportion are 25p units, with a number denominated 5p, 10p or 50p. Dealings are therefore always in quantities of shares, never in fractions. Some companies, as pointed out above, call the units 'stock'. Note that American companies use the term stock for their share capital, with some spelling it out as 'shares of stock'.

The Big Bang internationalisation of the UK market has, incidentally, started a trend to a general switch to the North American terms of Bonds for our fixed interest stocks and to Stocks for our shares.

Securities dealt in on the Stock Exchange fall into three broad groups:

\*   Fixed interest stocks of a type where the servicing is not dependent on the earning of profits but is met out of national taxation or local rates. Come financial rain or shine, boom or slump, tax and rate-payers fork out the money for interest and capital repayment. This is the so-called *gilt-edged* market.

\*   Stocks and bonds issued by overseas governments, municipalities and companies at fixed rates of interest. This is the *foreign bond* market.

\*   Fixed interest stocks and fixed and variable dividend shares where the interest or dividends depend on the earning of profits. This is the wide and diversified *companies* sector.

## GILT-EDGED

Called gilt-edged because for many decades before inflation began to erode their real value, they were looked on as absolutely safe for capital value as well as interest, such securities are loans raised by the UK government. Akin are the stocks of local authorities and counties, some public boards operating port, harbour and water services and specialised financial facilities, and government-guaranteed loans. There are also a few Commonwealth government and provincial issues. Some 400 or so different stocks make up this important, *public sector* market.

## FOREIGN BONDS

In pre-First World War days this was one of the most important markets, with active dealings in the stocks and bonds representing sterling loans to Russia and other European countries, South and Central American states, China, Japan and other foreign countries and cities. Defaults in the years subsequent to 1918 brought many reductions in interest rates and nominal values; and some bonds like the Russian ones became no more than low-priced gambling counters on hopes of eventual recognition of the debts. In more recent times, this sector of the market has been growing through the addition of overseas government and city loans, and company loans, raised on international markets in US dollars, deutschmarks, francs and other foreign currencies — called *Eurobonds* — and in sterling-denominated '*Bulldog*' stocks. This market, as shown in chapter 8, is a specialised one which is most suitable for the sophisticated investor.

Unlike the great majority of Stock Exchange securities, most foreign stocks are what are termed *bonds*. This means that unlike stocks and shares (ownership of which is recorded in registers) bonds pass from seller to buyer by hand and there is no official record of ownership. Attached to bonds are coupons which have to be cut off and presented to a paying agent to collect interest; when all coupons are used up, a 'talon' is exchanged for a new supply.

## EUROBONDS

In addition to overseas public sector stocks, a steadily growing number of UK, overseas and Irish companies have been raising finance by the issue of Eurobonds which get an official listing on the Stock Exchange. Currently, nearly 1,100 issues with a market value near to £120 billion are traded. Again, this is a specialist market of interest mostly to institutional investors.

## COMPANIES

Far and away the biggest by number, market value, variety and complexity is the company sector. Counting the main *officially listed* and expanding Unlisted Securities and Third markets, it takes in over 5,600 different stocks and shares of more than 3,000 companies, of which over 500 are overseas concerns incorporated in the United States, Japan, Canada, Australia, South Africa, Malaysia, Zambia, France, Germany, Holland and other territories. Included is almost every type of enterprise ranging from manufacturing, commercial and trading concerns; insurance, banking and financial services; shipping and public utilities to mining ventures and oil, tea and rubber producers operating in most parts of the free world.

Profit is the motivating force. With no taxpayers to provide the funds, payment of interest and dividends, together with the meeting of redemption commitments, depends on successful trading and operation. Again, there are groups and sub-groups of securities which can be broadly divided into those offering:
* A fixed rate of interest and dividend.
* A variable dividend, or equity.

There are clearly defined priorities for the payment of interest and dividends and the redemption of capital. The order of priorities is: fixed interest stocks (debenture and loan); share capital with preferential rights; and finally the equity, or risk, capital.

Where companies have more than one class of capital the risk rating of each type follows this order. Debentures and loan stocks are the safest, equity shares the riskiest, with preferential capital in between.

Fixed interest capital falls into three categories, the nature and rights of which are:

**Debenture stocks** are first in the priority ranking. Like a mortgage, they are secured on specific assets which are usually part or all of a company's factories, offices, other property, plant and machinery plus maybe liquid assets such as investments, stocks and debtors. Interest at a fixed rate is due on specific dates, normally half-yearly. With the rare exception of 'income' debentures, the interest is due whether profits earned are or are not enough to cover payment. Should the company fail to pay interest, because of losses or lack of cash, or it defaults in other ways such as inability to meet repayment of capital or sinking fund requirements when due, debenture-holders have powers to put in a receiver to run the business, to foreclose or to take other action to protect their interests. It is usual for responsible financial bodies such as banks, insurance companies or investment trusts, or individuals, to be trustees for the debenture stock; they can take the necessary steps to see that the debenture terms are followed, and even to take prior action if they consider that the stock is imperilled. Debentures may be:

*Irredeemable,* which means that only the company has the power of repayment so long as the issue terms are met. Such repayment does not normally happen until the company goes into liquidation; there is a general capital reorganisation; it merges with another company; or there is a takeover. Issue terms may specify repayment at par or at a premium: redemption terms might be, say, £105 for each £100 of stock. A current tendency amongst companies with spare cash is to offer to buy in stock at a figure above market prices, such as £75 per £100 as against a market value of only, say, £50.

**Redeemable** at par or at a premium on a specified date or dates, or over a stated period of years. For example, a single repayment date might be 30 September 1990, while multiple dates might be 30 September in any of the years 1990 to 1995 for part or all of the stock each year. Repayment options over a period of years may provide for redemption at premium rates. In this event, the terms might be, say: 1990 at 105; 1991 at 104; 1992 at 103; 1993 at 102; 1994 at 101; and 1995 at 100.

Though not very common in recent years, redeemable debentures may have a *sinking fund* which calls for the setting aside out of annual profits of (a) fixed proportions of the issue or (b) an overall amount to cover interest and repayment needs. The sinking fund is then (1) applied to buying in stock at market prices or repaying a proportion (by drawings) at par; or (2) accumulated to provide cash for repayment of the entire issue at a known date or dates.

There are a few *convertible debenture* issues with rights discussed later.

As with irredeemable stock, cash-rich companies may offer to buy in stock before redemption dates at prices above market levels.

**Loan stocks** usually rank after debentures for interest and capital repayment. While some issues are *secured* like a debenture, the majority are *unsecured* and in a liquidation rank with other unsecured creditors for any accumulated interest and repayment after any secured debenture stock. Interest is almost always a fixed rate payable half-yearly. The life is a fixed number of years or is spread over several years, either of which may be from as little as five to thirty or more. Trustees have similar powers to those generally applying to debentures.

**Convertible** loan stocks are a useful way to raise capital on cheaper initial terms than an ordinary loan stock or, when issued on a takeover, it is desired to give shareholders in the taken-over company the attraction of a continuing but deferred equity interest. The basis of a convertible is to give holders the benefit of a fixed income plus the option to switch into ordinary shares if the issuing company prospers. Conversion may be at one fixed date or (the more usual option) be spread over a number of years at a fixed price or at increasing prices per ordinary share.

**Subordinated** loan stocks, which may be convertible or non-convertible, are issued by banks and other financial companies. In most cases, the 'subordination' puts them after deposits and similar liabilities to customers in the event of liquidation. An example is Midland Bank $7\frac{1}{2}$ per cent convertible subordinated unsecured loan stock 1983/93 which on a winding-up would rank for repayment only after all creditors has been paid; otherwise, it was convertible up to 31 May 1983 at the rate of 21 £1 ordinary shares per £100 of stock.

**Eurobonds,** as noted earlier, are issued in various currencies by some larger companies, particularly those with international connections.

**Deep discount (or zero coupon)** stocks, an American innovation, have yet to catch on over here, though clarification of the tax situation of both borrower and lender has stimulated a little activity. Broadly, the interest rate is nil or well below normal rates; the issue price is far below that for a conventional stock; and repayment is at par of £100 per cent. Borrowers benefit from not having to pay interest during, say, a period when money is needed to develop a project which will not be revenue-producing for some time ahead. Lenders can benefit from the deferral of a high-rate income tax liability by deferring assessments until the time, such as retirement, when top tax rates may have fallen or be no longer applicable to their reduced incomes.

*Junk bonds* came into being initially to provide the bulk of the money for American managements' purchase of their companies in what became known as leveraged buy outs (LBOs). More recently they have been used to raise funds to fight off 'greenmail' operations by the target companies buying in big blocks of their shares acquired by arbitrageurs ('arbs') as the base for a well-trumpeted takeover operation. The feature — and the danger — is that most issues, particularly LBOs, have to carry high interest rates of up to 50 per cent or more than on first-class offerings in return for their high gearing relative to the equity capital, which can be as little as 10 per cent, or less, of the total capitalisation. Big profits and substantial cash flows are thus needed to service the onerous debt charges and to avoid the alternative of bankruptcy; hence the high yields demanded by lenders. So far junk finance has not been used to any noticeable degree in UK LBOs, at least by way of public issues, though banks are putting up this type of loan for management buyouts (MBOs).

*Warrants* give the right to subscribe for ordinary shares at a stated price or prices on a specific date or series of dates. Attached to a loan stock, as was almost the sole practice for some time, they are a titillator giving investors a fixed interest stock plus an option to become an equity shareholder. There has been, however, a trend to add warrants to equity issues, again to raise money on keener terms. They are mostly *detachable* from the parent issue and are dealt in in their own right. Some issues are, however, not detachable until after a specified time from the issue date of a loan stock and thus part of it: the stock is 'cum' warrants. Exercise terms of some North American natural resources companies' warrants are geared to market prices of gold, base metals or oil, which adds the attraction of a speculation on commodity price movements.

******

The high interest rates of recent years have inhibited companies from making debenture issues. The recent fall has, however, induced a return to this market, with some sizeable issues being made by well-known industrial companies and investment trusts. A feature of some stocks is the linking of interest rates or issue prices to the redemption yield on a specific government stock or average of two or three gilts.

The recent exemption from capital gains tax of profits on sales of debentures and loan stocks of UK companies is an encouragement to make such issues. They can now tempt high-rate income tax-payers with stocks at below normal interest rates issued at an attractive discount on redemption price; such, for example, as a 7 per cent (instead of, say, 12 per cent) stock at, say, £70 to give a 30 per cent tax free gain in ten years time. The gains tax exemption does not apply to stocks convertible into ordinary shares or with warrants attached to buy shares.

**Preference capital:** Although there are more than 1,300 listed and USM issues, preference shares were not a popular form of finance for some years. Dividend limitation when in force was, however, an incentive for some companies to make free scrip issues as a means to increase the income of their ordinary shareholders, while others have over the years made rights issues of high yielding shares to raise capital during difficult times. The greatest activity is currently in the allotment of preference shares as part of a takeover or merger deal, with such issues being convertible, redeemable or convertible/redeemable.

Whatever their nature, the position of preference shares in the capital hierarchy of a company is that they come after debenture and loan stocks but before equity (ordinary) shares for their dividends and for repayment in a liquidation.

Most issues have a fixed rate of dividend, payment of which depends on the earning of sufficient profits. Most issues are also *cumulative*, which means that if there are insufficient profits to pay the fixed dividend in one year the arrears are carried forward for payment out of any future profits; the unpaid dividends accumulate. A few issues are, however, *non-cumulative*, which means that an unpaid dividend is lost.

A company may have only one preference issue or, as with some water companies, anything from two to ten or more with various rates of dividend. The ranking of the latter for dividends and capital may be equal or in a priority order such as first, second, third and so on.

*Redeemable* preference shares are part of the capital of some companies. Redemption may be at par or at a premium at a specified date or dates; be by annual or other drawings or market purchases at the company's option; or may come into force on a merger or takeover. As with fixed interest stocks, companies with surplus cash have been tending to repay shares at redemption prices or, if there is a market discount, at a fair premium over recent market prices.

*Participating* preference shares, of which there are a few issues, after receiving a fixed minimum dividend get extra payments which may be related to payments on the equity shares or be a proportion of surplus profits. Holders may also be entitled to a share of surplus assets over repayment at par if the company is liquidated.

*Convertible* preference shares, as already mentioned, are issued by some companies on terms which are akin to those of convertible loan stocks.

*Preferred* shares are another name for a few preference issues which are otherwise similar to shares with the more usual description.

While £1 is the generally accepted par value for preference shares, there are par values of 50p, 25p or other figures, and some of £5 and £10. Stock is also to be found, especially amongst water companies; though quoted per £100 nominal value, such issues can be bought and sold in £1 units.

Dividends on preference shares, as explained elsewhere, are paid under the 'credit' method whereby income tax is not 'deducted' but is credited on the net distribution.

Although preference shareholders are part-owners of a company, they have normally little say in its operations. Only a relatively small proportion of such issues have full or partial voting rights equivalent to those of the equity capital. Votes by the majority come only in specified circumstances such as changes in a company's constitution. Examples of such changes are those which affect the preference shares' status such as an increase in borrowing powers; creation of additional preference capital; a change in the dividend rate; or failure to pay dividends for six or twelve months.

**Equity shares** which are commonly called ordinary shares, rank last in the company capital structure. They take what is left of profits and assets after all the demands of prior issues have been satisfied. As risk capital, they come out best if a company prospers just as they shoulder all or most of the losses if things go wrong. With over 3,000 officially listed, USM, Third, US, other overseas, and Irish issues dealt in, there is a wide and varied choice.

Companies are capitalised in different ways. They may have one or more issues of debentures, loan stock and/or preference shares, all of which come before the ordinary capital. They may have debenture and/or loan stocks plus ordinary shares, or simply preference and ordinary. Or as with the major risk ventures such as oil exploration and mining companies, whose success depends on finding a bonanza or on one profitable commodity, the entire capital is in ordinary shares.

Profits, as already mentioned, are allocated in order of priority of capital, with the equity coming last in the share-out. But if there is only ordinary capital, it gets the lot or stands the losses. This does not mean that all available profits are necessarily paid out in dividends, rather the reverse. Prudence dictates that part of the profits are ploughed back to help finance expansion and as a buffer against future losses or liabilities. In normal times, the average company puts up to one-half or more of its surplus to reserves. And, as happened some years ago, governments may impose restrictions which limit dividend increases to 10 per cent a year or some other level.

Equity shares come in two main classes. First are plain *ordinary* whose distinction is that they carry full voting rights; their owners, in theory at least, control the business. Second are shares which are voteless or have only limited voting rights like one vote per five or ten shares: they are often described as '*A*' *ordinary* or *non-voting ordinary*. The 'A' distinction has no legal definition and is simply the outcome of custom.

'A' shares may be the result of scrip issues (discussed later) or of the wish of owners of a private business on conversion to a public company to retain voting control through part only of the equity. As it is not always desirable for a minority portion of the equity to have voting control, there has been strong opposition to voteless 'A' shares, particularly from pension funds, insurance companies and investment trusts. The result is that the few remaining companies with 'A' shares are tending, or are being pressurised, to enfranchise them. The only advantage of such shares is that they get the same dividend as the ordinary but can usually be bought at lower prices to give somewhat bigger yields, reflecting their lower status.

There need be no limit to the accumulation of reserves out of profit retentions. Their total may, however, become disproportionately large in relation to the ordinary capital. The imbalance can be adjusted by *scrip* or *capitalisation* issues of new shares, which for instance may be one new for every two held — two shares become three. Nothing is, of course, added to the value of a holding. The operation is simply a reduction in reserves with a corresponding increase in issued ordinary capital.

**Accumulating ordinary shares,** sometimes known as *capital shares*, began to be created in 1973 as a tax-saving means of letting shareholders take their dividends in shares, though a small fraction of a penny is paid in cash to retain trustee status. The non-distributed part is used to pay for accumulating shares issued at the average middle-market price of the ordinary for a short period before the declaration of the dividend. The appeal is a compound growth in an equity holding. But it should be noted that as from the 1975/76 fiscal year dividends taken in shares are liable to income tax in the normal way. Investors liable at higher than the basic rate still have to pay the difference between the basic rate and the higher rate: in 1988/89 this is 15 per cent (40−25 per cent). The attraction is thus greater for basic rate only taxpayers; and greatest for tax exempt investors who can reclaim the tax credits.

Two developments have revived board room interest in providing dividend reinvestment options. First, a lead has been given by some major companies such as BAT Industries, Consolidated Gold Fields and RTZ. Secondly, cash is retained in the company coffers, which can help if money is tight. Thirdly, the tremendous growth in the number of small shareholders resulting from the privatisation flotations means that many of them are liable only to basic rate income tax, or are exempt and able to reclaim tax credits on their dividends. But, it must be noted, the accumulation portion could be liable to capital gains tax on sales of shareholdings if the profits exceed the CGT exemption limit: a small risk for many investors.

**Deferred shares,** of which there are very few issues, are in effect the reverse of the newer 'A' shares, the objective being to give them greater voting rights than the ordinary shares and/or a bigger share of profits remaining after paying a minimum dividend on the latter. There are rare cases — Peninsular & Oriental Steam Navigation Company is an example — where the whole equity is in deferred shares or stock. There are also very rare instances where 'deferred' actually means deferral of dividends for a number of years after which the shares become plain ordinary, ranking equally with the rest of the equity. Such deferred capital is usually issued on the takeover of another company or in payment for assets the profitability of which has to be established over a few years. 'Deferred dividend' shares can be attractive to high-rate taxpayers who want capital growth in preference to dividends.

**Common shares** is the American term for the equity. They may have a par value of $1 or some other amount. Or they may have *no-par value*, which means that they can be written into balance sheets at amounts decided by the directors.

\*\*\*\*\*\*

A simple, though not unusual, illustration shows how a British company might arrange its capital structure. The *authorised* (the total of each class which could be issued) and the actual *issued* capital are:

## SHARE CAPITAL

| Authorised £ | | Issued £ |
|---|---|---|
| | 5.6% (net) £1 cumulative | |
| 1,500,000 | preference shares | 1,500,000 |
| | 4.2% (net) £1 cumulative redeemable preference | |
| 1,500,000 | shares 1990/95 | 1,000,000 |
| 12,000,000 | 25p ordinary shares | 10,000,000 |
| £15,000,000 | | £12,500,000 |

## LOAN CAPITAL

| £ | | £ |
|---|---|---|
| | 7% debenture stock | |
| 3,000,000 | 1987/92 | 3,000,000 |
| | 10% convertible loan | |
| 2,000,000 | stock 1985/90 | 2,000,000 |

(Until what is called imputation tax was introduced, preference shares had a fixed *gross* dividend rate; income tax was deducted at the current basic rate from each payment. The change, which applies to all UK company dividends, was to a net rate with tax credit, as explained in chapter 11. Many companies changed the 'coupon' to the net amount after allowing for tax at the change-over rate of 30 per cent. A 10 per cent gross became 7 per cent net and the issue was re-described variously to note the change.)

Though the limits of loan capital and 5.6 per cent preference shares have been issued, the company has in hand £500,000 of redeemable preference and £2,000,000 (8,000,000 25p shares) of ordinary capital for future use if required. Beyond these limits further increases would have to be approved by holders of *all* the present share and loan capital. As the loan stock is convertible up to 1990 into 25p ordinary shares at the rate of one for each £1 of stock, £500,000 of ordinary capital has to be reserved to cover eventual exchanges.

The 'arithmetic' and the merits and demerits of each class of capital are dealt with in subsequent chapters.

An important development to be noted here is that after many years of agitation UK companies can now take powers under certain conditions to buy in or redeem their own shares. This means that although the powers are not so wide or flexible as those practised in the United States for many years, UK companies taking them can use excess liquid funds to reduce the share capital on which dividends are payable.

Action was sparse in the early days with few companies, and those mostly smallish ones, asking shareholders for buy-in powers. Some stimulation came after the Stock Exchange, in August 1985, tripled to 15 per cent the limit on the number of shares which could be bought-in in any one year; but again without any rush. It took the October '87 Crash to ram home to cash-rich companies that a dramatic drop in share prices was a chance to put surplus liquid funds to profitable use through buy-ins; and there was a scurry to take powers neglected up to then. Amongst the pioneers were General Electric Company (putting some of its fabulous cash mountain to work); Guinness; Courts (Furnishers); J. Rothschild Holdings (some 33 per cent bought-in up to mid-1988); Bradford Property Trust; and Warner Estates. The Bank of England recently added its influential weight to the benefits to share earnings of using surplus cash for buy-ins. Another strong argument in favour is the removal of temptations for itchy-fingered and size-crazy managements to lash out on wildcat, uneconomic, and illogical takeover sprees.

In addition to the attraction of an improvement in earnings per share on a reducing issued equity capital, buy-ins are a useful, and sometimes potent, weapon in fighting off takeover bids, as some American company targets have found. Such powers have in fact been particularly valuable to US companies being 'greenmailed' by arbitrageurs who build up big stakes with the publicly avowed intention of takeover bids, but with the real intention of being bailed out at a profit. Luckily for the 'arbs' and others who may benefit, the US buy-in rules are much wider and simpler than the UK regulations.

# 3

# The dealing business

A basic feature of the Big Bang upheaval is the re-classification of Stock Exchange membership. Out has gone the generations old simple division of *single capacity*, of broker or jobber with their clearly defined functions and with public contact strictly confined to the brokers. Now, *dual capacity* allows member firms adopting it to offer the whole range, or parts, of the Exchange's services — broking, jobbing and market-making; and extending to *triple capacity*, international security dealing, banking, money broking, new issues, investment management . . . all under one roof subject only to maintaining 'chinese walls' to avoid conflicts of interest. No longer is membership made up of individuals or member-owned private companies. Banks, money market and financial services groups, investment management companies, issuing houses and other approved firms can own up to 100 per cent of member firms with the doors open to overseas ownership — already there are American, European and Japanese corporate members. Despite the merging of activities under dual capacity two basic arms remain:

BROKERS whose job is to buy and sell securities for clients, advise on investments, supervise or manage portfolios, process the transfer of securities from seller to buyer, and participate in company flotations and capital raising operations. When acting as brokers they are remunerated by commission.

MARKET MAKERS (formerly jobbers) are stock and share traders with a likeness to wholesalers in other markets. They are principals whose profit or loss depends on the difference between the prices at which they buy or sell the securities in which they trade. The price difference is the *turn*, or spread.

The broad make-up of the new style Stock Exchange services is divided into:

*Agency brokers* providing the traditional service as agents paid on a commission basis. As they do not 'run books' as market makers there should be no conflict of interest; their concern is to get the best deal for their clients.

*Broker-dealers* are the new-style stockbrokers who make markets (job) as well as buy and sell stocks and shares for private and other clients.

*Discount brokers* provide no-frills dealing facilities only at reduced commission rates.

*Inter-dealer brokers* act as go-betweens providing market makers with a confidential service matching up sellers and buyers, mostly in gilt-edged stocks. They help market makers to lay off risks or to sell short without the knowledge of competitors.

*Primary dealers* are market makers in gilt-edged stocks who, because of the large volume of dealings and their function in Government borrowing, are under close supervision by the Bank of England.

*Accredited dealers* whose business is to try to match sellers and buyers in out of the way or rarely traded securities.

*Affiliates,* mostly solicitors and accountants, who pass on business to member firms in return for a share in the commission.

Although many firms are centred in London, there are one or more brokers in the major UK and Irish cities and towns. A number of London firms have in fact been expanding existing, or setting up new, country networks linked directly by screen and telephone to head office dealing and service rooms. Contrariwise, some provincial brokers have merged into groups with similar instant contact with their London trading rooms. Lists of names and addresses of brokers ready to deal for private clients can be obtained from the Secretaries of the various Exchanges as under:

LONDON: The Stock Exchange, London EC2N 1HP.
MIDLANDS and WESTERN: The Stock Exchange, Margaret Street, Birmingham, B3 3JL.
NORTHERN: The Stock Exchange, 4 Norfolk Street, Manchester M2 1DS.
PROVINCIAL: 4th Floor, The Stock Exchange, London EC2N 1HP.
  Note: This Exchange has members spread throughout the country.
BELFAST: The Stock Exchange, 10 High Street, Belfast BT1 2BP.
IRISH: The Stock Exchange, Anglesea Street, Dublin 2, Ireland.

The coming of nationwide electronic screen trading has cut floor business on the provincial exchanges to dealing in the securities of local companies, with major activities being the usual dealing and support services for investors and the bringing to market of local companies.

A new, and expanding, provincial activity is the provision of over-the-counter stockbroking services by building societies through link-ups with Stock Exchange member firms. Banks are also developing on-the-spot dealing facilities in leading shares.

Another fundamental, and somewhat unexpected, Big Bang change was a speedy desertion from the Floor where for many generations dealings took place face to face between broker and jobber. The only occupants left are the traded option 'crowd' whose dealings are by 'open outcry'. Now a broker gets up-to-the-minute prices from an electronic screen in his office. He or his dealers no longer have to get quotes from jobbers at their pitches.

The Stock Exchange Automated Quotations system — SEAQ — shows the latest prices for thousands of equities divided into three categories:

*Alpha* are the largest, most actively traded issues in which market makers show firm, continuous two-way prices during the mandatory quotation period (9 a.m. – 5 p.m.) all trades in which are published within five minutes on TOPIC, of which more later.

*Beta* are actively traded issues for which market makers display continuous firm two-way prices, but with trades not published immediately.

*Gamma* are less active stocks in which market makers are able to show continuous two-way quotes. Prices may, however, be only indicative for the minimum quantity though firm in any large quantities.

Out-of-the-way or unpopular issues are in a *delta* group with different dealing rules covering negotiated business and similar trades. Alpha and beta quotes, it should be noted, are actual dealing prices as against indications for the others.

From his screen-packed dealing room a market maker enters in his terminal two-way prices for the stocks in which he is registered, and his trades. From this information and that entered by other market makers, best price and, for alpha stocks, last trade data are fed to and displayed on the TOPIC service.

Teletext Output of Price Information by Computer — TOPIC — is an older colour TV service which shows competing bid and offer prices (the best current quotes being displayed in the Yellow Strip) from all market makers; and for alpha securities the price of the latest trade and volume data. Other features include company announcements as they are issued, up-to-date money market and foreign exchange rates, gold bullion prices and analytical data.

Investors benefit in various ways from this 'instant' service. Market information is available wherever there is a screen throughout the UK and Eire — and in the USA. First-hand prices are provided by the actual market makers. There is surety that the broker is getting the best market price at the time of dealing. Another valuable feature of SEAQ, incidentally, is that transactions are recorded and time-stamped, to provide a complete audit in the event of a dispute or an official enquiry into dealings in particular securities. Customers with access to the TOPIC screen can see the best bid and offer prices of all market makers' quotes.

*SEAQ International* extends the price service to the leading American, Canadian, Australian, Hong Kong, French, German, Scandinavian and other overseas stocks, which meets the needs of a growing international marketplace of which London is a vital part. Market makers can key prices directly into the system where they are brought together for comparison, with the 'Yellow Strip' highlighting the best available prices at any time. As with UK stocks, many of the international stocks quoted are on a firm dealing basis for a minimum number, but with market makers willing to deal in larger blocks at agreed prices.

*SEAQ Automatic Execution Facility* — SAEF — while not in action at the time of writing, will meet the call for even more sophisticated technology when it comes into the electronic network. Brokers will be able to enter orders to buy or sell securities with the order being automatically matched against the best quote held in the system — an advantage to all concerned. A broker/ dealer will be able to execute small orders quickly and without having to telephone market makers with a guarantee that they have been done at the best possible prices at any given time and with an 'audit trail' for any necessary check. The market maker will save time answering telephone calls while getting computer readable feeds providing data for his position-keeping. For the investor one telephone call covers getting the share price, his instructions to buy or sell and to have verbal confirmation of the carrying out of the order. And he is assured of having got the best price in the market at the time of dealing.

One custom which survived decimalisation is the Stock Exchange's adherence to fractions in its pricing system. For stocks, the fraction is as little as $\frac{1}{64}$ (roughly $\frac{1}{2}$p) with other fractions such as $\frac{1}{16}$, $\frac{1}{8}$, $\frac{1}{4}$, $\frac{1}{2}$ and so on. A price of $85\frac{3}{4}$ would therefore represent £85.75. Shares are quoted in pence and fractions for prices below £10. From £10 upwards the quotations are in pounds and fractions such as £12$\frac{1}{4}$ or £16$\frac{5}{8}$. Symptomatic of the decimalisation era is, however, its infiltration into 'big' prices with quotes like £12.20 creeping in.

Changes were, however, necessary in the recording of business in the *Stock Exchange Daily Official List*, to show for every security the closing quotation; lowest price and details of business done. Special symbols are added to prices to record the following:

‡ Bargains at special prices such as small parcels of shares sold below the normal quote and with the seller paying stamp duty. It also covers purchases or sales for 'new time', an operation explained later.

φ Bargains done on the previous day and not marked in time, or done after the deadline for closing the marking lists.

△ Bargains done with a non-member or executed in an overseas market.

Small lots of shares, particularly those with a normally difficult market, are liable to price differentials. A seller will have to accept less than a normal price and probably have to pay transfer duty for the buyer. The reason is the disproportionate cost of handling small lots.

Market makers may initiate business by bidding for or offering shares at a fixed price. They may want to square their book if they are oversold (are 'bears' or 'short') or they are carrying too many (are 'bulls' or 'long'); or they know of a possible buyer or seller.

Though market makers are eager to provide a two-way market in all listed stocks and shares, it is extremely difficult, sometimes impossible, to do so in some securities and circumstances. Factors which can limit the size of the market or an inability to quote are:

* The size of the issue. Some companies have hundreds of millions of shares listed. Others, like water companies and those with small preference or loan capital issues, may have only some tens of thousands listed, turnover in which is rare and in very small quantities. (The Stock Exchange now tends to withdraw listings where there have been no, or very few, deals over a year or so.)

* Where there are large family or other holdings which leave a relatively small proportion in other shareholders' hands.

* There are no sellers or early prospect of sellers,'and jobbers do not want to go short by selling stock they do not hold.

* There are no buyers around and jobbers do not want to take any, or more, stock on their books.

* Where an announcement, such as a dividend or takeover bid, which could affect the price is imminent. Even though this may be for an active share, the quote may be qualified by adding 'small' or 'not too many', or giving a quantity like 500 compared with a normal market number of 2,000.

While a dealing price may not be readily made, a market maker may still give a quotation which could be (a) as a basis for negotiation; (b) on a nominal basis; (c) as buyers only; or (d) as sellers only.

A broker accepting a 'basis for negotiation' quote has to disclose his business to the market maker, who will then try to find a counter-party to conclude a bargain.

A 'nominal basis' quote indicates that the market maker sees little chance of buying or selling. The broker can then ask for a proposition, suggest a basis on which he would deal, or state a firm price on which he would deal.

'Buyers' or 'sellers only', or 'one-way market', quotations arise because, as already shown, there are few shares in circulation, or there is a temporary technical situation due to jobbers wanting to square oversold (bear) or over-stocked (bull) positions.

Market makers' quotations are thus subject to a variety of factors. They may be 'close' (a narrow spread between bid and offered prices); 'wide' (a more than normal spread); 'nominal'; or subject to limitations. And where there is more than one market maker in the shares the 'touch' is the closest price between them, or the best bid of one and the cheapest offer of another.

When it comes to actual dealing, factors can be the size of the market and the size of the order. No problem should arise with reasonable numbers of alpha and beta stocks, and perhaps gammas, at quoted prices. But when the order is large in relation to the number of shares in issue, various expedients may be called for. The market maker may limit the number of shares he will buy or sell at his quoted price. In which case the alternatives are to accept and (a) to leave the balance to be done at the same price; (b) to indicate (or agree) a price for doing further business; (c) to ask for a proposition (bid or offer) in the balance; or (d) to have another go later with any indication of price and time limit clearly stated.

## CUM, EX and ALL

It takes time, as will be shown in chapter 6, for a buyer to be registered as the new owner and so to directly receive interest, dividends or other 'rights' to which he may be entitled. When such things are due or announced prices are adjusted to take account of their value. On the income side, this is usually some four to six weeks ahead for fixed interest stocks; and on the first day of the account following a dividend announcement for shares. Prices are then quoted 'ex'. Which means that the seller and not the buyer is due to receive the distribution. But if the price is *not quoted ex*, the buyer is entitled to the dividend to come.

For example, an 8 per cent fixed interest stock goes ex-dividend a few weeks before the half-yearly 4 per cent interest is to be paid. A buyer *before* this date will therefore be entitled to the interest and if he is not registered in time will collect from the seller. But if he buys at an 'ex' price the seller keeps the interest. The market price would be adjusted from say £76 to £72 ex-div. to allow for the payment. For a share quoted at 120p cum a 5p dividend the 'ex' price, all else being equal, would be 115p. Ex adjustments are the gross interest on fixed interest stocks and net after the tax credit for dividends.

Scrip issues, rights offers and other distributions affecting a price are similarly adjusted. The terms used are 'ex capital', 'ex cap.' or 'ex c.'; and 'ex rights' or 'ex r.'; or if a dividend or something else is involved, 'ex all'. The interest and dividend abbreviations are 'ex div.', or 'x.d.' and 'cum div.' or 'c.d.'. In practice, prices are rarely quoted 'cum' so that a buyer can generally assume he is entitled to all subsequent distributions unless the price is specifically quoted 'ex'. The Talisman settlement system, dealt with in Chapter 6, automatically makes adjustments for x.d. distributions, which saves passing cheques, through brokers, from sellers to cum. div. buyers.

**RULE 535**

The great bulk of dealings are in stocks and shares which have been granted a listing by the Council of the Stock Exchange and are therefore *officially quoted*. Dealings are, however, allowed in the *Unlisted Securities Market* and the *Third Market* (dealt with in Chapter 15); and under *Rule 535* which covers the following bargains:
*   In securities where the principal market is outside the UK and Eire; a quotation has not been granted in London, and dealings are not recorded in the Official List. This is rule 535(4)(a).
*   Of other public companies or corporate bodies not coming into the above categories in which specific bargains may be made with Council permission; included are securities of small local companies. Business in non-listed securities, particularly those of established unlisted companies, is actively encouraged so as to give holders the benefit of a market-place where business can be done at arm's-length prices. This is rule 535(2).
*   Of approved companies engaged solely in mineral exploration and which have not been long enough in existence to supply all the financial and other facts required for an official listing. Rule 535(3), this covers mostly oil projects.

Records of dealings in these categories are given as a Special List in the Official List and those for Thursday appear in Saturday's *Financial Times* which, however, does not currently include gilt-edged and other pure fixed interest stocks.

Under Rule 535 dealings are also allowed in the shares of suspended companies in two circumstances only: to allow a bear position to be closed or to allow a sale in connection with a deceased estate. In these cases dealings are not marked.

**LIMITS**

While dealing prices are often left to the discretion and market ability of a broker, a client may fix his own price and the amount of stock or shares he is prepared to buy or sell at. Limits can be:
*   Firm for a day or for a longer period such as the account, a month or 'until done' for a specified quantity of stock or shares.
*   For referral to a client at the bid or offer price at which he might do business.
*   Made by a broker with a firm order at a price at which a deal is not immediately possible, and made perhaps to more than one market maker.
*   Contingent on the sale or purchase at a stated price of one stock and the purchase or sale at a stated price of another. This may be relatively easy if the two stocks are in the same market such as gilt-edged and only one market maker is involved: this is called a *switch*. But it is more difficult, and may take more time to execute, if two markets are concerned such as the sale of a gilt-edged stock and the purchase of an insurance share. It is here that the flexibility of the dealing system comes in; it is possible for one market maker to make a firm proposition while the broker tries to deal with the other half of the order with another market maker.

Limits are often for prices only. They may however be for quantities, the whole of which the market cannot supply or absorb immediately. An out-of-the-way share in which dealings are infrequent or small is an example. Suppose the order is to buy 5,000 shares at 60p and the market maker, who does not want to go short, has only 3,000 on his book and cannot see where he might pick up the other 2,000. The 3,000 will be taken and a limit left for the balance for a specified time or indefinitely. The balance may come along in one lot or in a trickle.

## NTP

A market maker may sell stock even though he is short of all or part of the order and may not be too hopeful of covering himself quickly. He may then agree with the broker that the sale is 'not to press' (or 'NTP') for delivery. This means that the buyer cannot set in motion the 'buying in' machinery which can be used officially when there has been an unnecessary delay in delivery.

## OTHER MARKETS

Security trading is not entirely confined to the Stock Exchange. Though minute in comparison, there are other 'outside', markets in unlisted and listed securities. The main ones are:

**Over the counter** (OTC) run by specialist organisations or merchant banks who deal in the securities of companies (some quite substantial) which are not traded on the Stock Exchange. Some firms are market makers quoting buying and selling prices and running 'books' in specific shares. Others simply match buying and selling orders. And some carry on both types of business. A major aim of the *Third* market is to provide something of a controlled and more 'visible' market for OTC stocks which qualify for entry.

**Stock and share dealers** licensed by the Department of Trade and Industry who do business in all types of securities — Stock Exchange listed, Unlisted Securities Market and non-Stock Exchange quoted. Though these firms, as well as OTC traders, have their own comprehensive rules of conduct they are not governed by Stock Exchange regulations or in its compensation fund.

**Eurobond** trading by merchant and other banks and finance houses over the TV-screens and telephone in the growing number of Euro and other non-sterling currency stocks with an international market. Market-makers operate for each issue.

**Direct contact** with the secretaries of companies whose securities are officially suspended or cancelled, or where there has never been a listing, to find out if a buyer can be put in touch with a seller or vice-versa.

## PRICE POINTERS

Buying and selling stocks and shares, it will have been seen, is not a simple business of giving a broker an order and his being in a position to execute it right away. Points which help and save misunderstandings are:
* Stock and share prices are volatile. They can change widely over a day, even in seconds.

* Newspaper and other published prices are no more than a guide to quotations at a particular time, e.g. the previous day's close. And, depending on the method and time of collection, may vary from paper to paper.
* The *Financial Times'* daily lists of active stocks highlight (a) shares in which above average activity was noted the day before; and (b) the number of price changes in the most active shares on the day before that. On Saturday there is a list of the number and extent of price changes of the most active shares over a 5-day period to Thursday.
* Bear in mind when comparing gross and net share prices that the latter are free of brokerage, e.g. a net 101p is cheaper than a gross 100p plus 1.9p commission and VAT.
* If a broker is given discretion he can deal immediately at the best price.
* When a market maker has dealt, particularly in a large line, he is liable to alter his price to keep his book balanced.
* Securities, even the most obscure and smallest issues, can usually be sold — at a price. But in difficult markets they cannot always be bought; a lot of patience may be needed to pick up even a small quantity. Post-Black Monday dealing problems rammed home the great difficulty, even impossibility, of selling quite small lines of shares of some of the USM 'minnows'.
* Holding out for the last penny may mean missing the market; of eventually having to pay more or to take less. Don't be greedy.
* The market can be disturbed if a broker is asked to make constant enquiries about unexecuted limits. Leave well alone after the initial enquiry: the market maker will note the limit and approach the broker when he can do business.
* Do not divide a big buying or selling order between two or more brokers — it could lose control of the market.
* Limits should be clear cut and unequivocal as to the exact security, the quantity, the price and the length of time to operate. If for more than a few days, they should be checked — or revised — at regular intervals such as weekly, the start of each account or monthly; or before going on holiday, on a business trip or into hospital. Written confirmation can save misunderstandings.

# 4

# Buying and selling

In addition to the important price factor, stock market dealings fall into different categories, mostly to do with settlement of transactions. Just as it is essential to understand the pricing and dealing mechanisms, it is also imperative to know how and when payment will have to be made or received, or special transactions handled. Procedures depend on the nature of the security and transaction, and are:

## FOR CASH

Payment (settlement) is due on the business day following the day of purchase or sale of:
(1) UK government, local authority, nationalised industry, public board, Commonwealth government, provincial and corporation, and similar stocks. Also for traded options.
Exceptions, which must be arranged when dealing, are *forward bargains* for settlement on the account day (see below) of a current account when payment is due for investments made for such settlement; in other words, the sale of 'non-cash' securities to pay for the above type of stocks. Settlement may also be deferred for a maximum of 14 days when payment is to come from repayment of a short-term loan to a local authority or public board.
(2) New issues in the form of scrip; and renounceable allotment letters sent to holders of rights issues.
(3) Unless specifically done for the account (see below), bargains in US, Canadian, Hong Kong, Japanese and other overseas stocks are mostly for cash settlement or payment in, say, 5 days or 7 days.

## ACCOUNT SETTLEMENT

The Stock Exchange year is divided into accounts, most of which are normally for fortnightly periods and the balance, usually covering Christmas and other holidays, for three weeks. The normal account starts on a Monday and runs until Friday of the following week with settlement taking place ten days later, usually a Monday, the 'pay-day'.

This means that unlike cash transactions, there can be up to a fortnight's free run, a facility which short-term speculators use by buying and selling (or the reverse) within the account and receiving profits or paying losses on settlement day.

## AFTER HOURS

Official dealings begin at 9 a.m and end at 5 p.m. 'Unofficial' trading does, however, begin as early as 8 a.m. or 8.30 a.m. and continues (quite actively at times, particularly when Wall Street comes in) after the official close. After-hours deals are booked as 'early bargains' for the following day.

## NEW TIME

While the normal start of a dealing account is a Monday, it is possible to deal two business days ahead. Buying or selling 'for new' is possible on the last Thursday or Friday of the old account. This gives a run on a fortnightly account of twelve business days instead of ten. Naturally, something has to be paid for the privilege. But, depending on the price, the cost is no more than a penny or a few pence a share, such as 51p instead of 50p.

## PUT-THROUGHS

Put-throughs are usually simultaneous orders to buy and sell (or the reverse) the same security, emanating from one client, or from clients associated with each other such as members of the same family or associated companies. The broker consults an appropriate market maker and agrees with him put-through prices which are fair to buyer and seller. The market maker's 'turn' is smaller than for a normal transaction and may be as little as $\frac{1}{2}$p, depending on the price. A put-through may also start as a one-way buy or sell order for which a broker looks for a matching order. Subject to not upsetting the initial order, a market maker may himself take part of the 'line' at the put-through price.

## BED and BREAKFAST

'B and B' deals are a relatively simple and cheap way of mitigating capital gains imposts. Though mostly used to establish losses to set off against taxable gains, such deals can also be used to take advantage of any unused portion of the tax exemption limit by creating profits through an 'up' B & B transaction. The drill is to get the co-operation of a market maker willing to buy shares in the afternoon of one day and to sell them back the next morning at a small turn. Costs are the turn, which could be only a fraction of a penny depending on the share price; brokerage on the sale at scale rate or at a special rate in relation to the size of the deal; and transfer stamp duty at 0.5 per cent on the repurchase. The total, again depending on the size and nature of the 'B and B', can in fact be as low as $1\frac{1}{4}$ per cent (or even less) and little more than $2\frac{1}{4}$ per cent at most.

## CONTANGOS

The closing of a bought (bull) or sold (bear) position at the end of an account may be carried over, or continued, to the next account by a special arrangement which means closing the purchase or sale for the current account and reopening it for the succeeding one. Except in the case of bearer stocks, where financing can be easier than for registered securities, the overall total of each security for which facilities are required has to match each way.

The reason for 'matching' is the nature of the facilities needed by the two classes of operators. On the one hand are buyers ready to pay a rate of interest (or contango) for deferring settlement of purchases to the following account. Termed 'givers' or 'givers-on', they generally give the contango rate to, on the other hand, sellers wishing to defer delivery of sales and who, as takers of the rate, are called 'takers' or 'takers-in'. Success in a carry-over thus depends on the matching of givers and takers. Any balance either way means that unlucky bulls or bears who are 'thrown out' have to complete their bargains in other ways. They have to cut their positions at the best prices possible, or they have to try to borrow money or stock to complete their bargains.

Official completion time for carry-overs is the afternoon of the last day of the account; which means that unlucky operators without alternative means of settlement have to close their positions as best they can for 'cash' on the morning of the first day of the new account. Taking account of stamp duty and some profit for the market maker, the process involves taking less than a normal price on a sale and paying extra on a purchase. Successful transactions are accounted for at 'making-up' prices which are officially fixed at 3.30 p.m. on the final day of the account. A contract note issued by the broker sets out the two sides of the bargain at the making-up price. For (a) the giver it is the sale and repurchase; and for (b) the taker it is the purchase and resale.

A key cost is the contango rate which depends on interest rates generally; the two-way demand for carry-overs in each security; and the market rating of the security, with mining and other speculative shares costing more. Brokers may take a percentage on the contango rate for their services and also charge commission on each carry-over. Differences, after taking account of contango expenses, are paid or received on settlement day. Carry-overs are usually restricted to principals. Many brokers will not in fact handle them, or will insist on margins of up to 40/50 per cent being put up and maintained.

## CASH and NEW

This is another form of continuing a speculative transaction which is somewhat similar to a carry-over, or is an escape route when thrown out of a contango. Securities which it is not desired to take up are sold for cash on the last day of the account and bought for the new account; or, if a bear transaction, dealt with the opposite way. Costs are (a) the market maker's turn between selling and buying prices; (b) an additional payment for the facility; and (c) the usual broker's commission.

Taken together (and a good deal depends on the price spread of the particular share) the cost can be up to 10 per cent or more on the original buying price. Repeated over several accounts, the all-in cost can rise steeply and call for a large jump in price before breaking even, let alone making a profit. Cash and new is only for the optimists with long purses. In any case such deals are limited by Stock Exchange rules to seven accounts, or less if the broker insists.

# 5

# Having the option

Options in their basic form are nothing new. They have been around for several centuries as a means to hedge (insure) against rises and falls in prices; as a way to limit the cost of taking a view; or as bull or bear speculative instruments. The maximum loss is the all-in cost of the option, which is materially less than an outright purchase of the shares concerned, or as a floor under a bear sale. Two types of options have been available on the UK market since April 1978 — the old, *traditional*; and the new, *traded*.

## TRADITIONAL OPTIONS

Traditional options can be negotiated for any UK listed securities and, in theory, for any listed stocks on any recognised overseas stock exchange — and they can be single or double. For a *single option* a buyer ('giver') pays ('gives') money to the seller ('taker') for the right to buy ('call') or sell ('put') a security at an agreed price over a stated period. A *double option*, called a 'put and call', gives the right to buy or sell.

The option period is one, two or three months, usually the latter, or perhaps a longer time. While the initial intention may be to run an option up to the *exercise date* (the end of the agreed period), it can be dealt with in between on a *declaration day*, which is the last Thursday in the Stock Exchange account. Unlike a traded option, dealt with below, it cannot itself be sold.

Several factors are involved. *Striking price* is the market price at the time of making the bargain. *Time* is the period of the option. *Rate* is the charge made by the option dealer, with call rates varying from around 7 to 9 per cent on blue chip alpha shares to anything from, say, 12 to 20 per cent on gamma and very speculative or out-of-the-way counters. Puts can come a little cheaper, while doubles may cost between one-and-a-half times and twice singles. *Brokerage*, be it noted, is payable not on the option money but on the price of the underlying securities.

An example shows the impact of costs on this type of operating. A call is negotiated on 5,000 beta shares at a market price of 120p and option money of 13p a share with brokerage payable at what can be a usual rate of 1.65 per cent on the market value of £6,000:

| | | |
|---|---|---|
| Option money | | £650.00 |
| Brokerage | £99.00 | |
| VAT @ 15% | 14.85 | 113.85 |
| | | £763.85 |

The option money thus equalled 10.8 per cent and the all-in cost per share was 15.3p. In other words, the share price would have to go over 135p before a profit was in sight.

If an option is exercised there is usually no further brokerage; but the 0.5 per cent stamp duty has to be paid on taking up the shares; which means that the total cost would be just about 136p a share.

## TRADED OPTIONS

A significant extension of the traditional business which gives much more flexibility was the start in April 1978 of a traded options market. It gives the option buyer a double choice. First is the right to buy (call) or sell (put) shares at a specified price before a given date. Second, and most useful, is the right to *buy and sell the option* itself before its expiry date. A look at the 'call' option, the most active side of the market, shows how options are traded.

The minimum unit dealt in is one *contract* normally representing an option on 1,000 shares of the underlying security — the exceptions are a handful of high priced shares (over say £10) where the option is on only 100 shares. Units are not divisible into fractions such as 500 or 740 shares.

A contract has a limited life span set by its *expiry date*. Dates are fixed at three-monthly intervals to give three possible cycles over a year:-

January, April, July, October
February, May, August, November
March, June, September, December

with one of them being allocated permanently to the shares of each company introduced to the market. With the possible exception of a transfer from one cycle to another expiry dates thus always fall in the same month. An option's maximum life is three, six or nine months with all these months quoted. As one date expires a new one is added. When, for instance, the January date of a January, April, July cycle is reached it ceases to exist and an October option is added. . . and so on. Precise expiry dates are announced by the Stock Exchange and are stated on contract notes.

The contract gives the right to buy the underlying securities, if so wished, at the *exercise price*. Prices are fixed by the Stock Exchange on the following scale:

|      |      |      |      |
|------|------|------|------|
| 50p  | 110p | 200p | 330p |
| 60p  | 120p | 220p | 360p |
| 70p  | 130p | 240p | 390p |
| 80p  | 140p | 260p | 420p |
| 90p  | 160p | 280p | 460p |
| 100p | 180p | 300p | 500p |

Above 500p the scale rises at 50p intervals. The only exceptions during the life of options are adjustments to reflect capital changes in the underlying security such as scrip (capitalisation) or rights issues. A one-for-one scrip issue, for example, doubles the number of contracts — a holding of five contracts becomes ten when the underlying shares are marked ex-scrip. For an 'odd number' issue the adjustment is made by increasing the number of shares, with say a two-for-five distribution raising the total per contract to 1,400 (1,000 × 7 ÷ 5). No account is taken for dividend distributions.

At least two, sometimes three, exercise prices are established for each expiry date when a new class is first introduced. Options of a particular exercise price and a particular expiry date are termed a *series*, which means that each class is made up of several series. When the price of the underlying shares moves above the highest exercise price or below the lowest, new series at different exercise prices are added. There can thus be as many as five or more exercise prices operating at any time in respect of the options on the shares of a particular company. The price of the option is known as the *premium* and it is quoted in terms of a single share. As with actual underlying shares the premium varies from minute to minute and is subject to supply and demand and other market forces.

The option price is made up of two parts. First is the *intrinsic value* which only exists when the actual share price is higher than the option exercise price. For example, if the prices are 250p actual for the shares and 210p exercise for the option series, the intrinsic value is 40p. Second is the *time value* which is calculated on the time left before expiry. Hence, the longer the time to run the higher the time value is likely to be. An example shows these factors at work. A traded option is introduced in mid-January when the underlying share price is 200p. Nine separate option series could then be listed, as shown:

| *Expiry date* | *Exercise price* | | |
|---|---|---|---|
| April | 180 | 200 | 220 |
| July | 180 | 200 | 220 |
| October | 180 | 200 | 220 |

With the actual (underlying) share price at 200p, the prices of the traded options at the three respective exercise prices might then be:

| | 180 | 200 | 220 |
|---|---|---|---|
| April | 27p | 12p | 4p |
| July | 32p | 18p | 9p |
| January | 36p | 23p | 13p |

It is a natural corollary that the lower the exercise price the higher the cost of the option, as will be shown later. If the exercise price is below the underlying share price the option is said to be *in-the-money*; if higher it is *out-of-the-money*; and if the two prices coincide it is *at-the-money*. Of course, the reason why in-the-money contracts cost more than 'outs' is simply that the former have both intrinsic and time values and the latter have only a time value.

Putting the example into practice, a call option on one contract (1,000 shares) expiring in April at an exercise price of 200p would cost 12p a share or £120 plus dealing expenses compared with an outlay of £2,000 plus expenses for an outright share purchase. Much less money has to be laid out and the maximum loss (exclusive of expenses) is £120 should the actual share price fall below 200p. Should the shares rise, however, to say 240p two alternatives would be open. The option to buy the 1,000 shares at 200p could be exercised. Or the option itself could be sold. There would be no such choice in the traditional option market — the underlying shares would have to be bought at the option price of 200p and immediately sold again at 240p.

Another advantage is that if the underlying shares rose the 200p option would be attractive to other investors. Sticking to a rise to 240p the intrinsic value would have risen by 40p. But, depending on the time still to run, the option itself would still have a time value which might mean that it would be traded at say 48p, made up of 40p intrinsic value plus a shorter time value of 8p.

Traded options can be used to take advantage of a fall as well as a rise in a share price; they can be sold for the 'put' or bought for the 'call'. Compared with the call side already outlined, a holder of shares wanting to protect a position or a bear operator who considers the shares to be overvalued can be a *writer* (seller) of traded options. In this case, the writer receives the option money less expenses. Using the same figures as above, the shares would be 'put' at 200p, but as 12p would be received for the option the equivalent selling price would be 212p. If the share price fell the writer would be 12p a share better off on the sale or, alternatively, could buy back the option. If, on the other hand, the shares rose there would be a loss on buying back at a level above the option price; but the underlying shares would still be held, though at their higher price.

Unlike a buyer, who simply has to find the cost and expenses of the option, a writer has to provide security. This may be cover in the form of the actual shares themselves or any other asset approved by the Stock Exchange; or, if an *uncovered ('naked') writer,* a cash margin of at least 20 per cent of a day-to-day valuation of the underlying shares. To avoid risk of closure due to price fluctuations a naked writer may in fact be asked to put up, say, 35 per cent initially and to top it up on any subsequent fall below 30 per cent. Some brokers refuse, in fact, to transact naked business, which is not surprising when, as exemplified by widely publicised operations by some youthful speculators caught in the '87 crash, losses and bad debts can mount into hundreds of thousands or even millions of pounds.

Whether buyer or seller, the number of series available calls for considerable thought and working out before going into the market. Hence, if there is no definite objective such as an expiry date or an exercise price in mind, it is advisable to get a broker's advice on the most suitable action.

As a glance back to the table on page 26 shows, the range is wide. Taking the three April series, a purchase of the 180s at 27p is paying the equivalent of 207p a share, with corresponding figures for the 200s being 212p and for the 220s 224p. Accordingly, if the underlying share price at expiry date is 220p the 180s will show 13p profit and the 200s 8p profit, but there will be a loss of 4p on the 220s, subject in all three cases to expenses. On the other hand, it is notable that the higher the exercise price the lower the option cost.

The impact is demonstrated in the following hypothetical example which shows the profits or losses (excluding expenses) for the three April series at different actual share prices at the expiry date:

| Series | Option price | Share price at expiry date | | |
|---|---|---|---|---|
| | | 190p | 220p | 250p |
| 180 | 27p | L. 17p (63%) | P. 13p (48%) | P. 43p (159%) |
| 200 | 12p | L. 12p (100%) | P. 8p (67%) | P. 38p (317%) |
| 220 | 4p | L. 4p (100%) | L. 4p (100%) | P. 26p (650%) |
| P=profit  L=loss | | | | |

The 220 series demonstrates the wide range from minimum loss to maximum profit if there is a big rise in the underlying share price. Against such a fortunate turn as a rise in the share price to 250p, there must be a rise to at least 224p before there is any profit on this series. There is thus a twofold guideline in normal circumstances. Purchases of options with an intrinsic value (known as 'in the money') are a more conservative operational method than those having only a time value (or 'out of the money'). These positions are reversed for writers of options.

The ideal traded options market is one having a good trading volume and an ability to handle large orders easily. It is clear, therefore, that listings must be limited to the shares of companies with a substantial equity market capitalisation and with a free and active market in their shares. The market thus began with only ten leading companies, including British Petroleum, Commercial Union Assurance, Imperial Chemical Industries and Shell Transport. Subsequent additions, including two *gilt-edged* stocks, have raised the total to over sixty constituents; with more sure to come. And, a simple way to take an overall view of the equity market; there is the *Index Option* on the FT-SE100 Share ('Footsie') index.

*Traded put options* were introduced at the end of May 1981. Whereas *call* options cater for investors on the bull tack, looking for a rise, *puts* are for bears, hoping for a fall. Puts give the right to sell at a fixed price up to a future date and, as with calls, can be traded at any time during the currency of the option. This addition also makes it possible to take a combined bull and bear view in what is called a *straddle* — the purchase of both a call and a put traded option.

*Commission* is a fixed rate per bargain plus a variable percentage on the option money. While rates may vary between brokers, a representative scale is:

> *Buying*: £1.50 per contract *plus*
> 2.5% on the first £5,000 option money
> 1.5% on the next £5,000
> 1.0% on the excess

The total outlay on a purchase of 10 contracts at 20p per underlying share would thus be:

| | |
|---|---:|
| 10 contracts | £2,000.00 |
| Fixed rate @ £1.50 | 15.00 |
| Commission @ $2\frac{1}{2}$% | 50.00 |
| VAT @ 15% | 9.75 |
| | £2,074.75 |

to make an all-in cost of 20.75p per underlying share. *Selling* (exercise) charges are the usual rates for share deals. Charges on options in non-sterling currencies may differ, however, from the above and should be checked with the brokers before dealing. All transactions are for *cash settlement*. Individual positions are limited to 5,000 contracts (5m. underlying shares).

Price adjustments for ex-dividend positions should be noted. They can be irritating and loss-producing. The reason is that the shares underlying a traded option are in effect non-existent and do not qualify for payment. Yet, in view of their relationship to actual share prices, the option price, all other things being equal, is reduced correspondingly. Thus, if a dividend is 10p the share price will be reduced from, say, 210p to 200p ex dividend and the option price will also be cut by 10p; but with the option holder *not* getting the dividend, he loses 10p.

The *tax* position of both buyers and sellers is complex and depends on personal circumstances. It is sound policy, therefore, to get professional advice before starting to deal in traded options.

After a very slow start, turnover in traded options is now very substantial and growing on a widening appreciation of their uses by discerning — and speculatively minded — investors. The main advantages and attractions of T/Os are:

*Speculation:* A fixed sum of money put into a T/O will, depending on prices and time to run, give control over many more shares than an outright bull purchase or bear sale; always remembering that the option can become valueless. The profit or loss can be greater; if lucky or unlucky much greater. Also, the longer the time value the longer the run for the money. But whatever the outcome, the loss is limited to the cost of the contract.

*Profit protection* can be achieved by selling an actual holding at a definite gain and keeping an interest in the shares by applying some of the profit to buy a call option. The position then is that if the share price rises still further an additional profit can be made by selling the option or exercising it to repurchase the shares.

*The 90: 10 Strategy* can be used when it is thought that markets could become vulnerable to an overall downturn resulting from the possibility of a general election, a poor Budget, national or international economic uncertainty or some other adverse news. Capital protection is possible by selling all equity holdings and reinvesting the proceeds as to:

Up to, say, 90 per cent in short-dated gilts, a building society or a bank deposit, or in the money market.

The balance of 10 per cent or more in call options on individual shares or the FT-SE Index.

*Hedging* can be had. A put contract will give a hedge against a fall in price of a holding of volatile shares. Or a capital gains tax liability on shares showing a profit but thought to be due for a fall can be minimised or eliminated by holding them and covering the eventuality through a put option; such a move actually gives two options if the price fall is substantial — the put can be sold at a profit and the shares kept, or it can be exercised by turning in the shares and collecting an option profit.

*Anticipating capital receipts:* Purchase of a call makes possible the immediate purchase at their current price of shares for which funds for their payment will not be available for some time ahead but before expiry of the option.

*Overall views* on commodity or currency movements can be covered by puts or calls on the shares of companies directly interested. For instance, LASMO, British Petroleum and Shell provide a view on the course of oil prices, while Consolidated Gold Fields and Rio Tinto-Zinc cover rare and base metals.

Changes in the political situation in South Africa, together with movements in the Rand and the gold price, can be covered through local shares.

Otherwise, individual tactics can vary widely. At one end can be a low price 'snatch' purchase for a few pence of a call or put with only a few days to go to expiry date in the hope that something will turn up to avoid a complete loss. At the other end can be a long run of up to six or nine months to cover various happenings such as final or interim profit announcements, takeover chances and overall market movements, at, of course, much higher cost. In between, say 10 to 15 weeks 'time' can cover quite a few eventualities, particularly in volatile markets, for a smaller outlay.


The following summary of some of the technical terms used in this new market may help to a closer understanding of what it offers. The examples relate to 'call' options, and for 'puts' some of the terms operate in reverse: i.e., a put option is 'in the money' when the share price falls *below* the exercise price.

*Call:* An option to buy shares at a fixed price.

*Put:* An option to sell shares at a fixed price.

*Class:* All the options (with different exercise prices and expiry dates) on the shares of a particular company.

*Series:* All options within a class with the same exercise prices and expiry dates.

*Margin:* The collateral in cash or in certain specified recurities to be put up by a writer.

*Writer:* An investor who executes an opening sale of an option contract.

*Underlying shares:* The shares to which the option relates.

*Premium:* The price of an option.

*Exercise (striking) price:* The price at which the underlying share can be bought under the contract terms.

*Exercise notice:* A formal notification by a holder of a call option to buy (take-up) the underlying shares at the exercise price.

*Expiry date:* The latest date on which the option holder can exercise the right to buy the underlying shares.

*Abandonment:* Allowing an option to expire unexercised.

*Intrinsic value:* The difference between the price of the underlying shares and the exercise price when the latter is below the present price of the shares.

*Time value:* The value attached to options reflecting the difference in time between the present date and the expiry date.

*In-the-money:* When the exercise price of a series of options is below the current price of the underlying shares.

*Out-of-the-money:* When the exercise price of a series is above the current price of the underlying shares.

*At-the-money:* An option whose exercise price is approximately the same as the current market price of the underlying shares.

*Naked buyer:* A buyer who buys call or put options on securities not owned.

# 6

# Paper work is important

Once a bargain has been struck the paper work begins to flow. First is a *contract note* with the details depending as from 27 October 1986 on whether the transaction is a 'single' or 'dual' capacity deal and the unrestricted commission scales of individual brokers. The latter will depend, perhaps, on factors such as the size of each bargain, a customer's overall volume of business, the striking of individual broker's scales and the possibility that provincial firms with their generally lower operating costs could be in a better position to compete with London firms. The following example sticks to the pre-Big Bang official minimum scale, which many broker firms have broadly stuck to for private client deals of up to say, £50,000–£100,000.

Contract notes come in various forms and sizes. The details are, however, the same. After an introductory 'Bought (or sold) by order of . . .' or 'In accordance with your instructions we have bought (or sold) . . .' a *bought* note for 1,000 BZM Industrial will show:

|  |  | 27 January 1988 |
|---|---|---|
| (1) | 1,000 BZM Industrial plc | |
| | 25p ordinary shares @ 150p | £1,500.00 |
| (2) | Transfer stamp @ 0.5% | 7.50 |
| (3) | Commission @ 1.65% | 24.75 |
| (4) | VAT @ 15% | 3.71 |
| (5) | Contract levy | 0.80 |
| | | £1,536.76 |
| (6) | For settlement 15 February 1988 | |
| (7) | Time: 10.05 a.m. | |

This is for a single capacity (gross) purchase. For a dual capacity (net) purchase at the same price the details would be:

| (1) | 1,000 BZM Industrial plc | |
|---|---|---|
| | 25p ordinary shares @ 150p | £1,500.00 |
| (2) | Transfer stamp @ 0.5% | 7.50 |
| | | £1,507.50 |

Probably, if no brokerage is payable, the price would be higher, say, 152p.

A basic part of investment dealing is to know what the different items mean. They are:

(1) the *consideration* of £1,500 payable to the market maker for the shares bought from him.

(2) the government *transfer stamp duty* levied on most share *purchases* is currently 0.5 per cent. No duty is payable on gilt-edged, corporation and similar stocks; debentures and loan stocks; allotment letters for a rights issue or scrip issue; bearer securities; and US, Canadian and other overseas domiciled stocks and shares which are not on a UK register. *Convertible loan stocks are, however, liable to duty*.

(3) *commission* (brokerage) payable for the broker's services. Rates are theoretically negotiable; but for the average private investor the pre-Big Bang minimum scale is still largely applicable; and depends on the (a) type of security and (b) consideration. A typical scale is: *gilts* and similar stocks: 1 per cent on the first £2,500 consideration, 0.5 per cent on the next £5,000, 0.3 per cent on the next £12,500 and down to 0.05 per cent on over £100,000, plus by negotiation when the total exceeds £500,000; for *shares* 1.65 per cent on the first £7,000, 0.5 per cent on the next £18,000, 0.4 per cent on the next £50,000, 0.3 per cent on the next £175,000 and by negotiation over £250,000. All rates are subject to minimum charges which can vary from around £10 to £15 by 'no frills' dealing only discount brokers, to £15 to £30 or more for a full service. Where commission is shared with banks and other agencies rates may be more than on direct business through a broker member. Banks may also charge a handling fee of £5 or so per transaction.

(4) VAT at the current rate on the commission.

(5) Contract levy was payable on each UK share bargain over £1,000 as a contribution towards the expenses of the Takeover Panel (30p), and the Stock Exchange Securities Association and Securities and Investment Board (50p). The levy was abolished in August 1988 and will therefore not appear as a charge on future deals.

(6) the date when payment is due to or from the broker. It may be for the Account or for Cash.

(7) all contracts now give the time of doing the bargain as a check on its having been carried out on a 'best deal' basis at the particular time.

A fundamental point about this bought transaction is that the shares have cost not 150p each, or £1,500, but £1,536.76 divided by 1,000. The all-in cost is approximately 153½p. *A profit is not in sight until they rise to over this figure*.

Another important point is that the contract note should be safely kept. It will be needed for capital gains tax purposes if the shares are later sold at a profit or loss.

The next job is getting the physical possession of the shares from the seller to the buyer. Apart from providing your full names and address if you are a new client, this is the broker's task. The rare exception is a foreign company, such as one based in Hong Kong, where the buyer has to sign a transfer form.

## TALISMAN

Transfer of the greatest bulk of UK registered and listed company securities from seller to buyer has been simplified and considerably speeded up since 1979 by the introduction by the Stock Exchange of the Talisman system which applies to virtually all but gilt-edged stocks and new issues. Instead of passing along a sometimes winding pathway between market makers and brokers, shares sold now go into a pool from which shares bought flow out. Initially, all bargains are reported to a Centre computer system by both market makers and brokers, and the details are retained there to provide the information for future settlement. The basis for Talisman (Transfer Accounting Lodgement for Investors, Stock MANagement for Jobbers) is the registration of sold stocks into a Stock Exchange nominee company — SEPON Limited (Stock Exchange Pool Nominees) — to create a single holding of each issue and the subsequent transfer out to cover all individual bought bargains.

On the sold side, the broker sends a Talisman sold transfer to the seller for signature. On its return, he passes it, together with the share certificate(s), to the Centre where both are checked for good delivery for forwarding to the company's registrar for registration into a Sepon account. On account (settlement) day the stock is transferred to the market makers trading account and is then allocated to his various sold bargains in the 'shapes' (quantities) in which they were dealt, by a process of apportionment.

A major benefit of Talisman is that it smooths out peak periods of work for member firms, banks, institutions and registrars by allowing sold stock to be deposited at the Stock Exchange before account day. Any risks of fraud or misappropriation which existed under the old system of institutions signing blank transfers disappears. Sold transfers have SEPON Limited preprinted on them as the transferee. Registrars will reject any forms for Stock Exchange transactions not received direct from the Centre or on which the Sepon name has been altered.

On the bought side, the broker submits registration details — company name, number and type of security bought; and full names and address of the buyer(s) — to the Centre prior to account day. If there is any delay in submission of details, registration is made into a standby nominee name supplied for this purpose by the buying broker, who, when it becomes possible to complete the work, transfers the security from the nominee account into the correct registration name.

Clients wanting evidence that stock has been apportioned can ask for a *stock note* which gives the identical information as on the Talisman bought transfer. This identifies the bargain, specifies the registration details and, most important, contains an undertaking by the Stock Exchange that stock has been apportioned and is in process of registration. Once apportionment has taken place the stock is held to the order of individual buyers and bought transfers authorising removal from the Sepon account into the name of the buyers is prepared and lodged for registration. In due course, a new share certificate in the name of the buyer(s) is issued by the registrar through the Centre.

While transfers into Sepon are exempt from stamp duty transfers out are subject to the appropriate rate and this is collected centrally on behalf of the share buyer for passing on to the Inland Revenue.

Talisman irons out problems of dividends and rights accruing during the transfer period through its ability to allocate these to investors entitled to them from the details of bargains held at the Centre. Dividends on shares bought 'cum' received on the Sepon holdings are credited to the buying broker for passing on to his client who gets a certificate showing the necessary tax details. This means that, unless there has been a registration hold-up, sellers of shares 'cum dividend' do not receive the distribution direct and then have to pass it on through their brokers to the buyer. Capitalisation and other distributions received by Sepon are also passed on to buyers entitled to them.

To sum up the benefits for investors, Talisman:

* Reduces delays in receiving share certificates and any 'cum' dividends due.
* Reduces claims from a seller for dividends or other entitlements paid or sent to him but due to the buyer.
* Reduces time lags resulting from buyers being linked to dilatory sellers, through the apportionment process which allocates transfers on a date order basis.
* Results generally in buyers receiving a single share certificate in contrast to two or more which could dribble in under the old transfer system.

Rightly, the Stock Exchange claims that Talisman has provided a sound, workable introduction to further improvements to the settlement system both nationally and internationally.

Though Talisman has brought its various benefits, recording in company registers of purchases in the names of individual investors is unchanged. Each investor has an account which records purchases and sales and the balance owned. On receipt of a transfer, the seller's account is debited with the amount sold and a new, or existing, account for the buyer is credited. A certificate is then prepared for the buyer. A holder selling only part of his shares gets a new certificate for the balance. New certificates are sent to brokers, banks or other agents for passing on to their clients.

Plans are in hand, however, to develop an automatic system — TAURUS (Transfer and Automated Registration of Uncertifiated Stock) — doing away with certificates by means of direct computer registration of individual shareholders and so eliminating the present transfer system. Registrars will keep separate accounts for each investor who will get directly annual and other reports, dividends or interest and all other material, as under the present system.

Following extension to settlement of South African-registered shares, a Talisman system has been set up to simplify the holding and transfer of Australian, US and Canadian-registered securities. The basic benefit is the immobilisation of physical stock in the country of origin and its holding in safe custody on behalf of the UK investor whose interest is recorded in 'stock accounts' within the Stock Exchange computer system.

******

Handling of interest and dividend cheques can be simplified by completing *dividend mandates* supplied by the broker. They authorise registrars to pay distributions direct into specified bank accounts. The 'voucher' giving details of the payment is sent to the bank for eventual passing on to the investor. Many companies and borrowers encourage the use of mandates, which save loss and postage.

**SELLING**

Selling calls for a little more effort. The broker must be given crystal clear instructions on what is to be sold. Some company names are similar. A scrip or rights issue may have increased a holding. There is a notable difference between ordinary and A ordinary shares. If in the slightest doubt, check first with the certificate(s) which in any case will have to be sent to the broker. This is in fact a very pertinent reason for keeping accurate and up-to-date records of all share certificates and their location. They may be in the deed box at home (or the bank), held by the bank, or held elsewhere. It is simplicity itself if they are held by the broker in certificate form or in nominee names – he will do the delivering.

The first paper step after the sale is the contract note. Suppose the 1,000 BZM Industrial bought on 27 January at 150p are sold for 175p before the end of the account on Friday, 5 February. Such good fortune means that the two deals cancel out and no shares have to change hands. No further brokerage is payable, as bargains *closed* in an account attract commission on the initial transactions only. But under the 1986 Budget rule transfer stamp is still payable as already charged (a concealed tax!). The sold contract note would simply show the sale consideration of £1,750.00. The profit of £213.24 (£1,750.00 *less* cost of £1,536.76) would be due from the broker on settlement (pay) day of 15 February.

If, however, the sale was not made until 30 December 1988 at, say, 200p further brokerage would be payable and the contract note would show:

|  |  |  |
|---|---:|---:|
|  |  | 30 December 1988 |
| 1,000 BZM Industrial plc |  |  |
| 25p ordinary shares @ 200p |  | £2,000.00 |
| *Less:* Commission @ 1.65% | 33.00 |  |
| VAT @ 15% | 4.95 |  |
|  |  | £1,962.05 |

For settlement 23 January 1989.
Time: 11.42 a.m.

The net price realised was thus 196p a share and the profit was £425.29 (£1,926.05 *less* £1,536.76 cost) or 42½p a share. The contract should be kept for capital gains tax computations.

Although the account in which the sale was made ends on 13 January 1989 settlement is not due until the 'pay day' of 23 January. But before the broker can send a cheque he must have (a) the signed transfer form sent with the contract note and (b) the relative certificate(s). *Prompt attention to these details is essential if payment is to be received on time.* Failure to act will hold up payment.

If another investment is bought in the same account as a sale is made only the balance due to or by the broker will have to be settled. It is still essential, however, to complete the transfer details promptly.

## PAPER POINTS

Misunderstandings and tempers can be saved by giving clear-cut buying and selling instructions. Telephone orders should be repeated.

* Be sure about the security — name, type and amount — before giving an order.
* Keep the evidence of ownership — the certificates — in a safe place, at the bank or in a locked deed box. It is a tedious business to get lost certificates replaced.
* Sign and return all documents promptly.
* Joint accounts need signatures of *all* holders on transfers and other documents.
* Send certificates with a selling order or as soon as possible thereafter. Certificates lodged with a bank will be sent direct to the broker on giving the bank written instructions.
* Delay in completing sales formalities can hold up payment.
* When in doubt, ask — promptly. A broker or bank will know the answer. Delays, particularly with rights issues, can be costly.
* Unless quoted 'ex' when selling securities, be ready to hand over interest, dividends or rights received subsequently.
* Notify registrars immediately of changes of address. And sign printed notifications.
* Delivery of overseas registered securities can be simplified on subsequent sales by having them registered in broker's, bank's or other recognised *marking names,* who will pass on dividends, etc. Direct receipt of annual reports and all other communications to shareholders can easily be arranged by notifying the company registrars of your full name and address.
* Don't worry if securities are sold before receiving a certificate. Stock Exchange machinery looks after this. Once bought, stocks and shares can be sold at any time from a minute later to years ahead.

# 7

# Gilts with an edge

Gilt-edged stocks got their name because of their security. The gilt began to wear rather thin, however, when interest rates started to rise in the 1950s and it began to tarnish as inflation increasingly became a devastating way of financial life. Over the past thirty years or so, market prices of the older issues have at times dropped by up to 75 per cent or more; yields and interest rates on new stocks once soared from low single figures to 16 per cent and upwards; and real values of capital and interest have declined at a one-time unbelievable pace.

The reasons for a national debt and its growth partly explain the traumatic trends of recent years. Wars and the financial difficulties of kings were the basis. Though various expedients had been used in earlier days, the start of regularised government borrowing was in 1692 when £1 million was raised to help pay for the Grand Alliance and Spanish Succession wars. There was a leap during the Napoleonic wars and, with some ups and downs, the total was some £650 million by 1914. By 1919 the total was around £8 billion, near which level it stayed until 1939.

The scope of the debt was enlarged after 1945. The central government took on the job of raising part of the money for local authorities, the nationalised industries and other capital projects. New debt became partly or wholly recycled: it was lent on to other borrowers who had to pay appropriate interest and to provide for repayment of their loans. A significant feature of these capital-creating operations was that over the 21 years to March 1972, only *one-third* of the £19.7 billion total lent to other bodies was financed by increases in the national debt. The balance of over £13.1 billion came from surpluses of tax and other ordinary income over Budget expenditure.

It is pertinent to note here that sales of nationalised industries and writing off advances to lame ducks have greatly reduced assets held against debt; and further reductions will follow as privatisation ploughs ahead. There are, however, still a number of valuable assets 'on' or 'off' the books, amongst the latter being extensive state-owned properties acquired at prices well below current values. The problem is to get even an approximate indication of their extent and value – and their relation to the outstanding debt. That is a powerful reason to have an inventory of *all* the state owned assets. In simple words, what is the asset backing for the national debt — 100p in the £, 50p or 150p?

The economic and financial rot set in in 1973. The Heath government put light to the inflationary flame with an expansionist policy which touched off a borrowing boom that led to the subsequent property and secondary banking crashes. The Wilson and Callaghan governments fanned the blaze. The debt soared from around £37 billion in 1973 to £87 billion by March 1979 and then, despite protestations of trying to restrain new borrowing by the Thatcher government, to an estimated £190 billion nine years later; and this despite the receipt of billions from denationalisation sales.

Deficit financing, as this is called, is favoured by some economists and politicians as a way to stimulate business and curb unemployment. In hard terms, as seen in recent years, it is a financially unsound way to keep a government in being by means of money-wasting schemes and loss of, or not sufficient, control on spending. One school of thought considers that, with rare and strictly limited exceptions, financially wise and prudent governments should budget to cover ordinary expenditure by ordinary tax and other revenues, and even to show a reasonable surplus.

Borrowing should in fact be limited to finance for productive assets like the profitable nationalised industries now being sold off. Equally, capital receipts from asset sales should be applied to debt redemption, not used to cover up Budget ordinary deficits. The Treasury Mandarins and recent Chancellors of the Exchequer have, however, their own ideas on sound book-keeping and ways of papering over their financial sophism. A recent example explains. To loud trumpetings the 1988/89 Budget boasted a possible surplus of £2 billion for debt reduction. But this was only after setting off against normal expenditure £5 billion proceeds from privatisation sales. And, a figure tucked away as an offset to debt interest which does not attract public attention, are profits on the note issue which in recent years have averaged around £1 billion a year. Such profits are surely capital windfalls which could become deficits in persistent deflationary periods! So, in prudent financial terms, the 1988/89 *estimate* becomes a deficit of £4 billion (£5 billion + £1 billion − £2 billion)!

Some three-quarters of the national debt is in a variety of marketable securities dealt in on the Stock Exchange. The balance is mostly National Savings — savings certificates, premium bonds, savings banks deposits, savings bonds, index-linked bonds and Save-As-You-Earn plans — and the 'Floating Debt' as represented by short-term borrowing on Treasury Bills and Ways and Means advances. There are also debts due to the International Monetary Fund and to the United States and other overseas governments and lenders.

Although of limited interest to private investors, it is noteworthy that Treasury Bills have uses for short-term investment. Offered for tender each Friday, bills run for 91 days with the interest represented by the discount at which they are sold. The minimum tender is £50,000, though the denomination of bills is from as little as £5,000 upwards. This is very much a specialist form of investment which is dominated by the money market.

Private investor interest, National Savings apart, is concentrated almost entirely on the quoted sector — gilt-edged stocks. These are divided into two broad groups: redeemable and irredeemable, or dated and undated. These are in turn split into four market categories.
*     Shorts with lives of up to 5 years.
*     Mediums with lives of 5 to 15 years.
*     Longs with lives of over 15 years.
*     Undated with no repayment dates.
All stocks have fixed interest rates and one of their attractions is the variety of choice offered.

Gilts are normally quoted in thirty-two seconds (called the *tick*) of a £, such as 96-12, the 12 being the tick, to make a price of £96.375 (or £96⅜). In big deals the tick may be narrowed to one-sixty fourth or only 1.56p.

Two factors decide the choice of investment — yield and repayment date. Yield can be (a) flat (or running); or (b) redemption.

*Flat yield* is the simple calculation of multiplying the interest rate (or coupon) by 100 and dividing by the price. For example, the flat yield on an 8 per cent stock bought at £91½ per £100 of stock is:

$$\frac{8 \times 100}{91.5} = 8.743\%$$

or in round figures, 8¾ per cent.

In February 1986 the long-standing custom of including accrued interest in the price was ended. Now, the accrual is shown on the contract note as a separate item; it is *added* to both purchases and sales of gilts when dealt in *cum* interest and *deducted* when they are *ex* interest. For instance, if £2,000 of the above stock was bought when 58 days' interest had accrued, the contract note would show:

| | |
|---|---|
| £2,000 8% Treasury stock | |
| 2002/06 @ 91½ | £1,830.00 |
| *Plus* 58 days accrued | |
| interest | 25.42 |
| | £1,855.42 |

Similarly, if it had been sold at £91 the proceeds, also before brokerage, would be £1,820.00 plus £25.42, to equal £1,845.42. Interest factors to note are:

* Buyers are 'buying' their portion of interest accrued since the last half yearly payment. Sellers are receiving it for their period of ownership.
* As gilt bargains are for cash settlement within forty eight hours, two days' interest is added to the transaction date for calculating the accrual.
* The interest accrued is gross and has to be accounted for in annual tax returns.

*Redemption yield* takes account of the capital gain or loss on stocks bought below or above the repayment price, usually par; and where there are alternative dates on the last one. This complicated calculation is done by computer. Taking the same 8 per cent stock the gain of £8.50 per cent is spread over the maximum life to 2006 and the yield is increased to 8.909 per cent. Stocks bought above par do of course end up in capital losses on repayment and the redemption yield is lower than the flat return. For example, 12½ per cent Treasury stock 2003/05 bought at £129 would yield 9.690 per cent flat but only 9.139 per cent redemption after taking account of the £29 capital loss by 2005.

Normal market influences such as economic, trade and political factors apart, the general trend-setter for gilt-edged prices and yields is redemption date. The shorter the date the lower the yield. Comparison of yields on similar, or nearly similar, couponed stocks gives an idea of this life influence. The first example covers four 3 per cent stocks:

| Life | | Yield% | |
| Yrs. | Mths. | Flat | Redemption |
|---|---|---|---|
| 1 | 2 | 3.115 | 6.280 |
| 3 | 2 | 3.373 | 6.938 |
| 7 | 2 | 3.631 | 6.029 |
| undated | | 9.180 | — |

The lower yield on the 7:2 year stock reflects its attraction for capital gains tax-payers.

A second example covers three 10 per cent redeemable stocks all standing above par:

| Life | | Yield% | |
| Yrs. | Mths. | Flat | Redemption |
|---|---|---|---|
| 1 | 5 | 9.883 | 9.073 |
| 6 | 3 | 9.610 | 9.124 |
| 14 | 1 | 9.428 | 9.226 |

The coupon range is wide. At one end is $2\frac{1}{2}$ per cent Consolidated Stock — known as 'Consols' — the oldest issue which goes back to the last century and which at one time was the sheet anchor of safe investment. At the other end is $15\frac{1}{2}$ per cent Treasury Stock 1998 which was issued in October 1976 when Britain's post-war finances were at an ignominious low.

While flat yields can vary widely there are not the same differentials in redemption yields, particularly in stocks with lives of ten years and over. This is due to the liking of pension fund and other institutional investors for overall returns on their funds, with not too close an emphasis on either the income or the capital element.

The mavericks are the low coupon stocks such as $5\frac{3}{4}$ per cent Funding 1987/91 and British Gas 3 per cent 1990/95 the market prices of which are notably below repayment levels. They appeal to high-rate taxpayers because of the low income yield (liable to income tax) and the capital gains (exempt from tax) on redemption.

The tax free capital gains aspect is sometimes catered for when a new stock is launched. There have been several issues of low coupon stocks at substantial discounts to give low income-taxed interest but useful capital profits if held to redemption. For instance, a 3 per cent Treasury stock 1986 was offered at a minimum tender price of £$69\frac{1}{2}$ in March 1981 to give a flat yield of only some 4.3 per cent but a capital gain of a maximum £$30\frac{1}{2}$ per cent by repayment date at par on 19 May 1986.

A newer, unconventional type of stock is the *index-linked* launched in May 1981. Designed initially to try to meet some of the inflationary problems of pension funds, life assurance offices and friendly societies with long-term pension commitments, it is, as its name implies, linked to the retail price index (RPI). The initial issue of £1 billion Treasury Stock 1996 pays only 2 per cent initial interest, but this is upvalued in line with increases in the RPI, as is the redemption value of the capital sum. In other words, to an initial buyer at par the stock yields a 'real' 2 per cent after allowing for inflation. Other issues followed; but investor interest in ILs began to flag when inflation fell to around the 5/6 per cent level and conventional gilts became more attractive. However, in March 1984 the authorities gave in to market pressures and a fresh start was made with the flotation of another 2 per cent stock sold at £88$\frac{1}{2}$. But as before, popularity has continued to ebb and flow with the authorities responding to bouts of demand with up-lifted coupons of 2$\frac{1}{2}$ per cent and lives (at the time of writing) extending to 2024.

Another out-of-the-ordinary issue, in January 1981, was the 12 per cent Exchequer Stock 1985. The attraction for investors wanting hedges on the future trend of interest rates was that from September 1981 to September 1983 it was convertible at six-monthly intervals into 13$\frac{1}{2}$ per cent Exchequer Stock 1992 at reducing percentages per £100 of the convertible. For instance, whereas the conversion rate on 22 September 1981 was 99 per cent of the 13$\frac{1}{2}$ per cent, the ratio declined half-yearly down to 95 per cent in March 1983 and to a final figure of only 92 per cent in September 1983. Similar type issues with lower interest rates have followed.

In another category of unconventional operations, first launched in December 1980, tranches of existing gilt issues are taken up by the Bank of England, which then makes stock available to meet market demands at prices aimed to avoid runaways and to minimise upsets in the interest rate structure.

One government issue which calls for special attention is 3$\frac{1}{2}$ per cent Conversion Stock. In the simpler financial days when governments strove for balanced budgets some gilt-edged stocks were repayable by means of sinking funds. A percentage or fixed annual sum had to be provided in the expenditure estimates for purchases in the market or repayment of certain stocks. The only remaining sinking fund stock is 3$\frac{1}{2}$ per cent Conversion. When its average price over a period of six months is below 90, the equivalent of one per cent of the amount outstanding has to be applied in the following six months to buy in stock. It is a long time since the 90 level was exceeded. The sinking fund has in fact been at work since 1952 and the stock outstanding had fallen from £739 million then to around £143 million by 1988.

Naturally, as the amount is based on the Conversion Stock outstanding at each half-year end, the sinking fund cash is falling and so is the stock bought in. Despite this decreasing influence, the impact on the dwindling amount outstanding must be to push up the price, a point which the market took some time to appreciate. It does, however, explain why the yield is less than its apparent equivalent, 3$\frac{1}{2}$ per cent War Loan. Conversion Stock is a dated issue without a date which should of its own volition march steadily towards its non-sinking fund level of 90.

Timing of new issues in the gilt-edged market depends on several factors. The government may need money to cover a shortfall between ordinary revenue and expenditure which it may not be politic to finance by means of Treasury Bills or other short-term borrowing. Existing stocks fall due for repayment and have to be replaced wholly or in part by new borrowing — holders of the old stocks may then be offered conversion into new ones on straight exchange terms or with a sweetener of say £102 of the new for £100 of the old. Money may be required to lend on as loans to local authorities, the nationalised industries or some other project. Or, as has happened in recent years, it may be deliberate policy to meet ordinary expenditure deficits by borrowing instead of by taxation.

In fact, the public sector borrowing requirement (PSBR) as it is known, required funding of up to £14 billion a year in recent times and stock issues came thick, fast and big until the mid 1980s.

A potent consideration particularly prominent in recent times is the use of new issues to control the money supply. Short-term funds pile up in the money market and, unless there is some control, credit increases and with it inflation as too much money 'chases too few goods. Government stock issues thus convert what may be described as too much 'spending money' into loans for various periods of years. Banks, pension funds, life assurance offices and other financial institutions want on the other hand to invest some of their resources for future commitments which may be for very short periods or some tens of years ahead. New gilt-edged stocks are tailored to meet such needs — always, of course, with an eye being kept open so that repayment dates do not get bunched up into short periods.

A brief prospectus opens a new issue. It states the amount offered, the interest rate, the repayment date or dates and the issue price. Anyone can apply for any amount of stock in multiples of at least £100. As it was rare — at least, until recently — for an entire issue to be publicly subscribed immediately, the 'Departments' take up the balance. The latter include the Issue Department of the Bank of England, the National Debt Commissioners acting for the National Savings Bank and government departments with funds in hand. The portion so taken up then becomes what is known as a 'tap' issue which the Bank sells in the market as buyers come in ready to pay the 'tap' price. The latter is adjusted to market conditions or to suit monetary policies. The tap is turned on and off as considered desirable.

New issues of gilt-edged stocks can be made in three different ways:

* At a fixed price, with payment due in full in one amount. For example, if the issue price is £97 per cent, this amount is payable on application.
* At a fixed price, with payment being made by two or three instalments. For instance, a new stock offered at £95 per cent may be payable as to £30 per cent on application and the balance of £65 per cent some six or seven weeks later; or it might be £15 per cent on application, £40 per cent 18 days later and the balance of £40 per cent one month after that.
* By the much newer method of tender at a minimum price and with payment by two or three instalments or in full on application. If such an issue is undersubscribed the stock is allotted at the minimum price, with the Bank of England taking up the balance at the same price. But if the issue is oversubscribed all allotments are made at the lowest price at which any tender is accepted, with tenders at prices above the allotment price being allotted in full. For example, if the minimum price is £97$\frac{1}{2}$ per cent and there is an undersubscription, all applicants tendering this price or more will get allotments at this figure; but if there is an oversubscription and the lowest accepted tender is at £98 per cent, all stock will be allotted to successful applicants at £98 per cent. This type of issue was adopted following a serious embarrassment in February 1979 when, due to a sudden rise in gilt-edged stocks generally, there was a rush for two 'old-

style' issues which very swiftly rose to a substantial premium on the start of dealings.

* By auction, first successfully launched in May 1987. No minimum price is set by the Bank which expects to sell the whole of each offer at prices decided by the market (the bidders) which it does or what it considers to be the going rate.

Repayment dates, as already mentioned, vary widely. When there is only one date, such as 1994, there is no doubt as to the life of the stock. But where there are two dates, such as 1992/96, repayment will largely depend on the level of interest rates. If the coupon is, say, 9 per cent and 10 per cent would have to be paid on a replacement stock issued before 1996, the issue will run up to the last date. But if a replacement would cost only 8 per cent interest, repayment would be made at the earliest date. As redemption yields are normally calculated on last dates, earlier repayment increases the overall return on stocks bought below par.

Various factors affect market prices of gilt-edged stocks. Normal supply and demand effects apart, the most important influence for some time has been the degree of confidence in the existing and future economic outlook for Britain. If it is bleak, interest rates rise and stock prices fall. If it is good or thought to be promising, rates fall and prices rise.

Money rates in the US and other countries have been a notable factor in recent times. Gilt prices can move sharply in line with foreign rates, particularly those charged by American banks. A lot of 'hot' money swirls round the world to take advantage of changing interest rates and movements in and out of the UK have their impact on our own money and gilt markets.

Confidence is affected mostly by political changes and policies; whether our overseas trade (the important balance of payments) is running in surplus or deficit and whether the trend is up or down; changes in the value of the pound sterling against strong currencies such as the Japanese yen and the German D-mark; strikes and other domestic troubles; the trend of industrial production which should rise by at least 3 to 4 per cent a year to be of real value; the pace of inflation and the success or failure of attempts to get to grips with this damaging economic trouble-maker; and movements in short-term interest rates as money is 'tight' or 'easy'.

Although government and nationalised industries' stocks are the core of the gilt-edged market, there are other borrowers whose security is just as good, or almost as good. Cities, towns and county councils have always been borrowers through the medium of the stock market. Their quoted securities take two forms: stock issues, and short-term bonds with lives of one to five years.

Public offerings of blocks of stock — £1 million or upwards — were once a common means of finance for them. The trend since 1946 has, however, been to borrow from the government through the National Loans Fund, and by a 'tap' type of bond issue and short-term loans. Efforts to revive public stock issues have been spasmodic and short-lived. Most of both the old and new stocks have short to medium term lives with coupons ranging from low single rates to $13\frac{1}{2}$ per cent. Relics of the really cheap money days are some $2\frac{1}{2}$ per cent and 3 per cent undated issues of London and a few other cities.

*Bonds* are issued each Tuesday in batches on behalf of a number of councils at a common interest rate but in the names of individual borrowers. Greatest in number are one-year bonds, or *yearlings* as they are called, with individual councils taking anything from £250,000 upwards. Weekly offerings are under the control of the Treasury and Bank of England. Interest is based on current money market conditions; in very dear money days rates went over 17 per cent but are currently around 9 per cent to 10 per cent. Similar offerings are made of two, three, four and five-year bonds at correspondingly higher interest rates which are fixed for the whole term.

Dealings in yearling and other bonds are in minimum amounts of £1,000, with prices reflecting current interest yields and the unexpired terms. Local authorities also borrow direct from investors ready to lend on short-term mortgage bonds or on deposits for seven days or longer.

Issues of Public Boards and special finance companies set up with government approval have a kinship with corporation stocks. Their servicing may be well assured. Again, there are dated and undated stocks and bonds. Participants range from the Agricultural Mortgage Corporation to port authorities like the profitable Clyde and Forth, and the Metropolitan Water Board. Some issues are very small with infrequent dealings, and patience is needed to buy more than small amounts. Yields are generally, however, greater than on corresponding government stocks so that it can pay to dig around this market.

Although the 'old' division of the Commonwealth government, provincial and local authority sector of the gilts market is little more than a ghost of its one-time importance, it has had a revival through the issue of Bulldog sterling loans by Australia, Malaysia, New Zealand and Trinidad and Tobago. Several Rhodesia loans resulting from UDI settlement are amongst the old-timers. Bulldog loans of several foreign governments, as detailed in chapter 8, are also dealt in.

## GILTS GUIDE

Relative to other stocks and shares, gilts can be classified as safety first investments, that is so far as there can be any safety while inflation and other confidence destroyers could again hit interest rates and values for six — at any time. Points worthy of summarisation are:
* Choice of redemption dates is wide — from a few months to over 30 years.
* Government stocks are easy to buy and sell at close prices.
* Dealing costs are low. There is no transfer duty as with shares.
* Up to £10,000 a day can be invested in any one stock at low cost through the Department of National Savings; otherwise there is no limit to the amounts of individual stocks which can be held. Interest on stocks on this register is paid without deduction of income tax; which saves tax-exempt investors making repayment claims. Application forms are obtainable at main post offices.
* No capital gains tax is payable on profits from sale or redemption. Nor is there any relief on losses.
* Undated stocks, of which $3\frac{1}{2}$ per cent War Loan, $2\frac{1}{2}$ per cent Treasury, $2\frac{1}{2}$ per cent and 4 per cent Consolidated, $3\frac{1}{2}$ per cent Conversion and 3 per cent Treasury are the main issues, have the speculative attraction that one day a beneficent government may give them a date. Meantime, $3\frac{1}{2}$ per cent Conversion has a 'date' through its sinking fund.
* Gilt-edged funds run by some discount houses and unit trusts are a means for the uninitiated investor to operate in a highly sophisticated market. In

view of some recent problems, care is needed in selecting a soundly run and managed fund.

* Corporation stocks generally offer better yields than government issues. But the steady demand by the institutions tends to limit market supplies. It may, therefore, be easier to sell than to buy anything but small amounts of stock.

* Buyers of some Public Board stocks may need even more patience. But it can pay to wait for offers of stock. Yields can be up to two or more points better than on gilts.

* Interest on $3\frac{1}{2}$ per cent War Loan is paid without deduction of tax, which makes it a popular choice for non-taxpayers.

* Interest on some government issues is free of UK income tax to some overseas residents.

* Some gilt-edged stocks are available in bearer form, which is an attraction for foreign investors.

# 8

# Foreigners have a word for it

Foreign bonds divide very firmly into two sectors — the old and the new. There is a lot of difference between the two.

## OLD BONDS

These are mainly stocks issued by foreign governments and cities many years ago when Britain could provide them with finance out of world trade surpluses. Some, like Japan, have honoured their debts and, because they are redeemable at old rates of exchange, stand at substantial premiums. Some like Greece, have made funding deals which at least produce sterling income. Others, like China and Russia, have, however, been in total default for decades; their bonds are pure gambles that long deferred hopes of some settlement may come off — some day; though meantime some of the certificates have acquired value as collectors' items. Two exceptions to these groups are Ireland and Iceland which have post-war, fully serviced issues.

**'Bulldog' bonds** are the 1980s version of the old type of sterling foreign bonds issued in the UK. So far there have been two flotation methods. One is an issue at a fixed interest rate and fixed price. The second, and currently more accepted, method relates the interest rate or issue price to the yield on a UK gilt, or average of gilts, at a specific time on a specific day; plus a premium. For example, for a £75 million European Investment Bank issue the terms were based on a one per cent addition to the mean redemption yield on three comparable gilts, which came out as an 11 per cent coupon, £97.91 per cent price and gross redemption return of 11.27 per cent. Again, for a short term (1988) loan for Spain the interest was pre-fixed at 12 per cent with the issue price of £99.893 per cent based on only one UK gilt. Investors in 'bulldogs' have the choice of taking bearer bonds in multiples of, say, £1,000 or £10,000, or of registered stock transferable like UK gilts in multiples of as little as one penny. Such stocks are dealt in in the gilt-edged market at gilt commission rates.

## 'NEW' BONDS

A new form of international currency came into investment use in the late 1950s — Eurodollars. These are claims to US dollars owned outside the United States by companies, institutions and others. These dollars have grown over the years into a vast pool of money which has been lent by way of *Eurobonds* to a variety of borrowers of various nationalities. British borrowers include nationalised industries, local authorities, banks, insurance companies, and financial, industrial and other companies. Foreign participants range from provinces and cities to North American and European companies of wide variety. The early issues were denominated in US dollars. More recently, however, the currency mix has included deutschmarks, Swiss and French francs, Canadian dollars, Hong Kong dollars, Kuwait dinars and other currencies under the name of *Euro Units*. Euro-Yen issues are plentiful, while sterling-denominated loans feature in this dynamic and expanding market.

Issues are marketed by British, American, Swiss, German, French, Arabian, Japanese and other bankers, stockbrokers and financial agencies. Syndicates of banks, finance houses and stockbrokers are formed for each offering under the management of a *market leader* or leaders. Depending on the nature of the issue and the leader, the participants may be little more than a handful or may be several dozens. While a prospectus is the basis of the offer, the main public notification is an advertisement published after the issue has been subscribed, called a 'tombstone', which merely gives the name of the borrower, the amount and nature of the issue, and the participants. The latter can often read like a 'Debrett' list of world bankers and financial agencies as placers of the bonds amongst their clients and as holders themselves.

Subscription for Eurobonds is in the currency of issue. So also are the interest payments, which in the majority of issues means annually. Half-yearly (sometimes quarterly) interest payments are mostly confined to floating-rate note issues at rates usually fixed at a fractional percentage over what is known as the London Inter-Bank Offered Rate (LIBOR).

Eurobonds are not in the registered form usual with UK securities. They pass from hand to hand as bearer bonds. Interest is collected by cutting off coupons and presenting them to the paying agents in London or other specified centres.

Bonds have different lives. Some are repayable on one date; others have optional dates. Many are, however, redeemable by half-yearly or annual drawings. Lists of the serial numbers of drawn bonds are advertised and payment is made on presentation to the appropriate paying agent, usually a clearing or merchant bank. Fixed rate bonds are usually called *straights* ('bullets') to distinguish them from *floating rate notes* (FRNs). There is a useful sprinkling of *convertible bonds* which offer opportunities to move into the equity of the issuing company or, if it is part of an international group, into the shares of the parent company. Considerable ingenuity is in fact used by sponsors in tailoring issues to the particular needs of borrowers or to new forms of marketing.

There are also bonds with detachable *warrants* giving the right to buy shares in the issuing company at a fixed price and over a specified period. Issues of such bonds, usually pay a lower rate of interest as an offset to the 'spice' a warrant adds.

A number of Eurobond and other currency issues are listed on the Stock Exchange. A good deal of the turnover is, however, through what is termed a *secondary market* made up of banks, financial houses and stockbrokers spread over London, New York, Paris and other major centres. Each centre has *market makers* who are the principal traders in particular stocks and who make dealing prices.

## BOND POINTS

* 'Old' and Euro foreign bonds are a specialised market which needs careful study or expert advice.
* The market in most 'old' bonds is far from free. Sinking fund purchases make it virtually impossible to buy some issues.
* Occasional bursts of activity take place in Chinese, Russian and Bulgarian issues as gambles on possible recognition of bondholders' claims. Participation should be looked on as backing an outsider in the Grand National, unless the certificates are simply bought as collectors' items.
* Sophisticated UK investors are taking an increasing interest in Euro and similar bonds.
* Dollar-denominated Eurobonds can be a speculation on movements in the £ sterling against the dollar and other foreign currencies. Buy when the £ is strong; sell when it is weak.
* Eurobonds can be good investments for overseas residents.
* Convertibles are worth attention as (a) a currency hedge and (b) a safer way into overseas company equities.

# 9

# Figures matter

Profits, financial soundness, prospects and management are key considerations in the choice of any type of company investment. Ability to read and
interpret annual accounts and other financial statements are the starting point.

Despite the strenuous, sometimes frenetic, efforts of company boards to
simplify their annual reports the trend has unhappily been too much towards
over-simplification — confusion has become confounded. It may seem to be a
laudable objective to reduce a profits statement and balance sheet to the
smallest number of items and to push the details, often including key figures,
into a clutter of notes on following pages. The notes often however contain,
perhaps try to hide, facts essential to a reasoned assessment of results and
progress.

Also, although it may seem to be a trivial or minor criticism, reading some
company reports is made difficult and trying by the designer's fixation on
appearance in preference to utility by using inappropriate colour inks or
papers. It is difficult to read white ink figures on a light grey background or
black figures on dark blue paper. If colours are used, they must be strongly
contrasting. Type is also important. Many ageing shareholders have sight
problems which make it difficult to read fancy and small lettering; type faces
should be clear cut and easy to read. Equally, glossy paper gives off an
annoying glare when reading by electric light; matt paper is preferable.

Thought-provoking is the notable fact that some of the biggest, most
profitable and best managed UK companies produce the most informative,
straightforward, no-nonsense and least elaborate annual reports. Equally
thought-provoking is the tendency of some smaller, even relatively tiny
companies, sometimes struggling to survive, to go for expensive, picture-
laden, colour 'glossies' which give only the barest essential facts and figures.
For simplicity and informativeness it would be hard to find a better annual
report than that of Marks & Spencer, a leader in the elimination of frills in its
highly successful trading methods.

The aim in this chapter is to discuss the basic facts which should be clear in
annual accounts, or which should be extracted from them. The ways to use
such facts are dealt with in later chapters.

Two sets of figures are fundamental. Their content will depend partly on
whether a company trades solely on its own account or partly or wholly
through subsidiary companies. First is the *profit and loss account* which, when
applicable, is 'consolidated' to cover the trading results of the parent and its

subsidiaries. Second is the *balance sheet*, of which there will be two accounts — for the parent alone and a consolidated statement embracing the whole group. All three financial statements will give comparative figures for the previous year. Although the parent balance sheet should always be examined, particularly to note changes in the investment in subsidiaries, the much more important figures are the consolidated ones.

The consolidated accounts can come in two forms. One is the historical basis, which presents the figures as detailed in the company's books. The second, now very rarely seen following the decline in inflation, translates the historical data into figures which take account of inflation during the year. Each type of account should be drawn up on consistent bases year after year so that strict comparisons can be made; any changes in bases should be fully explained and, where feasible, comparative figures adjusted.

In days gone by when financial life was simpler and the stylists had not butted in, company accounts were two-sided. On one side of the profit and loss account (the right) income was set out in some detail and on the other side (the left) were charges against it such as interest on loan capital, depreciation, exceptional debits and taxation. The balance — the net profit — was carried down and set off against it were preference and ordinary dividends, transfers to reserves and the net balance added to (or deducted from) accumulated profits.

The balance sheet set out on the right-hand side the assets in adequate detail; it was fairly usual to show the gross cost of factories, plant, machinery and other fixed assets and to deduct accumulated depreciation. The left-hand side showed the sources of finance: the authorised and issued capital, accumulated reserves, loan capital, creditors in some detail, and special reserves for deferred taxation or some specific liability.

It could be argued that such detailed accounts were indigestible by reason of the quantity of figures. But they did give a straightforward summary of key figures which were there to see without having to turn to pages of notes for details. Though no brief is held for any North American superiority in accounting ability, it is a significant fact that some of the biggest United States and Canadian companies stick to the left–right form of balance sheet presentation.

The Companies Acts of 1981 and later years went a useful way to up-dating the form in which annual accounts should now be drawn up. This step, together with the accountancy bodies' Standard Accounting Practice recommendations, Stock Exchange Listing requirements, Statutory Instruments and EEC rules, is to be welcomed even though there must be reservations on the treatment of some items and the need for flexibility in individual application, particularly by companies which, by their nature, do not easily fit into standardised accounting moulds.

Almost all UK companies now use a tabular form, often condensing the facts too drastically. It is noted here that the drawing of attention to salient facts is most easily achieved by a 'highlights' table at the front of the report. However, as the task is to help towards an understanding of accounts, examples will be in tabular form and, though some are based on actual reports, they will be in round figures and take notice of the new requirements.

## PROFIT AND LOSS

Profitability being of prime importance, the first account to study is the *profit and loss statement*. This should show in reasonable detail the broad sources of income and expenditure, and how the profit (or loss) has been allocated. The type of basic statement that should be expected from enlightened companies which do not push too many essential figures into 'back page' notes is shown on page 53. A useful part of the account is the *statement of consolidated retained profits* which includes extraordinary income and expenditure which should not be part of the year's normal profit.

Features on the income part of the account are that in addition to its own trading profit, the group took in its £750,000 share of the profits of the associated companies in which it had a substantial equity interest; and received £250,000 from its trade and quoted general investments which, as shown later, stood in the balance sheet at a total of £1.5 million.

In the expenditure part, £1.3 million *depreciation* was provided to meet the using up of plant, machinery and other assets which eventually will have to be replaced by up-to-date equipment or scrapped as obsolescent. The imperative need to make adequate provision for replacement has been rammed home by the hyper-inflationary rise in cost in recent years, and is considered later.

*Directors' remuneration* is shown in the account as it must be disclosed somewhere, and what better place than the profit and loss account, though not all directors and accountants will agree? The interest cost of loan capital is self-explanatory as a charge against trading profit.

*Taxation* has long been a headache; with the actual rate, and so the charge, varying markedly between companies, even those in the same line of business. Main causes have been capital allowances of up to 100 per cent on expenditure on plant, machinery and buildings; stock appreciation allowances; foreign taxation; and disallowance of certain expenditure. The 1984 Budget brought, however, radical changes which should result in more even and rational annual tax charges, and consequently, in net profits. Stock relief was abolished and capital allowances reduced — on plant and machinery from 100 per cent to 75 per cent from March 1984, to 50 per cent from April 1985 and to nil from April 1986, with cuts on expenditure on industrial buildings to 50 per cent, to 25 per cent and to nil respectively. Compensatory reductions in main corporation tax were from 52 per cent to 50 per cent for the financial year 1983, to 45 per cent for 1984, to 40 per cent for 1985 and to 35 per cent for 1986 onwards. Put another way, there is a reversion to something like the old, well-used system of straight annual wear and tear allowances based on the cost of applicable fixed assets. (Our accounts example uses a 35 per cent corporation tax rate).

After providing £307,500 for the share of the minority interests in the net profits of subsidiary companies, £3,326,000 is left for shareholders. The two preference dividends take £126,000 and total dividends of 3p on the 40 million 25p ordinary shares absorb £1.2 million. This leaves a *surplus* of £2,000,000 million to be used for expansion.

*Extraordinary receipts and losses* can be a variety of items ranging from gains or deficits on sales of assets and profits on redemption of loan capital to foreign

## CONSOLIDATED PROFIT AND LOSS ACCOUNT

| | | |
|---|---:|---:|
| Turnover: | | £60,000,000 |
| *Less:* Cost of sales | £50,000,000 | |
| Distribution costs | 1,900,000 | |
| Administration | 1,500,000 | 53,400,000 |
| Trading profit: Group | | £6,600,000 |
| Associated companies | | 750,000 |
| Investment income | | 250,000 |
| | | £7,600,000 |
| *Less:* Depreciation | £1,300,000 | |
| Directors' fees, etc. | 300,000 | 1,600,000 |
| Profit before taxation and interest | | £6,000,000 |
| *Less:* Debenture interest | £210,000 | |
| Loan stock interest | 200,000 | 410,000 |
| | | £5,590,000 |
| *Less:* Taxation @ 35% | £1,956,500 | |
| Minority interests | 307,500 | 2,264,000 |
| AVAILABLE PROFIT | | £3,326,000 |
| *Less:* Preference dividends | | |
| 5.6% | £84,000 | |
| 4.2% | 42,000 | 126,000 |
| AVAILABLE ORDINARY SHARES | | £3,200,000 |
| *Less:* Ordinary dividends: | | |
| Interim 1p per share | £400,000 | |
| Final 2p per share | 800,000 | 1,200,000 |
| SURPLUS | | £2,000,000 |
| Extraordinary receipts (net) | | 300,000 |
| PROFIT RETAINED | | £2,300,000 |

STATEMENT OF CONSOLIDATED RETAINED PROFITS

| | |
|---|---:|
| Beginning of year-balance | £10,800,000 |
| Transfer from profit and loss account | 2,300,000 |
| Surplus on assets revaluation | 650,000 |
| Redundancy costs | (750,000) |
| At year end | £13,000,000 |
| Net earnings per ordinary share | 8.00p |
| Fully diluted earnings per ordinary share | 7.74p |
| Ordinary dividend (net) | 3.00p |

exchange adjustments and writing down goodwill and other intangible assets. Much argument has developed over the treatment of such abnormal non-trading gains and losses. One school claims that they should be part of the year's earnings and appear in the profit and loss account. Another claim, and one which is wholeheartedly supported, is that as fluctuating and probably non-recurring items they should be shown separately and not taken into the reckoning of distributable profits. By all means let them appear in the account; but clearly as distinct, separate items and in no way giving the illusion that they are normal gains or losses which will be repeated in future years. This treatment applies especially to any items described as *exceptional*, a term which surely indicates one-off profits or losses!

A conspicuous example in favour of putting non-normal, or ***extraordinary*** *items* below the line was thrown up in the 1980 figures of Tanks Consolidated Investments. Profits before taxation were shown as £12,279,185. But this included a net profit from exploration activities of no less than £10,747,594, made up of a very one-off surplus of £12,033,887 on the sale of part of an Australian diamond exploration activity, less losses of £1,286,293 on other ventures. In other words, the normal pre-tax profit was only £1,531,591 (£12,279,185 less £10,747,594) compared with a dividend payout of £2,518,250. If the whole of the £12,033,887 diamond profit was excluded pre-tax profits were only £245,298. Tanks directors were not responsible for this great distortion. They simply, if blindly, followed the incongruous rules which the auditors had no alternative but to accept.

Fluctuations in the external *value of sterling* can be another headache. A weak £ means that extra profits on sales in foreign currencies will be worth more in sterling terms — a strong deutschmark will, for instance, produce more pounds. But the reverse happens when the £ is strong. Exchange movements, of which there have been some substantial ones in recent years, particularly against the US dollar, can particularly affect the profits of international trading groups. Such fluctuations become extraordinary items when they affect the translation of foreign assets and liabilities from local currencies into sterling.

Companies which make a habit of putting as much as possible of windfall gains 'above the line' should be treated with caution, notwithstanding that company law and accountancy codes of practice have not been breached.

Last is the impact of the year's trading on the *ordinary shares.* The 'normal' surplus of £3,200,000 equalled a net amount of 8p a share or an indication of what could have been paid if the directors had not very prudently decided to keep almost one-half of the available profits in the business. If, as some accountants would insist, the extraordinary receipts were included the earnings would be 8.75p a share.

*Fully diluted earnings* are the amount available on the assumption that holders of £2 million 10 per cent loan stock converted into ordinary shares at the rate of 150 shares for each £100 stock. Such action would have increased the number of 25p ordinary shares in issue by 3 million to 43 million and would have eliminated the net cost of the convertible stock interest by £130,000 (£200,000 gross less £70,000 tax). Profit available for the increased ordinary capital would then have been:

| | |
|---|---:|
| Profit available for ordinary | £3,200,000 |
| *Add* loan stock interest (net) | 130,000 |
| Available for dividends | £3,330,000 |

and the earnings per share would be £3,330,000 ÷ 43,000,000=7.74p.

Calculation of the *ranking,* or cover, for interest and dividends on the various classes of capital is an essential exercise which, as will be evident in later chapters, is a 'must' requirement when assessing the merits of different types of security. The system widely used is *priority percentage* based on the profits after tax, which means taking loan capital interest at net cost. The resulting breakdown of the taxed profit of £3,592,500 (£3,326,000 available plus £266,500 *net* interest) is:

| Capital | Cost £ | Priority % |
|---|---|---|
| 7% Debenture | 136,500 | 0– 3.8 |
| 10% Loan stock | 130,000 | 3.8–7.4 |
| 5.6% Preference | 84,000 | 7.4–9.8 |
| 4.2 Preference | 42,000 | 9.8–10.9 |
| Ordinary | 1,200,000 | 10.9–44.3 |
| Reserves | 2,000,000 | 44.3–100.0 |

Interest on the debentures and loan stock, taking little more than 7 per cent, was thus covered about fourteen times by available profits while interest plus preference dividends absorbed less than one-ninth. Ordinary dividends took only 33 per cent and the balance of over 55 per cent was retained in the group. This exercise shows what may be termed the *income gearing*.

A matter of financial concern to shareholders in some companies is a lengthy delay between the announcement of an interim dividend and approval at the AGM of a final distribution, and their payment. Gaps of up to three or four months occur. True, advance corporation tax factors may be an excuse. But in these days of modern technology there is no reason why payment should not be made in days or a week or two at most. Many companies, large and small, can do it; so why not all?

## BALANCE SHEETS

A manufacturing company's financial position changes second by second. Raw materials are bought and with labour are turned into finished goods which are sold. The buyers (debtors) in turn sooner or later pay cash which is applied to paying working outlay, taxes, interest and dividends, and buying new assets. A balance sheet is, therefore, only a bird's eye view at a particular moment — the financial year-end. It is, however, very important in showing the degree of solvency, and the growth and status of the company's various classes of capital. Using the capital structure illustrated in Chapter 2 the consolidated statement for the imaginary company could be as shown on page 56.

These figures show a strong financial position and that the company is well placed for expansion. *Land, buildings, plant* and other assets essential to the business have been written-down by one-third of their cost at depreciation rates which should be detailed in a note on 'accounting policies'. Inflation has directed increasing attention to depreciation policies. Replacement costs have soared and continue to rise, with the result that a machine bought only a few years ago may cost twice as much or more to replace, let alone to buy something more modern. Thus, while depreciation rates based on historical cost may be adequate and be sound accounting procedure, the sums provided will fall short of current replacement cost. Prudence calls for additional provision, a matter discussed later. Under the new accounting conventions companies have the option, when considering the preparation of current cost

## CONSOLIDATED BALANCE SHEET

*EMPLOYMENT OF CAPITAL*
FIXED ASSETS:

| | | |
|---|---:|---:|
| Land, buildings, plant, etc. | £24,000,000 | |
| *Less* accumulated depreciation | 8,000,000 | |
| | £16,000,000 | |
| Associated companies | £2,500,000 | |
| Trade investments (at cost) | 500,000 | |
| | | £19,000,000 |
| GOODWILL AND PATENTS | | £1,000,000 |
| WORKING ASSETS: | | |
| Stocks and works in progress | £10,000,000 | |
| Debtors | 12,000,000 | |
| | £22,000,000 | |
| CURRENT LIABILITIES: | | |
| Creditors | £9,000,000 | |
| Taxation | 2,200,000 | |
| Dividends recommended | 800,000 | |
| | £12,000,000 | |
| NET WORKING ASSETS | | £10,000,000 |
| CASH AND INVESTMENTS: | | |
| Quoted investments (market value £1,500,000) | £1,000,000 | |
| Cash and short-term deposits | 4,000,000 | |
| | | £5,000,000 |
| | | £35,000,000 |

*CAPITAL EMPLOYED*

| | | |
|---|---:|---:|
| Issued ordinary share capital | | £10,000,000 |
| Reserves | | 13,000,000 |
| EQUITY INTEREST | | £23,000,000 |
| PREFERENCE CAPITAL: | | |
| 5.6% £1 cumulative shares | £1,500,000 | |
| 4.2% £1 redeemable cumulative shares 1990/95 | 1,000,000 | |
| | | £2,500,000 |
| LOAN CAPITAL: | | |
| 7% Debenture stock 1987/92 | £3,000,000 | |
| 10% Convertible loan stock 1985/90 | 2,000,000 | |
| | | £5,000,000 |
| | | £30,500,000 |
| Minority interests | | 1,500,000 |
| Finance lease obligations | | 2,000,000 |
| Deferred taxation | | 1,000,000 |
| | | £35,000,000 |

accounts (dealt with later), of writing up their fixed assets to current values and of putting the surplus to an earmarked reserve. The merit of such an adjustment is that annual depreciation charges are more realistic and larger sums are set aside to pay for replacements at current prices.

Unlike subsidiary companies, which are concerns more than fifty per cent owned and whose figures are consolidated, *associated and related companies* are those in which equity ownership is twenty per cent or more but not over fifty per cent and in which there is directorial or management participation. Under an *equity accounting* convention the appropriate share of profits is credited, as already shown, in the profit and loss account. Guesswork as to the progress of such participations is thus reduced or eliminated.

*Trade investments* are, however, participations made for strategic, supply or other reasons and in which there is no management say even though the equity holding may be more than twenty per cent.

When associated and trade investments are in quoted securities the market value should be disclosed: if they are unquoted the directors should provide their estimate of their current worth.

A praiseworthy accounting trend is to separate what are commonly called current assets into (a) working (or trading) and (b) cash divisions in order to show the 'liquidity' or 'illiquidity' of the group. The *relation* of working assets — debtors, stocks and work in progress — to current liabilities needs close attention. Unless there is a strong liquid position, a small surplus or a deficit (though not in every type of business) may be a sign of over-trading, weak financial control or the need for more capital.

A liquid deficit due to bank and other short-term borrowings exceeding cash and marketable investments also calls for thought, particularly if the borrowing is rising. Use of bank and other short-term finance is a normal procedure for merchanting and trading companies. But the general run of businesses should not rely too heavily on short-term borrowing for long-term needs that should be financed by share or long-term loan capital.

Two important items which do not appear in the accounts but which have to be the subject of notes are *capital commitments* and *contingent liabilities*. Contracts may have been entered into, or are contemplated, for the purchase of new plant, the building of a new factory or some other project which will have to be paid for after the financial year-end. The estimated cost of such future expenditure should be measured against the current liquid resources to judge whether the cash flow will be enough to pay the bills or whether new loan and/or share capital will have to be raised.

As their description implies, contingent liabilities, may never arise, but if they do they may be very costly and, as has happened, lead to bankruptcy or a financial crisis. They are often guarantees of bank loans or other liabilities of subsidiary or associated companies; bill discounting facilities; or capital commitments of other concerns.

A form of finance which has expanded widely is *lease and hire* of plant, machinery and other assets on which there can be substantial liabilities for 'rentals' over a number of years. Up to mid-1987 these liabilities could be shown 'off-balance sheet' and discoverable only by reference to the notes. Now, however, and not before time, they have to be written into the balance sheet as 'obligations under leases' or a similar description, with the assets financed by them included in the tangible assets and being written down in the normal way. Lease debts should, therefore, be added to other loan debt or creditors when working out the overall loan liabilities or net current asset position.

*Goodwill* and *patents* arise in various ways such as the purchase of assets for more than their tangible value, the promotional cost of new products or the development costs of products or processes exclusive to the group. But particularly outstanding is the very high goodwill that nowadays is frequently created in takeovers where the net tangible assets acquired are several times the cost in cash or in shares valued in the market at substantial to outstandingly large premiums on their par value. Rightly it has been laid down that such goodwill and other intangibles should be written off immediately against reserves or carried forward to be amortised out of profits over a reasonable period which, depending on their nature and individual company policy, may be five to ten years, or 25 years or more.

Cogent arguments are advanced for both one-off and instalment write-downs of goodwill, the impact on profits being the fulcrum. One-off elimina-tions from reserves or one year's profits boost future profits and earnings which will not suffer an annual charge. Contrariwise, the instalment method reduces available profits. So, other things being equal, one company's earnings are greater or less than those of comparable companies, with an effect on share market rating. The soundest method depends on the way goodwill has been or is created. If, for instance, it is a premium paid on a takeover or costly promotion of new products which will generate good profits over the years ahead, it is reasonable to write off the cost over the 'life' of the intangible asset in the same way as depreciation is provided on plant, machinery and other tangible assets.

A much wrangled-over problem is, however, merger accounting treatment on a takeover at a heavy premium on the worth of the net tangible assets. Until the accountants agree a goodwill code of practice and any necessary amend-ments are made to company law, it will be a case of 'anything goes' providing the auditors agree. Meantime, a controversial example of one-off write-downs comes from Saatchi & Saatchi, one of the world's biggest advertising and media groups, whose major asset is people who, like other humans, are liable to all the ills and to defect to pastures new. At 30 September 1987 all goodwill had been written off, but only by creating a *negative* goodwill reserve of £160.3 million after an amortisation charge of £2.8 million. This left net assets of £40.2 million for £99.5 million of convertible preference and £15.6 million of ordinary share capital; in other words a shortage of £74.9 million. Yet the Group's shares are so highly rated that their market value has at times been well over the half-billion pound mark.

*Research and development costs* should be charged against profits as incurred, with the possible exception of major expenditure the benefits from which will accrue over future years.

The bottom half of the balance sheet shows how a group is financed. Starting from the bottom, *deferred taxation* is a reserve set up to meet any future liability for tax held over by capital allowances and other deferrals. Recent tax policies have meant that deferments for many companies are substantial, and the question has been growing as to how much will eventually be payable. Accounting policy so far has been to limit provisions to liabilities likely to arise in the foreseeable future.

*Minority interests* are the share of the net assets of subsidiaries owned outside the group. They may be represented by fixed interest stocks, prefer-ence shares or ordinary shares, or a mixture. *Preference* and *loan capital* figures are self-explanatory.

This leaves the *equity* interest, which is the issued ordinary capital plus reserves built up out of retained profits and from other sources such as premiums on capital issued at above its par value. It is the basis of a fundamental calculation — the *net asset value* (NAV) of the 25p ordinary shares. Although the equity interest is shown as £23 million, goodwill and patents of £1 million should be eliminated. This leaves £22 million to which can be added the £500,000 surplus in the market value of the quoted investments. NAV per 25p share is thus:

$$\frac{£22,000,000 + £500,000}{40,000,000} = 56.25p$$

While NAV is by no means an assurance that if the group was wound up ordinary shareholders would get at least $56\frac{1}{4}$p a share, it is an indicator of worth and a measuring rod for growth and comparison with similar companies. Moreover, it is rare for it to be close to the market price of the shares — it can often be more, sometimes substantially more than the price, or it can be less.

*Capital gearing,* which is the ratio to each other of the different classes of capital, should also be worked out as an indicator of how the company is placed to raise new finance by means of loan capital or equity shares. The example shows fixed interest capital of £7.5 million (£2.5 million preference and £5 million loan) compared with £10 million ordinary. The gearing is thus $\frac{7.5}{10} = 3:4$. If reserves are taken into account the ratio becomes:

$$\frac{7.5}{10 + 13} = 1:3 \text{ (approximately)}$$

The gearing is low and there would be little or no difficulty in raising a substantial amount of new capital by means of debentures or loan stock. But if the figures had been the other way round, £23 million fixed interest and only £7.5 million ordinary, the gearing would be the high ratio of around 3:1, making an ordinary share issue the only way to get new money. While there can be no firm rule in view of the great diversity of companies, a gearing of more than 1:1 is about the highest for the average UK concern, property groups excepted. An alternative method of calculation is to relate only the loan debt to the ordinary capital and reserves.

So far the analysis has covered only one year. Valuable and necessary as this is, trends over a number of years are more instructive. Companies are now expected to give key details of results over a period of at last five years. Response varies considerably in detail and time. At one end of the gamut the period can be ten years or more, with detailed summaries of balance sheets, turnover, profits, dividends, capital spending and so on, plus key percentages such as the ratio of profits to turnover and capital employed. At the other end there may be no more than meagre details of turnover, profits, dividends and balance sheet totals for five years. An idea of the information necessary to assess progress and how it should be applied is given in the table overleaf which has been based, in simplified form, on figures of a well-known company with enlightened ideas on shareholder communications.

The overall picture is good. Turnover has more than doubled over the five years and, the 1985 hiccup apart, the ratio of profits before tax has remained reasonably consistent, though there has been some variation in the relation of pre-tax profits to shareholders' funds (capital plus accumulated profits and

## GROUP FIVE-YEAR RECORD

|                                        |        | 1983    | 1984    | 1985    | 1986    | 1987    |
|----------------------------------------|--------|---------|---------|---------|---------|---------|
| Turnover                               | £'000  | 113,000 | 141,000 | 161,000 | 211,000 | 240,000 |
| Profit before tax                      | £'000  | 11,300  | 14,700  | 14,100  | 20,300  | 28,700  |
| Net profit after tax                   | £'000  | 5,000   | 6,000   | 6,200   | 14,400  | 17,900  |
| Ordinary shares issued 25p             | '000   | 70,000  | 70,000  | 84,000  | 84,000  | 84,000  |
| Ordinary shareholders' funds           | £'000  | 37,000  | 49,000  | 65,000  | 75,000  | 86,000  |
| Total capital employed                 | £'000  | 71,000  | 92,000  | 114,000 | 129,000 | 142,000 |
| Pre-tax profit:                        |        |         |         |         |         |         |
| On turnover                            | %      | 10.0    | 10.4    | 8.8     | 9.6     | 12.0    |
| On ordinary shareholders' funds        | %      | 30.5    | 30.0    | 21.7    | 27.1    | 33.4    |
| On total capital employed              | %      | 15.9    | 16.0    | 12.4    | 15.7    | 20.2    |
| 25p ordinary shares — per share:       |        |         |         |         |         |         |
| Pre-tax earnings                       | p.     | 16.1    | 21.0    | 16.8    | 24.2    | 34.2    |
| Taxed earnings                         | p.     | 7.1     | 8.6     | 7.4     | 17.1    | 21.3    |
| Dividend                               | p.     | 3.00    | 3.30    | 3.30    | 4.00    | 4.75    |
| Dividend covered (times)               |        | 2.37    | 2.61    | 2.24    | 4.27    | 4.48    |
| Net asset value                        | p.     | 52.9    | 70.0    | 77.4    | 89.3    | 102.4   |
| Employment of capital:                 |        |         |         |         |         |         |
| Fixed assets                           | £'000  | 45,000  | 60,000  | 70,000  | 77,000  | 86,000  |
| Stocks and debtors, *less* creditors   | £'000  | 20,000  | 25,000  | 28,000  | 38,000  | 43,000  |
| Cash (net) and investments             | £'000  | 6,000   | 7,000   | 16,000  | 14,000  | 13,000  |
| Capital investments p.a.               | £'000  | 6,000   | 7,000   | 11,000  | 13,000  | 16,000  |

reserves). On the other hand, the pre-tax ratio to total capital employed has gone up over the period.

The importance of using pre-tax profits for comparisons is strongly brought out by the per-share earnings. Whereas tax reduced the 1983 figure to under one-half — from 16.1p to 7.1p per share — a lower proportionate tax bill, due partly to the reduction in the corporation tax rate to 35 per cent, resulted in a smaller cut from 34.2p to 21.3p in 1987. In the result, as also happened in 1986, dividend cover was appreciably improved and larger proportions of profits were retained.

Two developments other than trading results affected the balance sheet figures. Fixed assets were upvalued in 1984 by some £11 million and in 1985 shareholders were offered one new 25p ordinary for every five held at 90p, with consequent additions to issued capital and to reserves. Even allowing for these additions, the increase in net asset value from 52.9p to an almost doubled 102.4p is indicative of the growing strength of the group over the five-year period. Investment in new plant and other capital assets indicates that modernisation and expansion of productive resources are well in mind. Simultaneously, net working assets and liquid resources have more than doubled to a strong position from which to finance a good deal of further growth.

A liquidity snare which can be overlooked when current assets less current liabilities are shown as net current assets in the balance sheet is the inclusion in liabilities of bank loans and short-term borrowings which may or may not be secured on assets and be repayable at short notice. The property market collapse in 1973 and 1974 bought home the dangers of such 'concealed' debts. A simplified example based on the accounts of a well-known company typifies the differences shown up by a detailed balance sheet and the one actually presented to shareholders. The latter showed that net assets of £48 million were financed as follows:

|  | £'000 | % |
|---|---|---|
| Equity | 30,000 | 62.5 |
| Minorities and deferred tax | 8,000 | 16.7 |
| Loan capital | 10,000 | 20.8 |
| Total | £48,000 | 100.0 |

Notes to the accounts showed, however, that current liabilities included £8 million secured and £7 million unsecured bank loans, overdrafts and advances. Current assets included £3 million cash at bank. In other words, the *net* bank liability was £12 million. A further note showed that as much as £5 million of the loan capital was short term, which meant repayable within five years. The net loan position was, thus, that of a total of £22 million, only £5 million was long term: as much as £17 million was repayable within five years. The *real* position, as detailed below, was:

|  | £'000 | % |
|---|---|---|
| Equity | 30,000 | 50.0 |
| Minorities and deferred tax | 8,000 | 13.4 |
| Loans: Long | 5,000 | 8.3 |
| Bank and short (net) | 17,000 | 28.3 |
| Total | £60,000 | 100.0 |

Put another way, the equity interest (ordinary capital plus accumulated reserves) was 50 per cent instead of 62.5 per cent. It could, of course, be argued that the nature of a business is such that a large part of its trade is naturally financible by short-term borrowings. Equally, it should be borne in mind that unexpected losses or economic crises could lead to a money crisis through the calling-in of loans. The straightforward and most informative way is to set out the *gross figures in the balance sheet*. However, such is progress that the new accounting conventions provide for division into 'creditors — amounts falling due within one year' and 'creditors — amounts falling due after more than one year'; in other words, euphemisms for the clearer traditional 'current liabilities' and loan debt. Redundancy costs and trading losses of many companies reporting in recent times have amply stressed the importance of a clear-cut showing of the liquid/loan position, which can alter drastically in a very short period — and bring about bankruptcy.

The balance sheet, or a note, should also give the totals of *all* short and long period debt repayable annually for up to at least five years ahead and in five-year stages thereafter. Such details can throw up surprising, even alarming, results.

Another vital piece of information is the currency source of loan capital and borrowings. Fluctuations in sterling can mean losses — or profits — on repayment. If sterling falls repayments and servicing cost more. If sterling rises the cost is less. The impact is, however, eased if the overseas borrowings are secured on revenue-producing foreign assets.

*Off-balance sheet* finance is a newish artificial device to hide debts which calls for close examination. It takes various forms like sale and repurchase of assets at the year end; sale and lease-back deals; and supply of goods on sale or return. Most potentially dangerous is, however, the creation of a legally 'non-subsidiary' subsidiary finance company with a tiny share capital in which ostensible ownership is below 50 per cent and the legally 'controlling' majority is held by a complacent collaborator, often a bank or finance house. Moneys borrowed, which can run into hundreds of millions of pounds, are used to finance lease and other credit sales and other operations with the real parent company guaranteeing the borrowings. Neither the latter nor the corresponding debtors or other assets appear in the group balance sheet; which could look very different, perhaps shaky, if they were included. Not before time, the accountancy bodies are plodding away to formulate a standard which will ostracise such hoodwinking practices.

A relatively new financial aid is a **source and application of funds** statement, which is in effect a cash summation of the year's net transactions (see table overleaf). It shows how funds have been generated, distinguishing income from capital, and how they have been expended. Some statements are clear cut and easy to follow, with income items separated from capital transactions. Many are, however, jumbled up without the income/capital distinctions needed to show how a company has used (a) self-finance and (b) outside capital for expansion. It would be unwise to lay down a dogmatic pattern, as something depends on the nature of individual businesses, but an easily absorbed account could be as this simple example.

It is clear that this expansion-minded company has financed its growth by a mixture of operational retentions (£4 million), an ordinary share issue and borrowings. In the process, it has increased its liquid resources in anticipation of further growth or to pay for capital commitments in hand.

*Cash flow* was the forerunner of the source and application statement. Made up of the retained profits plus depreciation, it is a simple means of showing how much of the trading income has been kept in the business to be used for expansion. Unfortunately it is rarely used nowadays.

A recent addition to financial data which has some political significance is a **statement of value added**. The idea is to show how the surplus of turnover (plus any other income) over the cost of materials and services — the value added — has been applied as between the work-force, the government, the providers of capital, and provision for growth. An excellent example of such a summary is what Marks & Spencer call an 'Application of Group sales revenue' covering

## SOURCE AND APPLICATION OF FUNDS

|  | £ | £ |
|---|---|---|
| Profit before tax and extraordinary items | 6,000,000 | |
| Items not involving movement of funds: | | |
|   Depreciation | 1,500,000 | |
|   Foreign exchange adjustments | 100,000 | |
|   Other non-cash items | 150,000 | |
| Tax paid | 2,500,000 | 7,750,000 |
| Dividends paid: Preference | 125,000 | |
|           Ordinary | 1,075,000 | |
|           Minority | 50,000 | |
| | | 3,750,000 |
| NET FUNDS GENERATED FROM OPERATIONS | | £4,000,000 |
| Ordinary share issue — net proceeds | 3,800,000 | |
| Loan capital — net borrowings | 1,000,000 | |
| Other capital items (net) | 200,000 | |
| | | 5,000,000 |
| TOTAL NET FUNDS | | £9,000,000 |
| Investment in fixed assets (net) | 4,500,000 | |
| Investment in associated companies | 250,000 | |
| | | 4,750,000 |
| Working capital increase: | | |
|   Stocks and work in progress | 1,750,000 | |
|   Debtors *less* creditors | 1,500,000 | |
| | | 3,250,000 |
| Increase in net liquid funds | | 1,000,000 |
| TOTAL APPLICATION | | £9,000,000 |

the 52 weeks ended 31 March 1988, when sales, including sales taxes, totalled £4,974.3 million. This was applied as to:

|  |  | £m | % |
|---|---|---|---|
| Suppliers of merchandise & services | | 3,401.9 | 68.4 |
| Benefit of employees | | 396.8 | 8.0 |
| Central and local goverment | | 755.8 | 15.2 |
| Providers of capital: | | | |
|   Interest of loans | £ 21.2 | | |
|   Dividends | 135.8 | 157.0 | 3.1 |
| Replacement of assets and | | | |
|   expansion of business | | 262.8 | 5.3 |
| Groups sales, including sales taxes | | £4,974.3 | 100.0 |

Like the sources and application figures, this exercise shows that investors took out much less than the government and that a large amount was ploughed back to ensure the progress which would maintain and provide new jobs.

A further statement recommended by the Accounting Standards Steering Committee, but so far little used, is *money exchanges with government*. It should show the extent to which businesses pay and collect taxes, both on behalf of local as well as central government, and the grants and subsidies they receive. Distinguishing between amounts collected in an agency capacity and those directly borne, it should cover PAYE, VAT, corporation and similar taxes, rates and similar levies paid to local authorities, other sums paid, including social security, training levies and duties; and, on the receiving side, government grants, subsidies and other receipts. Such a statement would demonstrate the degree of interdependence between business and the State.

Last but far from least of the vital parts of company reports to read carefully is the *auditors' report*. As one highly respected City editor comments: 'The first thing I look at is the auditors' report: it can be the key to what is going on.' The great majority of reports give clean bills of financial rectitude. However, of late two developments have led to qualifications appearing in reports.

The first type of qualification is one of differences of opinion on the treatment of particular items in the accounts. These include items such as the bases of stock valuations, conversion of foreign currency transactions and depreciation; and the fact that the figures are presented on an historical basis. Differences largely arise because of the efforts of the leading accountancy bodies to lay down standards for a variety of procedures. As a result, auditors have to draw attention to deviations even though the procedures are perfectly sound financially and (a necessity) are consistent year by year.

Unhappily, the second type of qualification is serious and too often a warning that there is trouble ahead. The qualification, or series of qualifications, may draw attention to inadequate accounting records, deficiencies, misfeasances, over-valuation of stocks or other assets, omission of liabilities, stealing of assets, business misbehaviour of directors or employees, and other actions or lack of actions which have had, or may have, adverse effects on finances and operations.

A key qualification, which can be called a 'going concern' signal, concerns the financial viability of the company. The auditors may qualify their report by stating that it is 'subject to the renewal (or continuation) of the present bank facilities'. Or there may be some similar intimation that withdrawal of financial support could have unpleasant repercussions.

It is a fact that penal libel laws can inhibit or kill an auditor's adverse expression of opinion. But if there is something which clearly calls for attention, a warning signal, however it may have to be 'hedged', should not be beyond legal ingenuity. There have been too many scandals where the door has not been bolted before the horse got away with the loot or misdemeanour. An accelerating increase, particularly in the USA, of legal actions against auditors for alleged failure to spot and to draw attention to financial jiggery-pokery, mismanagement and misfeasances strengthens the argument for giving every possible warning signal; in extremes to refusing to approve the accounts.

Finally, treatment of *pension fund* contributions, assets and liabilities has come in for increasing discussion and criticism, and rightly so. Due to the rise in stock market, property and other values the assets of many company funds are worth more — sometimes substantially more — than their current and reasonably foreseeable actuarial liabilities, which in many cases have been reduced by redundancies and lower pay rises. In the result, one or more of several courses of action to deal with the overfunding are being taken. First, part of the fund is clawed back and credited to reserves or added to the year's profits. Secondly, a contributions holiday of one or more years is declared. Thirdly, contributions are reduced. Fourthly, current and future benefits are increased.

Government proposals that anything over a very conservatively valued surplus of five per cent can be applied in one or more of the above ways has been widely and rightly criticised as too low, with ten per cent advocated as the safe minimum. The impact of the first three treatments on a company's accounts are obvious — there is an abnormal increase in profits, particularly when a clawback is credited to one year's figures, and the earnings trend is distorted. Also, a traumatic fall in share prices could, as Black Monday's thunderous crash of October '87 rammed home, cause a pension fund to become under-funded and need topping-up to safe actuarial levels. Not before time this development has focused attention on the need for company employers to give employees and shareholders full financial facts about their pension funds; there has been too much coyness about this vital matter.

## CURRENT COST ACCOUNTS

Current cost accounts (CCA) are the inevitable response to inflation. Contrary to the accounts so far considered, which have been drawn up on an *historical* cost basis, CCA tries to present the facts on a current cost basis. Considerable research, amendments to various drafts and discussion, even heated argument, have gone into the setting down of guidelines in the preparation of CCA accounts. Even to-day, when ironically inflation is well down from double to low single figures, no clear cut accounting standards and statements of policy have been agreed; and further discussion and wrangling have been quietly pushed under the CCA carpet. Still, though CCA may be a dead or very feeble dodo, the key bases used to adjust figures from historical cost (HC) are worth recording: double figure inflation could return and with it a need to agree standard policies! Meantime, the Stock Exchange has dropped its insistence on publication of CCA accounts and few companies now waste time and money preparing such figures. The key adjustments are:

*Depreciation* is the first, and often the major consideration. Calculated only on historical costs, sums put aside for capital assets' replacements based on what the assets originally cost can fall far short of current, mounting replacement cost. A machine bought five years ago for £10,000 may, for instance, cost £20,000 or more to replace today. If it had an estimated life of ten years, the HC depreciation charge would be £1,000 a year. By the end of year five, only £5,000 would have been provided towards the price of a new machine. So even assuming, optimistically, the old machine could be sold for its written-down value of £5,000, no less than £10,000 of new capital would have to be found on top of the sale proceeds and the £5,000 depreciation provision to buy an equivalent new item of plant.

There is thus every inducement to provide extra depreciation to cope with the much higher potential liability. One way is to leave fixed assets at their net HC figure and to build up a CCA replacement reserve. Another way which is wisely being practiced by more and more companies is to revalue the assets annually and to provide depreciation on the higher, realistic total. Companies ignoring this vital need could be heading for a lot of trouble.

Although in a different category, associated and trade investments should also be CCA-revalued annually.

*Cost of sales adjustment* (COSA) is a second. Inflation pushes up raw material prices and other manufacturing costs. As materials are used up, their replacement cost rises. For instance, materials in stock may have cost £10 per unit but on sale of the product the cost of fresh stock to make another unit may have risen to £11. This would mean an artificially high profit on the first batch. COSA is therefore the difference, on an average basis, between the current cost of stock at the sale date and the historical cost. This adjustment, like the depreciation one, provides a *real* profit figure lower than the historical cost one in a period of inflation.

*Monetary working capital adjustment* (MWCA) is a third: this takes account of the charge (or credit) to maintain the net monetary working capital of trade debtors less trade creditors at current levels. If debtors exceed creditors, CCA provision is needed. But if creditors exceed debtors there will be some credit. In some cases part or all of a bank overdraft will be counted as a creditor.

*Gearing adjustment* is a fourth: this covers non-permanent capital such as finance from banks and other third parties, and will take account of set-offs like cash in hand and short-term investments. The idea is to apportion the adjustments for inflation between the shareholders' interest and other sources of finance.

It is, of course, impossible to generalise about the differences which comparison of CCA and HC profit and balance sheet figures can throw up, especially in periods of high inflation. With very rare exceptions it can be taken however that CCA profits will be less than HC ones or there will be losses; while balance sheet totals and the amount available to the equity capital will be greater — a paradoxical situation! A random sample from the accounts of four companies illustrates the impact of CCA on earnings and net asset-values of ordinary shares in 1983 when inflation was still a factor to reckon with.

| Company | Historic | Current |
|---|---|---|
| Imperial Chemical Industries | | |
|     Earnings per share | 65p | 39p |
|     Net asset value | 545p | 896p |
| Guest Keen and Nettlefold | | |
|     Earnings per share | 17.4p | 8.1p |
|     Net asset value | 294p | 331p |
| Imperial Group | | |
|     Earnings per share | 18p | 10.2p |
|     Net asset value | 123p | 186p |
| Bridon | | |
|     Earnings per share | 15.6p | 4.09p |
|     Net asset value | 156p | 231p |

## INTERIM REPORTS

Shareholders do not have to wait until after a company's year end for news of financial progress — or regression. Half-yearly reports must be issued with the minimum information required by the Stock Exchange being (1) net turnover; (2) profit or loss before taxation and extraordinary items; (3) taxation on profits; (4) minority interests; (5) profit or loss attributable to shareholders, before extraordinary items; (6) extra-ordinary items net of taxation; (7) profit or loss attributable to shareholders ; (8) rates of dividend(s) paid and proposed, and cost; (9) earnings per share in pence; and (10) comparative figures for the corresponding previous period. Included must be any significant information on the trend of activities and profit or loss together with an indication of any special factors influencing them. Unaudited figures must be referred to as such. A growing number of companies go one better by issuing quarterly reports, while many give more information than the required minimum, and add the previous full years figures.

Similar information has to be given in *preliminary profit* statements which normally precede publication of the full annual report and accounts by anything from a few days to several weeks.

## ACCOUNT CHECKS

The aim of the foregoing outline and examples has been to show the importance of reading the accounts sections of annual reports, however dull and mind-boggling they may seem. Features and figures to which special attention should be paid are:
* Auditors' report.
* Are accounts prepared on consistent bases year by year?
* Trend of turnover, pre-tax profits, earnings per share, dividends and net asset values over five years or more.
* Are turnover and profits rising faster than inflation?
* Priority percentages (or cover) for servicing loan, preference and equity capital.
* Proportion of capitalisation provided by (a) debentures and loan stocks; (b) preference shares; and (c) equity. Is (a) high or low in relation to (b) and (c)? What is the gearing of (a) and (b) to (c)?
* Total short-term borrowings repayable within five years.
* Bank and other short-term borrowings 'hidden' in current liabilities note.
* Extent of off-balance sheet liabilities needs critical examination; if substantial, look for another share investment.
* Amount of foreign currency borrowing and how matched by foreign assets.
* Liquid position. Are cash and marketable investments more — or less — than short-term borrowings?
* Total of capital and other commitments.
* Is the liquid position so tight that new loan or share capital will have to be raised?
* Read all notes to accounts.
* Compare net asset values with share prices. The multiples can be excessive — and dangerous — particularly in the case of market fashionable, small specialised and 'people' companies.
* Study the figureheads as well as the figures. Good financial facts should be backed up by first-class and forward-looking management.
* Take serious account of changes in top management. When some people move in as chairman or managing director it can be a promising sign, particularly if things have been going badly and the newcomers have

established sound reputations as 'company doctors' or 'change drivers'.
Again, when others with poor, sometimes downright bad records take
over it could be a warning to sell shares.

*   How is pension overfunding dealt with?

# 10

# Debenture and loan stock priorities

Details of the different types of debentures and loan stocks have been outlined in chapter 2. The task now is to see how to assess the standing of such prior class capital and to consider the merits and demerits of such stocks.

## DEBENTURES

Debentures rank, as already pointed out, first in the company financial hierarchy. Secured on specified assets, they are at the head of the queue for payout if a company goes into liquidation. While this is a comforting thought in general, it is not always a guarantee that the money is safe. Every now and again companies with debenture capital get into such difficulties that the assets do not realise enough to repay debentures 100 per cent or, in very bad cases, anything at all.

The first test is therefore the financial stock market standing of the company. Size is often a useful measuring rod, though it has not been unknown for some very large companies to sink without trace of any return to debenture holders. It can be a generally accepted fact, however, that the possibility of giants such as Imperial Chemical, Sainsbury, Unilever and leading brewers like Allied-Lyons, Bass and Whitbread getting into difficulties is unthinkable. There are also many relatively small companies which have first rate-cover for their debenture issues. Size apart, the tests are capital and interest cover.

**Capital cover** is most often a first and floating charge on the fixed and all other assets of the company. It may, however, be restricted to specific assets such as, say, some of the tied houses of a brewing company. Where there is more than one debenture issue it is fairly common for all stocks to rank equally for capital and interest or, as the law puts it, *pari passu*.

A capital cover exercise can be worked from the sample balance sheet outlined on page 56. This shows net assets of £35 million, which is not, however, the cover for the £3 million 7 per cent debenture stock. The security is the total assets, so the £12 million of current liabilities have to be excluded. Also, as goodwill and patents would probably be worthless on a forced liquidation, assets would exclude their £1 million valuation. The assets cover would thus be:

| Fixed assets          | £19,000,000 |
|-----------------------|-------------|
| Working assets        | 22,000,000  |
| Cash and investments  | 5,000,000   |
| Total                 | £46,000,000 |

which would produce cover of:

$$\frac{£46,000,000}{£3,000,000} = 15.3 \text{ times}$$

If there was a second debenture of £2 million 10 per cent stock ranking *pari passu* with the 7 per cent issue, the cover for the combined stocks would be:

$$\frac{£46,000,000}{£3,000,000 + £2,000,000} = 9.2 \text{ times}$$

Two caveats on the use of cover figures are necessary. First, as assets are based on going concern values as shown in annual accounts, they would realise something different, particularly on a forced sale. A highly specialised factory could, for instance, be worth its balance sheet value to a prosperous, going concern but be very difficult to sell even at a knock-down price in the event of closure. Offices in a busy city centre might, on the other hand, be standing in well below market values. Secondly, as they may not be ascertainable from the published accounts, no allowance can be made for preferential creditors such as employees' pay and taxation.

When it comes to **interest cover** a gross basis is used, not the priority percentage method. The starting point is the profit before taxation. Keeping to the sample profit and loss account of page 53, the surplus before tax, interest and minority was £6 million and the 7 per cent debenture interest £210,000 gross. Interest cover was thus:

$$\frac{£6,000,000}{£210,000} = 28.6 \text{ times}$$

If there was also a £2 million 10 per cent issue the figure would be:

$$\frac{£6,000,000}{£210,000 + £200,000} = 14.6 \text{ times}$$

After a lengthy period of quietude the debentures issue market has been stimulated into activity by the drop in interest rates; which makes this type of finance more attractive. Some large industrial companies and investment trusts have led the way with medium to large placings or offerings at interest yields of up to one per cent or so above similar life gilts. This renewal has helped to increase market supplies of good stocks and to offset a shrinkage in the amounts of outstanding older issues through three types of operation — persistent buying of good class debentures by pension funds; companies with overflowing cash coffers repaying early or buying in their own stocks at above market prices; and early redemptions to clear the way for capital reorganisation or for newer and longer borrowing operations. Exemption from capital gains tax on profits on *straight* UK stocks should encourage the issue of new debenture (and loan) stocks at discounts and low interest rates.

As with gilt-edged stocks, debentures, as noted earlier, come in irredeemable, redeemable, short, medium and long form. Irredeemables are a relic of the days long ago when the pound rode high, wide and handsome, the British Empire was intact, we traded profitably overseas, interest rates were low and stable, and inflation was a bad dream of neurotic economists. The government could then borrow at 3 or $3\frac{1}{2}$ per cent for years to come and 4 per cent for ever and a day on an industrial debenture was a good investment for widows, orphans, *et al*. The traumatic change began in the 1950s. Interest rates began to creep up, with the pace accelerating with awareness that inflation was becoming an increasing menace. Investors not only demanded higher interest but also insisted on time limits on their lending. Dates became imperative.

Dates are one specific time or spread over several years such as say 1992 to 1997. Yields can, therefore, be flat (running) or redemption. A 6 per cent stock repayable in 9 years can be bought at, say £72 to give a flat yield of 8.33 per cent and a redemption yield of over 11 per cent. A debenture portfolio can thus be arranged to give a relatively low flat yield and a high redemption profit, or to produce capital sums over a period of years by picking stocks with a run of repayment dates.

While there are not very many shorts left, there is still a fair choice of medium and long-term debentures available. Yields naturally depend on the borrower's rating; but the general run is around a point more than on corresponding gilt-edged stocks. Once more, the patient investor ready to wait for stock to be offered can get above average yields from some of the smaller issues, particularly those of out-of-the-way concerns such as water undertakings.

## LOAN STOCKS

The catchment area here is wider and more varied. Many companies of all sizes have one or more secured, unsecured or convertible loan stock issues resulting from a cash-raising operation, a takeover or a conversion offer. Like debentures, the investment rating has to be capital and interest cover in association with the size and standing of the issuing company.

**Capital cover** partly depends on whether the stock is secured or unsecured, and if secured, whether a debenture ranks in front of it or 'shares' *pari passu* in the assets and profits. Priorities may also arise where there are two or more loan stocks all secured or all unsecured. If the stock is secured with no other charge in front of it, cover is calculated on the same basis as set out on page 70.

But if a debenture ranks first, the capital position of £2 million stock, again based on the sample balance sheet on page 56, would be:

| | |
|---|---|
| Total assets | £46,000,000 |
| *Less* 7% Debentures | 3,000,000 |
| Available | £43,000,000 |

to produce cover of:

$$\frac{£43,000,000}{£2,000,000} = 21.5 \text{ times}$$

Another assessment method would be the total required to cover both debenture and secured loan stocks. The two together, totalling £5 million, would be covered:

$$\frac{£46,000,000}{£3,000,000 + £2,000,000} = 9.2 \text{ times}$$

The position is very different, however, if the loan stock is unsecured: it then ranks with the ordinary creditors. Again assuming £3 million debentures ranking ahead, the assets position would be £43 million available to cover the loan stock *plus* creditors and other liabilities of £12 million, or a total of £14 million. The capital cover would then reduce to:

$$\frac{£43,000,000}{£14,000,000} = 3.1 \text{ times}$$

Similar criteria apply to **income cover**. Interest has priority over preference and equity dividends. Again, however, it should be the gross charge against pre-tax profits and using the same sample company the cover after debenture interest would be:

$$\frac{£6,000,000 - £210,000}{£200,000} = 29 \text{ times}$$

or if the total debenture and loan interest is applied:

$$\frac{£6,000,000}{£410,000} = 14.6 \text{ times}$$

These examples are based on an obviously prosperous company in a sound financial position. But what of the less sound companies and those on a downward path? The choice demands great care, particularly amongst unsecured stocks. Yields can be a useful, though not certain, indicator of rating. The old maxim of 'the higher the yield the greater the risk' should be applied.

Life range for loan stocks, as to be expected, is wide, with repayment dates varying from one fixed time to spreads over several years. The tendency, as previously mentioned, for companies with surplus cash or the wish to reorganise their loan structures to seek earlier repayment is worth investigation or same crystal-gazing. With success depending on the offer of a tempting premium over market price, it can be profitable to look around for companies likely to buy in their loan stocks. An example was an offer in 1986 by Imperial Group (after its takeover by Hanson) to buy out holders of four of its loan stocks at a cost of £118 million. With two of the issues — 6.9 per cent and 7.5 per cent stocks — standing at £73½ and £76½ in the market, repayment at par of £100 showed useful gains.

## CONVERTIBLES

Convertibles offer a mix of two different types of investment at opposite ends of the capital spectrum — a fixed interest stock with the option to switch into an equity. It is not surprising, therefore, that they are a popular form of investment and company finance, and that listings, including preference issues, have a market value near to £15 billion.

Each issue has two dates or sets of dates. The first is the *repayment* time of a specific year or a spread over several years. The second is the *conversion* date or series of dates spread over two, three, four, five or more years. Sometimes the two dates coincide. More often, however, the conversion range is shorter than the repayment term.

Conversion rates may also vary. Some issues may have a single conversion rate of, say, one share per £1 of stock, 150 shares per £100 of stock or one share per £1.25 of stock. Other issues have graduated rates which might be per £100 of stock, say, for 100 shares in year one, 95 shares in year two, 90 shares in year three and, perhaps, so on for additional years. Conversion terms are thus geared to an anticipated continuance of expansion and prosperity. The longer action is deferred the higher the cost of the ordinary shares.

A few issues are only *partly convertible*, the rights being limited to say only 50 per cent of the stock. The result on conversion is that a holder gets his ration of ordinary shares but is left with a 'rump' of pure fixed interest stock. The question may then be the profitability of retaining the latter. The answer will depend on the yield on the net cost of the rump after deducting the value of the ordinary shares from the original cost, and the desirability of keeping a fixed interest stock for income.

A conversion issue may have a condition that if a certain proportion such as 75 per cent is converted the company has power compulsorily to convert the balance or to pay it off. While such action can indicate that a company is so successful that its ordinary shares are the better investment, it may not please investors wanting a good fixed interest yield. All they can do, however, is to accept the situation.

A profitable variation is an uplift in the conversion rate in order to clear off a loan stock in readiness for a new capitalisation programme. A good example was Rolls Royce Motors' offer to raise the rate on its 8 per cent 1997/2002 convertible from 100 shares to 125 per £100 of stock provided that holders acted within a specified time. As there was an immediate and substantial increase in the value of the stock, it was well received by holders.

Action on a conversion date depends on individual investment objectives. Is yield the primary need? Is a 'safe' option on an equity interest the aim? Or is it a case of having the two options and playing it by ear as conversion dates come round?

Before considering factors bearing on a decision, account has to be taken of the *conversion premium* or *discount*. Market prices of convertibles have an extra criterion, which is the value put on the option to switch into ordinary shares. It may be substantial for a prosperous, highly regarded company but little or nothing, even a discount, for one doing poorly. An example shows the arithmetic:

A company's 10 per cent convertible stands at £121 and its ordinary shares at 178p; and £100 stock is convertible into 54 shares. It would thus cost 54 × 178p or £96.12 to buy 54 shares. But the cost of £100 stock would be £121. The premium on the ordinary would therefore be £121 less £96.12 or £24.88 which would give a figure of:

$$\frac{£24.88 \times 100}{£96.12} = 25.9 \text{ per cent premium}$$

Three basic factors affect the decision just as much as they play a part in the investment choice in the first place. First are the flat and redemption yields on the stock as a pure fixed interest investment. Second is the ordinary share yield. Third is the premium (or discount) on conversion. All three vary considerably with, as always, much depending on each company's market standing and prospects. Loan stock flat yields can vary from around parity to up to double or more the return on the ordinary shares; and in some cases can be lower. Seven examples give an idea of the range of permutations:

| Coy | Stock | | Conversion | | Prices | | Prem. | Yields % | |
|-----|-------|-------|------------|--------|--------|------|-------|----------|------|
|     |       |       | No. Shs.   | Period | Stk. £ | Shs. p | %   | Stk.     | Shs. |
| A   | 9½%   | 2000/05    | 105     | 1983/93 | 126   | 94  | 27.6  | 7.54  | 3.78 |
| B   | 9½%   | 1992/2001  | 124     | 1984/92 | 192   | 163 | −5.8  | 4.95  | 3.59 |
| C   | 8¼%   | 2003       | 55.555  | 1987/03 | 139   | 219 | 14.3  | 5.94  | 2.12 |
| D   | 9%    | 2002/07    | 80      | 1986/02 | 148   | 174 | 6.3   | 6.08  | 3.08 |
| E   | 10%   | 1990/95    | 54      | 1982/90 | 88½   | 83  | 97.5  | 11.30 | 2.27 |
| F   | 13%   | 1994/99    | 33.33   | 1983/89 | 150   | 410 | 9.8   | 8.67  | 5.57 |
| G   | 11%   | 1993/98    | 107.156 | 1981/93 | 155   | 153 | −5.6  | 7.10  | 6.50 |

All of the stocks yield more than the shares. Apart from the 'loss' due to the premiums involved on conversion, investors putting the emphasis on income can thus defer action until the final conversion dates. Companies usually notify stockholders in advance of each conversion date and set out the advantages and disadvantages of taking action. A notice might, for instance, give these facts based on market prices:

| CAPITAL VALUE: | | |
|---|---|---|
| £100 8% stock @ £73 | | £73.00 |
| 76 ordinary shares @ 73p | £55.48 | |
| Balance of stock redeemed at par | 1.20 | £56.68 |

The difference of £16.32 on a conversion would mean a decrease in market value of 22.4 per cent for those who converted at that point.

| GROSS INCOME: | |
|---|---|
| Interest on £100 stock @ 8% | £8.00 |
| Dividends on 76 shares | £6.52 |

The loss of £1.48 income would equal 18.5 per cent. (But it would not take account of any future dividend increases.)

Decisions have to be made as final conversion dates get near. Any premium on conversion will have been falling as the deadline approaches. The choice therefore becomes clear-cut — to continue a fixed interest stock for income, or to join the equity shareholders. For many investors the answer will depend on circumstances at the decisive time. And it may be underlined if the stock is redeemable on the last conversion date.

*Conversion* into equity shares of the issuing company is the general rule for sterling issues. Some recent offerings have, however, novel options such as into the shares of another company of which the issuer has a big enough holding to cover a full conversion. Some examples, in each of which the issuer has a right to pay cash instead of handing over shares in order to avoid watering down its holding, are:

Associated Newspaper 6 per cent 15 year sterling bonds convertible into Reuters B shares at £11.20 each.

Bond Corporation, the Australian conglomerate, 6 per cent ten year bonds convertible into Allied-Lyons ordinary at 420p a share, with an option for holders to redeem stock after five years to give an annual return of 10.43 per cent.

General Cinemas, a US organisation, 15 year debentures convertible into 333 Cadbury Schweppes ordinary shares per £1,000 of stock.

**Dual currency convertibles** are a useful means to combine the fixed interest/ equity formula with the option to move into overseas company shares. There are for instance some *sterling-dollar convertibles* issued by American companies and a few Dutch and German groups. Denominated in sterling, they are convertible into the shares of the overseas parents in similar ways to the more general convertible stocks. An attraction for investors who want a hedge against a fall in sterling is the ability to convert into an equity quoted in US dollars or some other foreign currency at stated rates of exchange which can be comfortably above current rates. The convertible will tend to move in line with the rise and fall of the parent shares. Gains and losses can, therefore, be made on a foreign share while staying in a sterling security. There is also a good choice in the Eurobond sector, with most of the issues being Japanese stocks.

The sharp improvement in sterling in late 1977 brought an 'inversion' of the dual convertible. British companies began to issue Eurodollar bonds convertible into *their* ordinary shares. The appeal was more to the overseas investor taking a view on the future of the UK economy and its impact on a few leading companies.

*Euroconvertible loan stocks*, of which there is an interesting choice, differ somewhat, it should be remembered from UK domestic issues in so far as interest is mostly paid only once a year instead of half-yearly. Quoted prices, like those for UK gilts, are 'clean' of accrued interest, which is accounted for in the total cost or proceeds. No ½ per cent stamp duty is payable on purchases, as with sterling convertibles. Settlement is usually seven days after purchase or sale. Holders can normally convert at any time once the first action date comes round. Many issues give holders 'put' options to sell back bonds to the issuer. On the other hand, the issuer may have powers of compulsory redemption at around par if market dealings over, say, 28 consecutive trading days are at par or at a specified premium on par.

## WARRANTS

For all practical purposes warrants are options to buy shares some time in the future. Depending on the time to run, they generally command a premium on the existing share price. If, for example, the exercise price is 100p and the shares stand at 100p, the warrant price may be 5p, 10p or more, depending on its life and prospects for the particular company. But if prospects are poor, the warrant may be unsaleable or stand at only $\frac{1}{2}$p or 1p as a gamble on a turn-round in fortunes. Should there be no advantage in exercising the option on the expiry date, the warrant is simply torn up. Warrants are usually attached to loan stock offers and may be detachable or undetachable from the loan stock. In the latter case they cannot be sold separately from the stock.

A promising field is provided by investment trusts, a number of which have reasonable size issues. There are also warrants of North American mining groups and European and US banks giving purchase rights to gold and base metals at fixed prices.

An investment trust example shows the profit potential if the share price moves up substantially during the life of the warrant. One share can be bought at 484p at any time up to 1995 and current prices are 447p shares and 124p warrants. Assuming a doubling of the share price to 894p, the profit on a straight purchase would be 100 per cent, but the gain on the warrant would be 231 per cent to a value of 410p (894−484p).

Warrants are a useful speculative media which have the advantages of being a cheaper way to take a view than by buying the shares. It must be remembered, however, that their life is limited to the exercise date or dates and that they can become worthless.

## PRIORITY POINTERS

In view of the extensive ground which has had to be covered, it should be useful to summarise some of the key facts about fixed interest stocks:

* Debentures are the safest form of company investment.
* But as their interest is fixed they are not inflation-proof.
* Redeemable debentures and loan stocks standing at discounts are useful investments for high-rate income-tax payers.
* Irredeemable debentures can be attractive in dear money times when yields are high. Prices rise as interest rates fall.
* Unsecured non-convertible loan stocks generally yield more than debentures and can be good income providers.
* Convertibles are good buys for those wanting options on the two worlds of fixed interest and equities.
* Convertibles priced at premiums of over, say, 10/15 per cent on conversion value should have not less than three to five years to run before final conversion date.
* Debentures and loan stocks of cash-rich companies have chances of being bought in at prices above market levels.
* Dual currency convertibles are a cheap way to take a view on American and European stock market booms and as a hedge against the ill-effects in UK markets of an adverse general election result, rising deficits on overseas trade or persistent rises in inflation.
* Warrants have a use as longer-term options.

# 11

# Getting the preference

Preference shares, as noted in chapter 2, are first in the pecking order of company *share* capital; they have prior rights over the equity. There was a period when the number of issues was dropping because of redemptions and the growing popularity of loan stocks as a form of finance. More recently there has, however, been a fair replenishment through scrip and rights issues and takeover offers, with a good proportion of the newcomers being convertibles, redeemables or convertible/redeemables. Persistent buying of old and new issues by life assurance offices and pension funds attracted by the relatively high yields tends, however, to continue to restrict market supplies. It can, therefore, be a longish business to pick up fair-sized lines of smaller preference issues.

Though most of the *convertible* issues are relatively small, there are some attractive propositions worth searching out. As with loan stocks, new conversion terms add spice to the convertible preference sector. United Biscuits, for instance, has a 25-year Euro preference issue with a 'rolling' investors' put option during years 5 and 10 of its life. Between 1993 and 1998 the shares can be put (sold to UB) at a price rising from £119.45 to £149.38 per £100, and UB can call them in during this period at similar prices. Again, Chesterfield Properties gives holders of its 5.25 per cent preference (convertible basically into 13.245 ordinary per £100 of shares) some takeover protection through stepped-up terms of 13.986 ordinary if a predator comes along before August 1989, and decreasing annually to 13.423 before August 1992.

Broadly, the special factors to take into the calculations are the same as for convertible loan stocks — conversion terms and dates; repayment date(s) if redeemable; the premium (discount) on the ordinary share price; and the comparative yields.

Assessment of preference shares starts with the same criteria as for loan capital — capital and dividend cover. It should, however, take account of two general considerations. First, because of their position in the capital structure, such shares by and large yield more than loan capital. Secondly, if there is more than one issue, priorities must be considered. For instance, if there are first, second, third or more issues, do they rank in order of priority or equally?

**Capital cover** arithmetic can be based on the sample balance sheet on page 56. The starting point is the assets left after meeting the calls of the prior charges and current and other liabilities, and eliminating goodwill and patents. The detailed working is:

| | | |
|---|---:|---:|
| Fixed assets | | £19,000,000 |
| Net working assets | | 10,000,000 |
| Cash and investments | | 5,000,000 |
| | | £34,000,000 |
| *Less:* Debentures and loan stock | £5,000,000 | |
| Minority interests | 1,500,000 | |
| Deferred taxation | 3,000,000 | |
| | | 9,500,000 |
| Available for share capital | | £24,500,000 |
| An alternative calculation would be: | | |
| Ordinary capital and reserves | | £23,000,000 |
| *Plus:* Preference capital | | 2,500,000 |
| | | £25,500,000 |
| *Less:* Goodwill and patents | | 1,000,000 |
| Available | | £24,500,000 |

Assuming that the £1.5 million 5.6 per cent preference shares have priority over the 4.2 per cent redeemable issue their capital cover would be:

$$\frac{£24,500,000}{£1,500,000} = 16.3 \text{ times}$$

and the cover for the £1 million redeemable issue would be:

$$\frac{£24,500,000 - £1,500,000}{£1,000,000} = 23 \text{ times}$$

But if the two issues ranked equally — and this would be a more conservative way to arrive at the cover for the redeemable issue — the outcome would be:

$$\frac{£24,500,000}{£1,500,000 + £1,000,000} = 9.8 \text{ times}$$

Before looking at **dividend cover** a change which took place as from 6 April 1973 should be noted. Dividend taxation was notably altered. In place of the income tax which had been deducted at basic rates from dividends, a tax credit system was introduced as part of an alteration in the method of paying corporation tax. Dividends had henceforth to be declared net of income tax.

The impact on ordinary shares was minimal. But on preference shares it meant an actual or nominal re-rating of dividends depending on whether companies altered the rates to a net basis or simply accepted the nominal change. Some who changed now describe the shares as, say, '4.9 per cent (formerly 7 per cent) £1 cumulative preference shares' or give some other indication of the new situation. The immediate effect was that as the 1973/74 basic tax rate was 30 per cent, a 10 per cent gross preference dividend became a 7 per cent net dividend and the investor got a tax credit for 3 per cent.

This was all very well while basic rate was 30 per cent, but the problem came in the following tax year when it was increased to 33 per cent. What was the tax credit rate? And what about companies which had actually reduced dividend rates to net figures? Was a 10 per cent rate already reduced to 7 per cent to be further reduced to 6.7 per cent (10 less 3.3)? The answer was No. Netting stayed on the 30 per cent basis. As a result, the former 10 per cent gross became 7 × 100 ÷ 67 or 10.45 per cent for personal tax purposes. Tax-exempt investors reclaimed 33 per cent, not 30 per cent!

Credits naturally alter in line with changes in basic tax rates which have moved from 35 per cent in 1975/76 back down to 30 per cent for the years from 1979/80 to 1985/86, to 29 per cent for 1986/87, to 27 per cent for 1987/88 and to 25 per cent for 1988/89 with hopes expressed of further cuts to 20 per cent — always providing the economy keeps on improving and inflation doesn't get too much out of hand!

Tax changes make no difference to preference shareholders on basic tax rates — net payments are unaltered at their fixed percentage. But tax-exempt investors get repayments which vary with basic rate changes. For example, repayment on a net dividend of £70 was £30 at the 30 per cent level, £37.69 at 35 per cent, and £25.90 at 27 per cent; but will be only £23.33 at 25 per cent — 25/75ths of £70.

The following table shows the gross equivalents of net dividend payments at the respective 1987/88 and 1988/89 tax rates of 27 per cent and 25 per cent; and of hoped-for future rates down to 20 per cent.

### GROSS PREFERENCE DIVIDENDS

| Net | Income tax rate % | | | | | | |
|-----|------|------|------|------|------|------|------|
| %   | 20   | 21   | 22   | 23   | 24   | 25   | 27   |
| 4.0  | 5.00  | 5.06  | 5.13  | 5.19  | 5.26  | 5.33  | 5.48  |
| 4.5  | 5.62  | 5.70  | 5.77  | 5.84  | 5.92  | 6.00  | 6.16  |
| 5.0  | 6.25  | 6.33  | 6.41  | 6.49  | 6.58  | 6.67  | 6.85  |
| 5.5  | 6.87  | 6.96  | 7.05  | 7.14  | 7.24  | 7.33  | 7.53  |
| 6.0  | 7.50  | 7.59  | 7.69  | 7.79  | 7.89  | 8.00  | 8.22  |
| 6.5  | 8.12  | 8.23  | 8.33  | 8.44  | 8.55  | 8.67  | 8.90  |
| 7.0  | 8.75  | 8.86  | 8.97  | 9.09  | 9.21  | 9.33  | 9.59  |
| 7.5  | 9.37  | 9.49  | 9.62  | 9.74  | 9.87  | 10.00 | 10.27 |
| 8.0  | 10.00 | 10.13 | 10.26 | 10.39 | 10.53 | 10.67 | 10.96 |
| 8.5  | 10.62 | 10.76 | 10.90 | 11.04 | 11.18 | 13.33 | 11.64 |
| 9.0  | 11.25 | 11.39 | 11.54 | 11.69 | 11.84 | 12.00 | 12.33 |
| 9.5  | 11.87 | 10.03 | 12.18 | 12.34 | 12.50 | 12.67 | 13.01 |
| 10.0 | 12.50 | 12.66 | 12.82 | 12.99 | 13.16 | 13.33 | 13.70 |

The 'numbers' impact on preference share issues whose coupons were changed from gross to net rates at the 1973/74 basic income tax level of 30 per cent were, for instance, in percentages: 5 to 3.50; 6 to 4.20; 7½ to 5.25; 8 to 5.60; 9 to 6.30; and 10 to 7.00.

The new system underlines the advantage of using the priority percentage system of calculating preference dividend cover on a net of tax basis. Using once again the sample company, the profit figure of £3,592,500 given on page 55 would be apportioned as to:

| Capital | Cost £ | Priority % |
|---|---|---|
| Debentures and loan stock (net) | 266,500 | 0 – 7.4 |
| 5.6% Preference | 84,000 | 7.4–9.8 |
| 4.2% Preference | 42,000 | 9.8–10.9 |
| Balance — ordinary | 3,200,000 | 10.9–100.0 |

Loan capital interest and the 5.6 per cent preference dividend take less than one-tenth of taxed profits, while addition of the 4.2 per cent preference payment makes the total absorbed still less than one-ninth of available profits.

## PREFERENCE POINTERS

Investment in preference shares can be worthwhile for those seeking reasonable safety and good yields. But attention should be given to the following points:

* Unless of the rare participating type, a fixed dividend gives no protection against inflation, though the generally high yields are some compensation.
* So long as the companies are prosperous, dividends come in half-yearly.
* Cumulative preference shares with dividend arrears can be good speculations if the issuing company has a chance of getting back to the dividend list; arrears of dividend will have to be paid before any dividend can be paid on the ordinary shares.
* Though few in number, convertible and redeemable preference shares of companies going through a bad time but with fair hopes of recovery are worth attention for yield (where dividends are being paid) and capital gain when the good times return.
* Some of the older redeemables have no fixed repayment dates, and action is at the company's option or an event such as a merger. Newer issues tend, however, to have a definite redemption date or dates spread over several years. Both old and new may also be redeemable at a single premium or a rising scale of premiums as the years go by.
* With more and more companies wanting to clear the way for loan stock issues, there is the possibility of (a) redeemable shares being paid off at the earliest date; and (b) non-redeemable shares being paid off at par or a small premium. This adds a speculative attraction to the likely candidates.
* Check on voting rights. Shares with votes can be in a strong or strategic position in a takeover bid which will have to take cash account of such rights.
* There can be no hard and fast rules on cover; much depends on individual companies and their business. But by and large the minima for reasonable safety should be three to four times for dividends and three times for capital.
* Convertibles have the attraction of a fixed income and the chance to switch

into the equity of a prospering company. The latest conversion date should, however, have at least three years to run, particularly if the 'premium' is more than 5 to 10 per cent.

* Be patient if few shares of an attractive issue are on offer. It can pay to leave a buying limit and take shares as they come along.

# 12

# Sharing the equity

Last in the profits and assets queues is the equity. What is left after meeting all prior charges belongs to this risk capital — the ordinary shares. Figures emerging yearly and half-yearly thus have a direct impact on the share price; though, as will be seen later, not always in the way that logic would seem to dictate. They also provide the data on which to work out the key investment arithmetic that should be applied before buying or selling.

Continuing the profit distribution tally of our sample company it will be remembered that under the priority percentage method the taxed profit was £3,592,500 and that prior charge interest and dividends took £392,500, or 10.9 per cent, to leave £2,000,000 for the 40 million 25p ordinary shares. Over 89 per cent of available profits belonged to them, with £1,200,000 being used to pay a 3p net dividend and £2,000,000 being kept in the business. *Net earnings* per share were 32 per cent or the more readily grasped figure of 8p. As it is an almost academic factor with companies which pay out only part of their available profits, it is not necessary to go into a somewhat intricate calculation whereby the tax formula called advanced corporation tax (ACT) can partially alter the earnings ratios. For all practical purposes, the net figure for normal use is the one shown as earnings in the company's annual accounts. This fact is slowly being realised by hair-splitting analysts who have ignored the realism of their American counterparts who have been put off taking realistic views on UK company shares whose earnings have been re-worked on a 'full' tax basis.

One year's earnings do not, however, make an investment summer. Trends over a period of years are much more important and decisive. Are they up, down, sideways or fluctuating? Equally important, because of the factors affecting the annual charge, they should be looked at both before and after tax, together with the number of times dividends are covered by the taxed figures. A straightforward example taken from the accounts of an industrial company shows how earnings and dividend cover can vary. Here are the figures in pence per share for five consecutive years:

|                | Yr. 1 | Yr. 2 | Yr. 3 | Yr. 4 | Yr. 5 |
|----------------|-------|-------|-------|-------|-------|
| Pre-tax        | 9.8   | 9.8   | 9.6   | 13.0  | 14.2  |
| After tax      | 5.4   | 4.9   | 4.5   | 7.4   | 8.5   |
| Net dividend   | 1.1   | 1.2   | 1.3   | 1.5   | 1.6   |
| Dividend cover | 4.9   | 4.1   | 3.5   | 4.9   | 5.3   |

The need to make comparisons through pre-tax earnings is stressed by the fact that whereas the tax charge rose from 45 per cent in year one to 53 per cent in year three, it fell to 40 per cent in year five.

**Price–earnings ratio** is an important indicator where the after-tax figure is used. This is the number of times the per share earnings divide into the share price; in other words, the number of years it would take for earnings at the current rate to add up to the present share price. Taking the above year five's 8.5p earnings the PE ratio on a price of 85p would be $85 \div 8.5$ or 10. On a price of 75p the PE ratio would become 8.8, and at 95p it would be 11.2.

PE ratios can be a good indication of the stock market assessment of the current standing of a company and its prospects and/or financial soundness. A high PE ratio, such as 20, 25 or more, is an indication of good, above-average prospects or a recovery phase which may gain momentum. A low PE ratio, such as 3.5 or a little higher, indicates that prospects are thought to be poor, profits are in a static phase, or there are doubts about the financial position. PE ratios are also a useful way in which to compare the relative standing of companies in the same industry, such as brewing, chemicals, retail stores and so on.

**Yield** is another important indicator which comes into all investment assessments. What income will be produced? For fixed interest and fixed dividend securities it is a known gross amount related to the par value and price. For equities it is invariably a varying amount from nil upwards, depending on annual dividends and the share price.

Equity dividends should be calculated on the gross basis — which was easy before the tax credit system started. Now, however, the net payment has to be grossed up before the yield can be worked out. For example, a net dividend of 6p at a tax rate of 25 per cent would become a gross amount of:

$$\frac{6 \times 100}{75} = 8p$$

while the gross yield at 150p a share would be:

$$\frac{8}{150p} = 5.33 \text{ per cent}$$

The table overleaf shows the gross equivalents at various basic tax rates for a range of net dividends. The tax range covers the 1987/88 and 1988/89 basic rates of 27 per cent and 25 per cent respectively; and looks forward to the promised land of future cuts down to 20 per cent.

**Net asset value** is the next calculation. As shown in chapter 9, this is the sum of the net assets after meeting all prior charges; but, and this is simple caution, after deducting intangible items such as goodwill and patents. Referring back to the sample company, the amount left for the ordinary was clearly set out as £23 million — £10 million in 25p shares plus £13 million accumulated reserves. Eliminating £1 million goodwill and patents and adding the £500,000 surplus of market value over cost prices of investments, the net amount left of £22.5 million equals 56.25p a share.

## GROSS ORDINARY DIVIDENDS

| Net pence | Income tax rate % | | | | | | |
|---|---|---|---|---|---|---|---|
| | 20 | 21 | 22 | 23 | 24 | 25 | 27 |
| 0.5 | 0.62 | 0.63 | 0.64 | 0.65 | 0.66 | 0.67 | 0.68 |
| 1.0 | 1.25 | 1.27 | 1.28 | 1.30 | 1.32 | 1.33 | 1.37 |
| 1.5 | 1.87 | 1.90 | 1.92 | 1.95 | 1.97 | 2.00 | 2.05 |
| 2.0 | 2.50 | 2.53 | 2.56 | 2.60 | 2.63 | 2.67 | 2.74 |
| 2.5 | 3.12 | 3.16 | 3.20 | 3.25 | 3.29 | 3.33 | 3.42 |
| 3.0 | 3.75 | 3.80 | 3.85 | 3.90 | 3.95 | 4.00 | 4.11 |
| 3.5 | 4.37 | 4.43 | 4.49 | 4.55 | 4.60 | 4.67 | 4.79 |
| 4.0 | 5.00 | 5.06 | 5.13 | 5.19 | 5.26 | 5.33 | 5.48 |
| 4.5 | 5.62 | 5.70 | 5.77 | 5.84 | 5.92 | 6.00 | 6.16 |
| 5.0 | 6.25 | 6.33 | 6.41 | 6.49 | 6.58 | 6.67 | 6.85 |
| 6.0 | 7.50 | 7.59 | 7.69 | 7.79 | 7.89 | 8.00 | 8.22 |
| 7.0 | 8.75 | 8.86 | 8.97 | 9.09 | 9.21 | 9.33 | 9.59 |
| 8.0 | 10.00 | 10.13 | 10.26 | 10.39 | 10.53 | 10.67 | 10.96 |
| 9.0 | 11.25 | 11.39 | 11.54 | 11.69 | 11.84 | 12.00 | 12.33 |
| 10.0 | 12.50 | 12.66 | 12.82 | 12.99 | 13.16 | 13.33 | 13.70 |

While NAV is an important indicator of overall progress or recession, it should be used more as a background to turnover, profit and profit margin trends. A dynamic company may have an inspiring profit trend but a low NAV. The task is to get the right balance between earnings and net asset values. Mostly, the emphasis should be on earnings, preferably backed up by a good NAV.

It cannot be too strongly stressed that net asset value is the position of a going concern at a particular moment, the balance sheet date. Subsequent happenings like a general trade slump, a world crisis or a deterioration in management can quickly alter a financial position. A liquidation can hammer home the difference, often large, between a 'going concern' and forced sale values of factories, plant and other not easily realisable assets.

Enforced closures or sales of once profitable assets, reduced export earnings, foreign competition and other adversities hit many companies in 1980 and 1981. Bankruptcies and desperate struggles for survival, with or without financial rescue operations, were common. Not surprisingly, trading and capital losses ate, sometimes horrendously, into the net worth of the unfortunates, with an impact on the net asset value of their ordinary shares. A not unusual example was the drop during 1980 in the NAV of Stone-Platt Industries from 136p to 99p a share, and a subsequent flop to nil when the group went into receivership. The lesson, therefore, is that until shaky companies are again making good profits, earnings are the more vital factor than net asset values. But more of this in later chapters.

# 13
# The changing market

Many factors, singly or in combination, affect the course of stock and share prices — for individual securities, particular sectors or the market as a whole. They range from events relating to individual companies to world economic and political crises. Their impact may be temporary or lead to lengthy up or down trends. Three overall influences have, however, been at work for a good few years:

(1) There is no longer a dividing line between investment and speculation. Economic, political and trade imponderables have put the fixed interest sheep and the equity goats into the same pen.

(2) Markets are being increasingly dominated by the pension funds, insurance offices and other institutional investors with their slide rule professionalism and, at times, their unhappy tendency to sheep-like mass action. It is estimated that the proportion of UK-quoted ordinary shares held by individuals fell from 54 per cent in 1963 to 47.4 per cent in 1969, to 37.5 per cent in 1975 and to only 28.2 per cent in 1981. On the other hand it is estimated that at the start of 1988, $20\frac{1}{2}$ per cent of the adult population, or 9 million people, were shareowners compared with only about 7 per cent in 1979. Public sales of British Telecom, British Gas and other privatised companies accounted for a large proportion of the increase, the estimate being 6 million people, or 13 per cent of all adults, with 6 per cent (8 per cent including the Trustee Savings Bank) owning no other shares. Three per cent of the total held shares in the company for which they work.

(3) Inflation has played havoc with values and yields, and led to temporary and long-term distortions.

Specific factors which affect equity markets are political crises; ideological money-wasting legislation; nationalisation, actual or threatened; balance of payments deficits on overseas transactions which lead to panic action such as borrowing from the International Monetary Fund to stave off national bankruptcy; high and persistently rising unemployment; strikes and other damaging industrial action; over-expansion of the monetary supply with the need for higher interest rates and restrictions on credit and bank lending; financial scandals like the costly collapse of the secondary banking and property booms; soaring and dramatically falling prices for crude oil; national or world-wide over-production or under-demand in particular industries such as steel and shipbuilding which in turn affect supply industries; and intensified competition (not a bad thing in itself) in specific industries such as is happening in the supermarket and other retail markets. Finally, and so hurtfully noticeable in recent times, are the manipulations of stock market entrepreneurs and arbitrageurs; plus programme trading by American financial houses.

External troubles such as wars, revolutions, political upheavals, economic problems and stock market gyrations in other countries can also affect the UK market, even if only to cause a passing shudder or fractional uplift. America's Wall Street can have a more than momentary effect on other stock markets as happened so dramatically in October 1987: when Uncle Sam turns we all turn and perhaps fall out of bed with a nasty thump. A bull market can, however, be running in London while a bear slide is on in New York. It is a noteworthy fact that UK investors, particularly investment and unit trusts and companies on the takeover trail, were well to the front in 1978 picking up US shares after a long down-drift which substantially undervalued many prosperous companies: this process has accelerated substantially since the suspension of exchange control in October 1979. Contrariwise, in 1983, the Americans began moving into the London market in an increasingly big way as buyers of leading UK company shares which, on their way of calculating values, were cheap compared to their US counterparts. As a result, Americans are now substantial holders of Imperial Chemical and similar top company shares; and, at times, are the market pacemakers.

Bird's-eye pictures of the world's leading stock markets are provided by daily indices, some of long standing, others fairly recent tools. Most used and quoted of the UK indices are the Financial Times Industrial Ordinary, Government Securities, Gold Mines, and Fixed Interest indices which are based on small but representative numbers of securities. The Industrial index covers, for instance, only 30 leading shares, but it has the advantage of extending back to 1935 and is subject to substitution when a constituent is no longer representative, or is a takeover victim. Two takeover changes were the disappearance of Imperial Group and Distillers following their absorption into, respectively, Hanson Trust (already a constituent) and Guinness which became a new member along with Royal Insurance joining National Westminster Bank as the second financial sector representative.

More widely based are the FT–Actuaries indices which were started in 1962. Despite their shorter life, they have the merit of covering 24 sectors of the industrial and oil markets in a 500-Share index and a total of 34 sectors and 710 shares in an All-Share index which includes a financial group, investment trusts, mining finance and overseas traders. The All-Share therefore provides not only sectional trends but also a much wider view of the whole equity market than the FT 30-Share. There are in fact times when the 500-Share and the All-Share move in a contrary direction to the FT 30-Share index. Sharp contrary price changes in one or two of the constituents can also disproportionately distort a movement in the latter.

A new ordinary share index — Financial Times–Stock Exchange 100 — was launched as a joint effort in January 1984. Designed to meet the needs of two new markets — Traded Options and London International Financial Futures Exchange (LIFFE) — it provides a minute-by-minute index of price movements. Components are 100 of the largest companies measured by market prices and accounting for almost 70 per cent by total market value of UK equities; in other words, a large part of the market. It is a weighted arithmetic index with a base of 1000 representing the summed market values of the constituents at 30 December 1983, when individual valuations ranged from

£276 million for Scottish & Newcastle Breweries to £7,422 million for British Petroleum. Prices are taken from the Stock Exchange Automated Quotations (SEAQ) computer system which recalculates the index as changes take place. The up-dated 'Footsie' indices are then fed into TOPIC and other information services for the use of subscribers.

It is perhaps apt here to bring in psychology. Whenever an index, particularly the FT-30, nears a round figure like 1500, the pundits start speculating about it crossing (up or down) the 'psychological barrier' of what is supposed to be some magic figure. This may make exciting talk, but it is no more than a nice round number. The market, in essence the big institutional investors, goes its own way, motivated by the simple age-old stimulator of more buyers than sellers — or the reverse!

Looking at the industrial shares market over the postwar years, the FT-30 has moved with yearly swings mostly not exceeding 20/30 per cent. Naturally the biggest, and sometimes the swiftest, moves have been reactions to major developments such as, on the downside, the Heath/Barber monetary debacle of the 1970s and an American tipster's forecast in 'Black September' 1981 of a coming world stock market cataclysm, when there was a then record slump of $22\frac{1}{2}$ per cent. On the upside, boosters have come from favourable budgets; a slowing down in inflation; increases in industrial output, productivity and profits; improving balances on overseas trade; and a strengthening pound. In broad terms the lows and highs of the FT-30 were: 1946/59: 100 and 339; 1960/69: 253 and 522; 1970/79: 146 and 559; 1980/86: 407 and 1426; and 1987: 1232 and 1926.

Because of its wider spread, the FTA-All Share is a better indicator of market trends since its launch in 1962. Yearly movements were from a low of 84 in 1962 to a high of 181 in 1969; a low of 62 in 1974 and 1975 and a high of 284 in 1979; a low of 313 in 1980 and a high of 842 in 1986; and a record-shattering range of 788 and 1239 in 1987, a year which started at 835 and finished at 871! As the FTA-All share chart of annual highs, lows and means shows, the swings (apart from 1974 and 1975) were not excessive up to 1986. Also, since 1974 the *mean price level* has been persistently upwards — which does lend support to the cult of the equity as a gainful long-term investment policy. But a sobering pause for breath is needed. The second chart picturing the 1987 movements of the three equity indices shows how Black Monday can hit where it hurts.

Time alone will tell which of the three equity indices is the most representative of share movements. But for what it is worth at this early stage of Footsie's life, it is interesting to compare the cumulative increases of the runners over the $4\frac{1}{2}$ years to June 1988:

| End Year | FT-30 Share | | FTA-All Sh. | | FTSE 100 | |
|---|---|---|---|---|---|---|
| | Index | Inc. % | Index | Inc. % | Index | Inc. % |
| 1983 | 775.7 | — | 470.5 | — | 1,000.0 | — |
| 1984 | 952.3 | 22.8 | 592.9 | 26.0 | 1,232.2 | 23.2 |
| 1985 | 1,131.4 | 45.9 | 682.9 | 45.1 | 1,412.6 | 41.3 |
| 1986 | 1,313.9 | 69.4 | 835.5 | 77.6 | 1,679.0 | 67.9 |
| 1987 | 1,373.3 | 77.0 | 870.2 | 85.0 | 1,713.0 | 71.3 |
| 1988* | 1,483.2 | 91.2 | 963.0 | 104.7 | 1,857.6 | 85.8 |

*Six months to 30 June

**Figure 1: FTA All-Share Index — highs, lows and means**

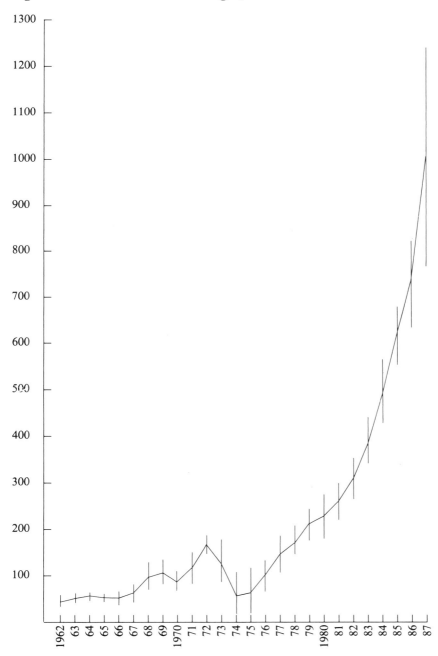

**Figure 2: FT Indices — highs, lows and means 1987**

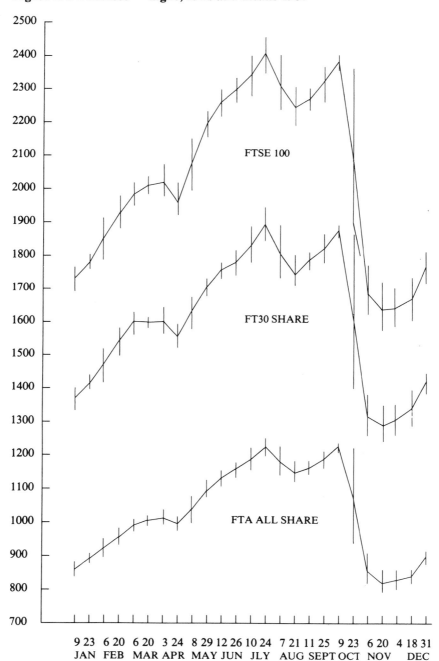

**Figure 3: FT Gold Mines Index — highs, lows and means 1987**

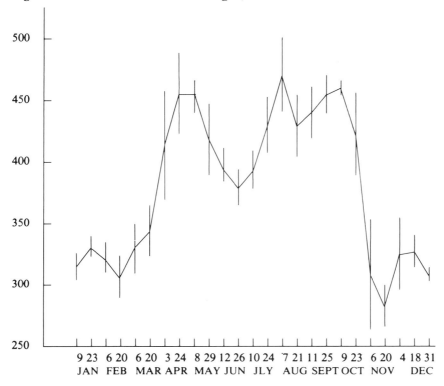

**Figure 4: London Bullion — highs, lows and means 1987 (in US$)**

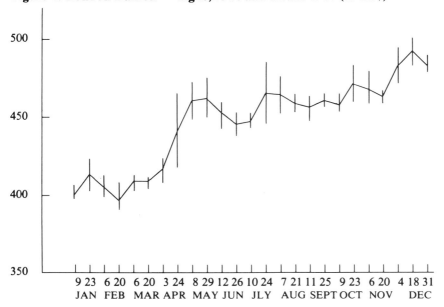

Compared to the equity indices, the FT-Government Securities index has performed somewhat more staidly, though at times showing quite sharp ups and downs, mostly reflecting changes in interest rates and/or fluctuations in sterling. From a post-war high of 114.0 in 1949 it was down to 64.2 some twenty years later with intervening fluctuations between 72.1 in 1973 and an all-time low of 49.2 in January 1975 when the money squeeze was really on and interest rates had raced up to then undreamed-of heights. Yearly swings thereafter were between 55.9 and 65.2 in 1976, and over 1977/81 a low of 60.2 and high of 79.9. Wide changes in interest rates in 1982 increased the 'gap' to 61.9 and 85.8. Thereafter the range was: 1983: 77.0 and 83.7; 1984: 75.7 and 83.8; 1985: 78 and 84.6; 1986: 80.4 and 94.5; and 1987: 83.7 and 93.2.

As is to be expected of a speculative sector, gold mining shares fluctuate widely and mostly — though not all the time — in line with the price of the metal. In 1980, for instance, when gold hit an all-time top price of US$850 an ounce, the FT-Gold Mines index moved between 265 and 559. Then, after a crash back in the metal to under US$300 with a later recovery to US$400/450 plus, the index roved between 181 and 735 over 1981/86, with a gamut of 262−498 in 1987. An inescapable fact in 1987 was that — as the next chart illustrates — share prices, after moving more or less in line with gold itself, fell right down the mine shaft after Black Monday. Share prices had got too much out of step in the general euphoria and moved back to more realistic levels. But as the Gold Mines index is made up of South African shares any ironing out of the Apartheid imbroglio and a lifting of sanctions will surely push up the value of the Rand and with it of South African shares.

All these indices are in cash terms. They take no account of inflation. London stockbrokers BZW (formerly de Zoete & Bevan) put realism into market movements through an exercise based on 30 leading equities and a selection of gilts. The base date is December 1918. The equity index after *adjustment for cost of living* rose, for example, from 270 at end-1958 to a peak of 477 ten years later, only to fall to 106 — almost its starting point — in 1974. It then recovered somewhat erratically to 306 in 1984 and on to 339 by 1985 and — a reassuring coincidence in view of Black Monday — ended both 1986 and 1987 at 396. By contrast the Gilt index, also adjusted for cost of living, more than doubled to 239 by end-1934 before dropping down with only a few up hiccups to 138 by 1946, to 25 in 1967, and to a miserly 3.2 by 31 December 1987.

Another BZW exercise shows how £1,000 invested on 1 January 1946 in equities, gilts and Treasury Bills with *gross* income reinvested would have grown. By December 1987 the 'cash' worth would have been: equities £156,604; gilts £8,264; and Treasury Bills £14,060. After cost of living adjustment the growth would have been reduced, however, to: equities £12,501; gilts only £596; and Treasury Bills £1,015. Another comparison of a £1,000 starter with *net* income reinvested would have produced £5,798 from the equity portfolio or over ten times the £546 from a building society investment.

March 1987 brought the launch of an ambitious new benchmark for global investors — the FT-Actuaries World Indices. Made up of individual indices for 24 different countries, a series of regional indices (such as Europe, North America, Pacific Basin) and a world index, the data are in three separate currencies — US dollar, sterling and local. The basis is the price of some 2,450 equity stocks which represent well over 70 per cent of the total market of the world's main stock exchanges. A major use for the index, and individual country indices, is the measurement of performance by investment trusts and unit trusts, pension funds and other institutional investors with holdings spread in particular areas or widely around the free world.

The moral of all statistical exercises is loud and clear. *Successful investment is a fluid business: the target is to be in the right market at the right time.* Which means (a) constant attention to a portfolio; (b) research; (c) courage to back one's views; (d) sitting on cash at times; (e) bucking trends; (f) scouring the bargain basements and rubbish heaps; (g) adaptability; (h) patience; (i) no jobbing backwards to what might have been; and let's face it, (j) some luck.

Reverting to London's nerve-racking fall in October 1987, it is worth recalling the old aphorism that 'when Wall Street sneezes London catches a cold'. As it happened, Wall Street's sneeze spread the cold beyond London to stock markets all round the world, even to the highly-rated Tokyo, Hong Kong, Sydney and to emerging favourites such as Kuala Lumpur and Singapore, all of which have at times suffered sympathetic falls and attacks of nerves. Yet while world stock markets were slumping, or at best drifting downwards, companies throughout the world were maintaining production and profits, even increasing one or both. And, other companies, particularly in the UK, were pulling out of recession or returning to profitability after squeezing out, often financially painfully, water which had begun to undermine their productivity during a long *laissez-faire* and often loss-proof period. This pattern will continue to be repeated while domestic and international stock markets are moved up and down by short-term rather than long-term happenings and prospects. The internationalisation of world markets with 24 hours a day dealing is already intensifying, not reducing, the inter-reaction.

What then is the investor, particularly the courageous, to do when markets go for a burton? Get out while the going seems to be good? Sit tight for recovery? Or step in at what might be considered bargain, near-rock bottom prices? A vital consideration is to judge how much of the selling is panic-inspired or is forced selling to meet losses. Such factors, combined with a fall in normal buying, are, it must be appreciated, those which result in wholesale and indiscriminate slaughtering of prices; market makers tend to read all brokers as sellers. No hard and fast rules of action can be laid down when markets go haywire. But, as a generalisation, crashes can be opportunities for alert, courageous buyers with cash in hand to start picking up first line shares in one or more markets on the view that sooner or later the sheep will be sorted out from the goats.

Many examples could be given of spectacular scoops 'if only one had known' — and also of hanging on too long for the maximum profit. Great Universal Stores ... Tesco ... Glaxo ... Rugby Portland Cement ... BTR ... Imperial Chemical Industries ... Courtaulds ... these are a minute sample of companies which have performed well over the years and which have well rewarded investors who got in when their shares were neglected or pooh-poohed as having few or no prospects. On the other side of the coin are spectacular failures such as Rolls Razor, and London and County, and other secondary banking shares which faded out completely or fell to a tiny fraction of their high and over-boosted peaks. There was also the much-publicised Australian nickel mining venture, Poseidon, whose shares raced up in a few weeks from a few shillings to over £100 and subsequently crashed back to below their starting level. And in our once so staid gilt-edged market the widely held $3\frac{1}{2}$ per cent War Loan rattled down from £109 in 1946 to an abysmal £$19\frac{3}{4}$ in 1974.

Many market forecasting systems and theories have been expounded and operated for almost as long as there have been stock exchanges. Computers have added to the production of all kinds of data and the proliferation of scientific techniques, particularly in America, the land of expertise. Some systems, like charts which record price movements and from which it is claimed that the use of certain theories make it possible to forecast future trends, have survived the test of time. Others range from intricate 'models' to way-out theories that sunspots, yes sunspots, have a bearing on market movements. There are also 'random walk' theorists and learned papers have been written on 'random selection' by throwing darts at a newspaper page of share prices. An obvious reaction to most of these ideas is that if they did accurately forecast general or particular movements, and were widely used, it could become impossible to act because all users would want to buy or sell simultaneously.

While overall market, sector and individual share charts are useful as records of what has gone before and as signals of highs and lows, they should be used only as back-ups to two basic tools — research and instinct.

Objectives will determine the extent of research, and the data generally available is dealt with in chapter 22. Annual reports and Extel cards (statistical data on companies produced by Exchange Telegraph) are the best and simplest means to take a view on individual companies: the facts to look for are outlined in chapter 9. These should be backed up by the records of high and low prices in *The Financial Times, The Times, The Daily Telegraph* and some other newspapers; and, for securities not quoted by such publications, in the monthly handbooks which most stockbrokers can supply to clients.

Market instinct is something you have or have not. It can, however, be nurtured or developed by keeping abreast of financial and economic news and market reactions. But let it be noted that despite its highly developed and collective instinct, the market does not always get things right. It can over-react, which may be a buying or selling chance. When a partner of an astute and particularly able merchant banker was asked what motivated him the answer was: 'Seventy-five per cent instinct and twenty-five per cent fact'. The aim for ordinary investing mortals is probably nearer to seventy-five per cent fact and the rest instinct.

A variety of ground rules and aphorisms have come over the years from self-made millionaires, professional speculators and the market. Andrew Carnegie, who made a vast fortune from steel, advised putting all eggs in one basket and watching the basket. At the other end of the scale many pundits believe in spreading the risks and having no more than ten to twenty per cent in one share or market sector. Naturally subject to the capital available, the middle course is:

* To concentrate at any one time on no more than five to ten securities which have been well vetted, or on a particular group such as stores, investment trusts, finance companies, gold and base metals ...
* To be ready to move smartly into other shares or groups.
* Not to concentrate on shares only. There are times to be in gilt-edged and other fixed interest stocks.
* And times to be substantially or wholly liquid — in cash.
* Sell into strength, buy into weakness can pay off.

* To check the market before buying. It may be narrow, making it hard to buy (or sell) a fair quantity. Is the quote wide (for example, such as 60–70p) or narrow (for example 65–67p)? Is it an active counter or a matter of negotiation? Is a line of shares on offer? Might a 'tap' develop on signs of a buyer?
* To remember in these inflationary days that there is no absolutely safe investment. Everything is a speculation.
* Don't be greedy. Every stock and share has a maximum price — at some time. Leave something for the other fellow to go for.
* To realise that a bell doesn't ring when the market hits top or touches bottom. Make up your mind on a fair buying or selling price, or to start operating.
* When the gurus (the know-all economists of Wall Street and Throgmorton Street) publicise their market forecasts don't panic into selling all or rushing in to buy. They can be very wrong. It can pay to ignore their pontifications or, perhaps, even to do the reverse.
* To think in terms of *percentage* rises and falls. A rise from 10p to $12\frac{1}{2}$p is 25 per cent. A rise from 100p to 110p is only 10 per cent.
* It is rare to get in at the bottom or out at the top. It is a miracle to do both.
* Don't risk missing out on a good thing by holding out for the extra penny.
* If a dud share has been picked, cut the loss quickly: the money can be used more profitably elsewhere.
* Never job backwards. Forget what might have been 'if only ...' Look to what might be.
* To keep moving, particularly when a share looks like getting bogged down in a narrow price range.
* Investigate before investing. Time spent on reconnaissance is seldom wasted, says an old proverb.
* Where possible, compare price earnings ratio, yield and profit trend of the selection with those of similar companies and the trade sector averages.
* Be doubly careful buying glamour shares. Be satisfied with reasonable profits, especially quick ones. The market can go mad in particular shares or sectors with many chickens eventually coming home to a beggarly roost.
* To realise that the market quite often expects too much by way of profits or other developments from companies. When analysts' optimistic forecasts translate into realities a price fall can be an opportunity to buy into a good company.
* That a good company without market friends is worth attention. Price recovery may take time, but it will come with realisation of the under-valuation of recovery prospects.
* That rights issues can be a cheap way to buy into a good company. Selling by holders can depress the price. Once the issue is out of the way there is often a recovery.
* That shares of bid-for companies can be worth picking up on the initial offer in the hope of a higher bid later.
* That if a share bought as a long-term investment rises 30 per cent or more in quick time find out what goes on and think about taking a profit — or buying more.
* Don't speculate on the account unless ready to cut a loss or take up the shares if the quick turn doesn't materialise. Contangos, and selling for

cash and buying for new can be very costly ways of financing hopes deferred.
* To take part at least of a big, quick profit. It reduces the cost of what is left.
* To keep in hand enough profit to pay capital gains tax. And perhaps a little more to build up a cash reserve for taking up rights issues or some sudden inspiration.

With these general guidelines in mind it is timely to look at the more mechanical side of dealing. But first some comments on a potent market mover — *tips*. Tips can be good honest expressions of opinion with no other motive than to direct attention to undervalued securities such as recommendations by stockbrokers, City editors or research-minded friends. Or, despite the efforts of the Stock Exchange Council to stamp on such practices, they may be attempts to engineer up prices or to sell a line of shares. So, it is simple commonsense to think of two market sayings: 'Where there's a tip there's a tap'; and 'when a pal whispers in your ear buy so-and-so's, sell 'em as fast as you can'. Inside information can be very valuable, but it can also be a dangerous thing on which to act. *Insider trading* is rightly heavily frowned on and can lead to damaging enquiries by the Stock Exchange and the Takeover Panel: it can also mean heavy fines or imprisonment.

A noteworthy development is the recent proliferation of 'newsletter' tipster services, some of which charge pretty heavily for their advice. While established publications are competent, honest efforts, without a trace of insider operations or motives, the reliability and disinterestedness of some of the newer, flamboyant productions may be questioned, especially when they recommend USM, Third Market or OTC shares with limited markets; or they operate from European or American bases and hard-sell non-UK over-the-counter stocks or, as has happened, 'paper' companies with no business or assets.

In practice it can pay to wait before buying on a newspaper or widely broadcast recommendation. Market makers, rightly expecting an increased demand, will mark up the price. But once the initial rush is over and there is little or no follow through they will tend to lower their quotes, partly or wholly to replenish their books or to close bears in shares they have sold short. It can in fact happen, particularly in generally dull markets, that a tip does not generate enough business to affect the actual dealing price; and it is not unknown for a price to fall on a tip.

*Averaging* is a much debated tactic. Opinion leans heavily towards averaging *up* when prices are rising but is chary of averaging *down* when they are falling. Before consideration of the arguments for and against such operations it is worth looking at examples, starting from the assumption that a favourable view is held of a particular share which may take some time to show its real paces.

The first buy is 1,000 shares at 100p all-in. The price rises and, as the shares still look cheap, a further 500 are bought at 110p. A total of 1,500 shares are then held at a cost of £1,550, an average of about 103p, or nicely below the market level. The rise continues and a further 500 shares are bought at 120p to give this position:

| 1,000 shares | @ 100p | £1,000 |
|---|---|---|
| 500 shares | @ 110p | 550 |
| 500 shares | @ 120p | 600 |
| 2,000 | Totals | £2,150 |

The doubled holding has cost an average of 107½p, or pleasantly less than the current quotation. *So long as the price rises, averaging up beats the market.*

Supposing, however, that instead of rising after the first buy of 1,000 shares at 100p the price falls to 90p, at which level 500 more are bought and that on a further fall to 80p another 500 are added. The position then becomes:

| 1,000 shares | @ 100p | £1,000 |
|---|---|---|
| 500 shares | @ 90p | 450 |
| 500 shares | @ 80p | 400 |
| 2,000 | Totals | £1,850 |

The doubled holding has cost an average of 92½p, or quite a bit above the latest price. *The overall loss is increased by averaging down on a falling market.* The paper loss, instead of being confined to £200 on 1,000 shares, has increased to £250 on 2,000 shares priced at only 80p. Averaging down must, therefore, be faith in one's judgement in picking a share which is substantially undervalued and which will eventually prove its worth. If the judgement — or hunch — proves right and the price later goes to 150p the 2,000 shares (now worth £3,000) will show a profit of £1,150 on averaging down against only £850 on averaging up deals.

Working on the adage that 'the first loss is the smallest', seasoned operators will cut their position if the initial buy drops sharply. But they are not always right. The wisdom of averaging down comes back to having courage to back a possible long-term winner. Conditions at each particular time will decide whether it is wise to continue buying on each sharp fall.

Another problem is to decide when to sell or to start selling. The answer depends partly on whether the operation is viewed as a long-term holding or as a short-term speculation. Also, on whether there is a quick, sharp rise; the movement up is slow and bumpy; or there is a persistent fall. A market aphorism says: 'run a profit, cut a loss'; but when do you stop running and when do you apply the knife? Such advice excepted, there are only two certainties. A successful cash bid apart, there is no knowing when the top is reached. The bottom is nil.

An old Stock Exchange axiom is that money cannot be lost by taking a profit. Successful operators also claim that fortunes are made by selling too soon. Assume, as occasionally happens, that a price soars to double or more very quickly; that 2,000 shares costing £2,000 become worth £4,000. Investment or speculation, selling 500 at 200p (for £1,000) reduces the cost (capital gains tax excluded) of the 1,500 balance to a net £1,000 or from 100p a share to 66⅔p, which considerably strengthens the position.

A prudent way to deal with a speculation on the way up is to decide to sell a proportion of the holding on a rise of so much. For example, from a purchase of 2,000 shares at 100p it is decided to sell one-fifth (400 shares) on each 20p rise. If anticipation turns to reality the position would be:

| Original buy | 2,000 @ 100p | £2,000 |
|---|---|---|
| Sale of | 400 @ 120p | 480 |
| Balance | 1,600 @ 95p | £1,520 |
| Sale of | 400 @ 140p | 560 |
| Balance | 1,200 @ 80p | £960 |
| Sale of | 400 @ 160p | 640 |
| Balance | 800 @ 40p | £320 |

If a fourth sale was made at 180p, to yield £720, there would be a profit before gains tax of £400 and 400 shares would be left standing in at nothing against a market value of £720, to make a total gain of £1,120. It could be argued quite rightly on hindsight that if no shares had been sold the 2,000 would be worth £3,600 at the date of the fourth sale, or a paper gain of £1,600. Naturally, action must be dictated by the primary motive — out-and-out win or lose, or cautious speculation.

*Jobbing* is another way to try to reduce the cost of a holding or to speculate in a particular share. Success largely depends, however, on picking shares which move fairly widely over relatively short periods; which is not easy. A simple example would be an initial purchase of 2,000 shares at 100p, of which 1,000 were sold at 120p and then bought back at 105p all-in-cost. The position would be:

| 2,000 bought | @ 100p | £2,000 |
|---|---|---|
| 1,000 sold | @ 120p | 1,200 |
| 1,000 left | @ 80p | 800 |
| 1,000 bought | @ 105p | 1,050 |
| 2,000 left | @ 92½ | £1,850 |

Provided the price continued to fluctuate and the timing was near enough right to make a gain on each operation, jobbing could continue indefinitely. But before launching on such a venture, costs should be kept well in mind. In addition to brokerage and stamp duties there is the market's turn on bid and offer prices. Break-even point might therefore call for a price change of anything around 7 to 10 per cent. On the other hand, a sale of shares paid for creates what is known as a *covered bear* position. If the two deals are done within the account, there is no brokerage on the repurchase: the market's turn and stamp duty is the only 'cost'.

Not all speculations are for a rise, or on the bull tack. It is also possible to go short, to *sell a bear*. Only those with courage and long purses, professional operators like jobbers, or speculators with very certain knowledge of bad news on the way will, however, take the bear tack. It is easy enough to sell shares one does not own hoping that the price will fall before delivery is due. But it is a very different proposition being able to buy them back lower down during the period open, usually the current Stock Exchange account. If the price rises instead of falls by the last day of the account the only normal option is to buy back and face the loss. The alternatives, which are not always open or practicable, are to try to arrange a carry-over or 'cash and new' deal, as explained in chapter 4. *Going a bear is not an operation for the general investor or speculator;* it is best left to the professionals. The traded options market does, however, provide a way of backing a bearish judgment in some shares by writing a 'call' option or buying a 'put' option.

There can, however, be an exception, as already mentioned. Delivery of shares already held is not due until the end of the account in which they are sold; and in some instances it may be held over. The covered bear is then in the position, if the price falls, of being able to buy back without any delivery worries. He simply buys back his own shares.

*Switching* from one holding to another can bring regrets — and self-congratulations. Which reaction depends on whether sales are at the bottom or top and purchases at the top or bottom. It is difficult enough to hit one deal correctly, especially in an active share, and even harder to pull off the double. It can be tempting to buy the new shares first and to put off selling the old until the last minute, or the reverse; which is dicing with the market. The effective way is to deal simultaneously, and to hell with what happens afterwards.

Dealing at the best price is a perennial headache for which there is no ever-certain relief. Judgement and that rare quality, a feel for the market, can however, help. For instance, it is not very clever to sell on a generally dull day unless it is thought that even duller days lie ahead. Contrariwise, if markets have been roaring ahead for some days it may pay as a buyer to await a reaction as bulls are tempted to take profits.

Some very general rules can work — *at times*. They are:

* If the market is optimistic, the first day of a new account can be a poor buying time because of short-term bulls opening a two-week position. Wait till the quick-turn buyers are out of the way.
* A dull start to a new account may, however, be a good buying time, especially if there is no specific reason for the lethargy. The bears may be out, helping to push down prices.
* The last two days of a strong, ebullient account may be a good buying time. Short-term operators may be selling to close their bull accounts.
* The last two days of a dull account may be good for selling. The bears may be buying to close their positions.

One solution of the price problem, which may or may not work profitably, is to give a broker *limits*, as outlined in chapter 3. In the case of a switch the limits can be *contingent* on selling one share at a stated minimum price and buying the other at a stated maximum price.

Selling one investment to provide money for buying another can bring regrets and self-castigation for being too quick off the mark. The security sold may go up and the one bought go down. Or, on the cheerful side, movements may be the reverse. Both may, of course, rise. In which case it may be asked: Am I better or worse off?

A key factor in the answer is the relation of prices. Say 1,000 shares of A are sold at 150p net for £1,500 and 3,000 of B are bought at 50p all-in. B have to move only one-third to equal A's price changes. If each rises 10p, A to 160p and B to 60p, the latter will be worth £1,800 against only £1,600 for A. The switch will have shown a paper gain of £200 on 'what might have been.' Rightly, of course, if A rises to 160p and B falls to 40p the paper loss will be £400—£1,600 less £1,200. Only a long-term view will show whether the switch was wise or foolish.

# 14

# Portfolio creation and management

Various factors ranging from luck to prescience can contribute to building up a successful investment portfolio. Three fundamentals do, however, help:
* First: Riches, though indubitably helpful, are not a prerequisite. A few hundred pounds can get the ball rolling. Many substantial portfolios have grown from tiny beginnings.
* Second: Plough back the profits after setting side enough for capital gains tax. *Capital should be sacred.*
* Third: Flexibility is vital. However successful a policy or particular share may be there comes a time to switch to something more promising.

Otherwise, financial and family circumstances will determine the investment mix and changes which age may dictate. What is appropriate during working life may need modifications when pensions take over from higher level earnings. Non-workers below pension age may have investment objectives different from those of substantial money-earning investors.

## IN THE BEGINNING

Investment tactics for those starting out in life without the benefit of inherited wealth should begin with the simple and traditional. Before launching into stocks and shares first build up the proverbial nest egg and get into the excellent habit of regular saving.

Young, single people should think ahead to the 'capital cost' of marriage — the so-called 'deposit' on buying a house on mortgage and furnishing it, together with family protection. Depending on their scale, part or all of regular savings should be in quickly realisable form such as Savings Certificates, and/or a building society. In fact, the latter is a must if marriage lies ahead; a building society will usually give preference for a mortgage to an investor already on its books.

Life assurance, in addition to the financial protection it gives, has three particular appeals to the young. First, the younger the starting age the lower the premium rate or the greater the cover obtainable for the money. Second, it is a good form of compulsory saving for family protection and a retirement fund. Third, short-term and convertible type policies give the maximum cover at the lowest cost with the option to take a longer-term view when financial circumstances make it possible to pay larger premiums.

Reduction of the top income tax rate from the 60s plus of recent years to 40 per cent (1988/89) and the change in the capital gains impost to what in effect lumps it in with income tax means that, at least from the tax angle, differentiation between an emphasis on income or capital gains is not the factor it used to be. However, unless income is a prime requirement, capital appreciation should have priority; after all there is still the incentive of the CGT exemption limit which, for 1988/89, means an extra tax free £5,000 to add to personal and other income allowances, as illustrated in the taxation chapter.

Lump sums of accumulated savings can be invested directly in individual stocks and shares; but because of brokerage costs, the minimum single purchase should be not less than £1,000. Smaller lump sums (£250 to £500 minimum) or monthly savings (£25 minimum) can, however, be invested indirectly through the savings plans of a growing number of investment trusts and a majority of unit trusts, as detailed in chapter 21. Investment trusts, it is noteworthy, can have a useful edge on unit trusts because their shares can usually be bought at discounts of up to 20 per cent or more on their net worth — £80 buys say £100 of varied investments — to enhance long-term growth prospects.

Convertible loan stocks and convertible preference shares should also be well up on the starting list. While they may not give the chances of quick-fire appreciation offered by ordinary shares, they are a safer way into the equity market at a time when capital is growing and risks should be minimised.

The time to bring individual company equities into the portfolio will naturally depend on individual circumstances. It could be from the start, if job prospects are good and secure, and an increasing earned income will leave surpluses over normal outgoings. On the other hand, if capital must be kept handy for emergencies, the extra risk involved in direct investment in ordinary shares should be deferred until some £2,000/£5,000 is spread over investment and/or unit trusts and convertibles. The search must then be for shares with capital growth chances.

A promising sector for long-term appreciation and speculation is natural resources — base metals, gold and platinum, oil, rubber and foodstuff shares — the prospects for which are covered in chapter 19. The conservative equity investor should have at least 15/25 per cent of his portfolio in this sector, while the risk-taker might think of a stake of up to 50 per cent.

More and more companies now offer divided reinvestment in shares at a price fixed on the average market quotes over, say, five days from the ex-dividend date. This is a useful and simple way to accumulate shareholdings, possibly at advantageous prices. For instance, the 'striking' price in one case was 854p a share compared with 905p market on 'take-up' day.

Shareholders in some companies can enjoy appetisers in the form of discounts on purchases of their products or cut-price travel facilities. These can be useful tax-free additions to dividends. But the companies selected should be sound, profitable and prosperous concerns. Some stockbrokers make a speciality of cataloguing companies which offer such facilities.

## MATURE TACTICS

A happy fact of life for successful people is that their earned incomes increase with age and that some of their heavier outgoings like mortgage repayments and children's education eventually stop. They have, unless they take on new commitments, more to save. They can concentrate more on building up capital for retirement. As so often, a key consideration is individual circumstances —

length of time to retirement, prospective pension and whether index-linked to inflation, and the cost of a new way of life.

Tax-saving bond schemes have attractions provided it is appreciated that Chancellors of the Exchequer have unpleasant tendencies to stop up tax loopholes. Hence, while some portion of annual savings might go into bonds which produce capital sums around retirement age or give tax-free incomes, the major choice should be stocks and shares; and, unless investment income is needed while still at work, the emphasis — and hope — should be on capital growth. Here is food for thought:

Risks can be minimised by searching out (lots of patience needed) low coupon redeemable debenture and loan stocks standing at good discounts on their repayment prices some ten years or so ahead. Index-linked gilt-edged stocks, with their inbuilt inflation-proofing, are also well worth attention, and are easy to buy.

Convertible loan stocks and preference shares of sound, progressive companies, though somewhat riskier, will, however, usually offer better growth prospects. Sterling-dollar convertibles provide degrees of currency protection and a hedge against adverse political and economic upheavals in the UK.

Investment trusts, with their already mentioned discount attractions, are high on the list for equities.

Then follow direct purchases of other companies' equity shares.

Warrants, whose number and variety are on the increase, are the 'option' way of buying shares some way ahead. If the choice is right the eventual cost of equities can be usefully below their market price at the time of exercising the warrants, after allowing of course for their cost. If the choice is wrong the maximum loss is limited to the cost of the warrants.

Strategy will depend, as ever, on individual circumstances and prospective needs; and should be flexible. It can, for instance, be concentrated entirely on fixed interest and convertible stocks, at least until a strong capital base has been built up. At the other extreme everything can go into equities right from the start. In between it can be a cumulative progression through the above groups.

## AND NOW RETIREMENT

Investment strategy on retirement will be largely dictated by the adequacy of pensions to meet living costs. The first step should, therefore, be to draw up an income and expenditure budget — and to allow for inflation. After this, one consideration for anyone 65 or older should be the wisdom of putting part of any capital into an immediate or deferred annuity on his or her own life; or, if a married man, into a joint or survivorship annuity to continue provision for his wife in case of earlier death. (Current practice is generally for some part of a lump sum retirement payment to go automatically into an annuity.)

Portfolio investment is, however, the main concern here. Individual circumstances and capital available will decide the best strategy. There may, for instance, be no need to deviate from pre-retirement policy if pensions and investment income are enough to cover foreseeable needs. This would particularly apply where pensions allow for inflation. But should total income be barely enough or inadequate, a new emphasis would be necessary. The extreme would be to invest everything in fixed interest securities, with a spread over long-dated gilt-edged, public board and water stocks; and company debentures, loan stocks and preference shares. The compromise would be to try for some inflation protection by diverting one-quarter or one-half to reasonably good-yielding equity shares of sound progressive companies. Also, to include some high-yielding convertible stocks or shares.

A fixed interest-equity spread is the answer where pensions need relatively little topping up. Assuming that some thousands of pounds are available, the disposal could be:

| | |
|---|---|
| Fixed interest | — one-quarter |
| Convertibles | — one-quarter plus |
| Equities | — the balance |

And, at the risk of being boring, some of the equity portion should be in investment trusts.

Another plan would be the allocation of enough capital to ensure the income needed to pay house standing costs — rates, insurance, heating, lighting, maintenance — the *must* expenses which, unhappily, go up and up. The simple formula would be to invest the 'basic costs' fund in fixed interest stocks such as long-dated gilts, debentures, loan stocks and preference shares. But this would not cover inflation. So, a compromise would be to split the fund, say, one-half or three-quarters between such stocks and the balance in equity shares of companies which, so far as human foresight goes, have prospects of paying increasing dividends.

But whatever the investment layout, do keep some money — a thousand or more — in a building society or high interest deposit account to cope with emergencies or for the odd junket or cruise.

## PROGRESS REPORT

Portfolios should be watched for progress, weaknesses and changes. But they should not be fussed over by making daily valuations or everlastingly asking stockbrokers for prices and opinions. The shortest-term valuation of price charting should be weekly, with a monthly full-scale evaluation. A useful working routine is to:

* Keep handy as an *aide-mémoire* a card or paper listing for each security: (a) the amount held and (b) the all-in cost price.
* Tabulate across a card or paper: (a) cost and (b) end-week or end-month prices of each holding, to show progress.
* Make a monthly (or quarterly) valuation showing for each security:
    Amount held.
    Cost: all-in price and amount.
    Value: price and amount.
    Gross annual income.
    Yield per cent on *current value*.

Computer-orientated brokers provide up-to-date valuations at short notice or by arrangement at regular intervals. The main consideration is that, although cost price is always of concern, attention should be concentrated on: (a) current value and (b) gross yield on each investment. These are the data on which to decide on changes — whether at a profit or a loss.

And always be ready to change course in anticipation of slumps and booms in markets. There are times to be liquid and in fixed interest stocks, and times to weigh into equities.

# 15

# Stock Exchange newcomers

New securities come to the Stock Exchange in various ways, some in large chunks, others in tiny driblets. By far the largest are public issues, offers for sale and rights issues to existing shareholders. Because of their nature, the latter, together with takeover offers, are covered in the following chapters.

Issue fashions change, usually in line with current financial and market conditions, and sometimes in a follow-my-leader way. Though relatively quiet for some time before, the launch in November 1980 of the Unlisted Securities Market (USM) set off an increasing flow — at times a spate — of newcomers, sometimes two or more in a single day. There have also been a substantial number of calls, some running up to hundreds of millions of pounds, for new capital from shareholders of already listed companies. Whatever the nature of each type of newcomer, it has to be understood and its merits have to be assessed on the information given in a prospectus or other offer document.

## PUBLIC ISSUES

These are now mostly made by government and other gilt-edged type borrowers. Not often in recent years has a *new* public company been floated by public issue or have existing companies raised money this way.

A government stock prospectus is a very brief document. Its main features are restricted to the amount of stock to be issued; the issue price and whether payable in full on application or by instalments; dates of half-yearly interest payments; redemption date or dates; and minimum application amount.

A little more information is given in a corporation loan prospectus. In addition to the amount to be issued, subscription terms, interest and redemption dates and minimum application, it will state that the stock is secured upon all the corporation's revenues; that annual provision will be made for redemption; and will give the purpose of the issue, which will usually be for capital needs. It will also give details of the population, rateable value, current rate in the £, product of a one penny rate, and the total outstanding debt. This type of borrowing is now almost a museum piece.

## SALES BY TENDER

These are in effect auctions with reserve prices. Once the almost sole preserve of water companies, the method has spread into the gilt-edged and company sectors. It is now an accepted new issue medium for all and sundry. The basis is the offer of fixed interest or equity securities at minimum prices with applicants having to estimate — or guess as can happen — the lowest price to bid to get an allotment. The margin for gilts and water company debenture and preference offers is normally small, sometimes a fraction of a point. For example, if the minimum price is £98.50, successful bids would probably be around £99 or £99.25. On the other hand, if the highest bids for a gilt were below £98.50 the Bank of England would take up the stock and put it on the 'tap' list; but underwriters would have to meet their commitment on a water stock. Water issues are usually short-term preference stocks with, say, five to ten years life, though debenture offerings are making a comeback. Pension funds, life offices and other institutions are far and away the major subscribers for water and gilt issues. Private investors interested in bidding should consult their stockbrokers about prices at which to tender.

Fireworks, controversy, frustration and criticism centre, however, on issues other than by water companies. Back in the early 1960s the tender method was used, largely to curb stags and to hit a striking price fair to companies and investors alike; in other words, to apply free market motivation. Some flops, and much criticism, pretty well put paid to the method and, with rare exceptions, it did not get going again until the launch in October 1980 of the Unlisted Securities Market. Revival was prompted by the huge premiums at which fixed price share offers opened on the start of dealings. Somebody was getting fixed pricing wrong: either issuing houses were underpricing their offers or unlucky applicants were paying much over the odds when dealings began. So tenders had a run, but not for long — fixed price offers again became the front runners. The ideal is, of course, to get an offer fairly priced for all parties; have an over-subscription of no more than a few times; and for dealings to begin at no more than, say, some ten per cent premium and to stay at such a level until the company's trading results call for a realistic re-assessment. Until other means to avoid excessive opening premiums are found, tenders are — in theory, at least — the fairest method; but issuing houses are chary, or wary, of using them. .

## OFFERS FOR SALE

This is the more used way of bringing new companies to the market. Unlike a public issue of 'virgin' shares, an offer for sale is of existing shares which have been bought or subscribed by an issuing house (a merchant bank or stockbrokers) at an agreed price or for a round sum and offered on at a slightly higher price which will cover expenses and give a profit on the deal. The public offer price may be fixed or by tender.

Some offers involve the raising of new capital, in which event the new shares alone or together with some of the old shares are the subject of the offer. Occasionally, *secondary offers* are made of already listed shares which a big holder (or holders) wish to sell in order to reduce their interest or to raise money to pay inheritance tax. Outstanding examples have been government sales of British Petroleum shares, three at fixed prices and one by tender, with the last, in October 1987, a victim of the Black Monday and a flop of flops, of which more elsewhere.

The Stock Exchange insists on a great deal of information being given in an offer prospectus, the assessment of which is dealt with later.

## PLACINGS

These are what the name implies. New securities or blocks of existing ones are sold, or placed, at stated prices to financial institutions and private investors. The Stock Exchange insists on a placing ceiling of £15 million on the main (Listed) market and £5 million on the USM. When the amount exceeds £2 million the lead broker is limited to placing no more than 75 per cent amongst his own clients and, to give a somewhat wider spread of initial shareholders, to have a co-sponsor broker for the balance, with the market maker's portion being a bare 2.5 per cent. Placings often result in hectic first day dealing at fancy premiums on the initial price. A prospectus is an essential part of the operation.

## INTRODUCTIONS

These are a rarely used method of getting a market listing in stocks or shares of previously unquoted public companies with a fair spread of holders. Unlike offers for sale or placings, there is no offer of a specified amount of securities. Some holders may, however, undertake to make some stock available at agreed prices. Some introductions are, however, of securities already listed on another recognised stock exchange; where an already listed company segregates part of its assets by a distribution of shares in a subsidiary or associated company; or, as has been happening of late, a listing of the shares of American or other foreign companies which want the prestige of a UK quotation. Newcomers in the overseas category have been growing apace and now include some of the biggest and most prestigious North American and European companies; which means, as mentioned elsewhere, that the market value of overseas stocks is far ahead of that for UK companies. Such additions are a necessary step in the development of an international stock market which, it is anticipated, will have no geographic frontiers and will be trading 24 hours a day.

## UNLISTED SECURITIES MARKET

A new development launched in November 1980, which has been gathering pace and popularity, is the Unlisted Securities Market (USM). Appreciating the fact that a variety of established and new companies would like to have a market for their shares without going to the relatively high expense of getting an official listing, the Stock Exchange set up the USM. Prior to this move, dealings in shares qualifying for the new status had to be outside the market, with the Stock Exchange missing the business, or under rule 535 (2) with its clearance formalities for deals. (An early effect was the move of some '535 (2)' companies into the USM.) Now, only a few years after the start, the shares of approaching 400 companies with a market value of almost £8 billion are traded in this lusty, sometimes turbulent, new market.

While applicants have to sign a general undertaking somewhat similar to that required for an official listing, and outlined later, certain other requirements are not so extensive, with a saving in costs. For instance, a small box giving little more than the company's name, capitalisation and sponsors instead of a two, three or more page prospectus, sharply prunes advertising costs. Similarly, compared with the normal minimum of 25 per cent for an official listing, the minimum voting equity capital in public hands need be no more than ten per cent.

Three ways of entry are placings, offers for sale, and introductions where at least ten per cent of the voting equity is in public hands. Though the latter method does not call for an accountant's report, an Extel 'pink' information card giving basic facts about the company and key financial statisics has to be produced. An accountants' report is, however, necessary for placings, while an offer for sale may have to be underwritten and a prospectus advertised in at least one newspaper.

Advantages of a USM 'quote' include opportunities to raise additional share or loan capital; to be able to offer marketable 'paper' in takeover or merger deals; to enhance a company's status as a result of the necessary financial vetting by its sponsors and being under the watchful eye of the Stock Exchange; and to enable existing holders, often the founders of the business, to realise cash through the sale of some of their shares at a fair, arms-length market price. While many participants are new technology and electronics companies, the ever-broadening range includes dance school, casino and other leisure activities, oil exploration, clothing manufacturers and retailers, property developers, food production and so on. As USM companies progress, and at least 25 per cent of their voting equity moves into public hands, they can apply for a full official listing, a move which the Stock Exchange encourages and which is happening. Till then, dealings in their securities are recorded in a separate section of the *Daily Official List* and brokers' contract notes specify that the bargains have been done in the USM.

The USM, it should be stressed, is a very volatile market where, because of the often small number of shares available for trading, price movements can be wide, sometimes violent, and it can be difficult to sell or buy more than a relative handful of shares. With some exceptions, it is not the place for the proverbial widows and orphans.

## THIRD MARKET

This was launched to provide some sort of 'central' dealing facilities for flotations not qualifying for the two senior markets. Admission requirements are minimal and entrants include grass roots start up companies with little or no track record to mining and oil exploration ventures. Rightly, they are labelled with heavy wealth warnings and by and large are only for gamblers ready to lose their shirts. Shares of some 50 companies are currently traded.

*******

Whatever the nature of a cash-raising operation, including rights issues to shareholders, a Bank of England release date has to be obtained for anything involving £3 million or over. This is to avoid indigestion in the market; and it can mean the building-up of a sometimes lengthy queue for a 'date'.

## PROSPECTUS VETTING

An essential part of bringing new company securities to market by public issues, offers for sale, placings and some introductions is a prospectus. Drawn up by the sponsors — usually a merchant bank or stockbrokers — it has to give sufficient financial and other information required by the Companies Acts and the even stricter Stock Exchange to enable investors to assess the merits of the securities offered. A prospectus should be thoroughly read, with close attention being given to the small type. Information and figures which matter are:

*Nature and growth of the business.* The key facts to ponder are the length of time established; solidity; standing in the particular industry; adequacy of factory or other accommodation to meet current needs and foreseeable expansion; dependence on any patents or manufacturing processes which could be outmoded by new, rival or less costly production methods.

*Management* is one of the most important and vital contributions to the success of any business. It is essential that the directors and personnel who have successfully built up the company should continue with it, preferably on long-term service contracts. It is equally important that if one or more of the founders is ageing, new or younger management is being trained to take over.

*Sponsors* should have a good track record of issue business and be well-known in the financial community. New issue business is not confined to the City of London; there are some highly regarded provincial houses.

*Capital structure* is important, particularly the proportion of any debentures, loan stock or preference shares. What are the borrowing powers? And the total amount of secured or unsecured bank loans? What are the annual and other repayment terms of *all* loan or borrowed capital?

*Offer terms* should be reasonable in relation to the net assets applicable to the shares, the profit record and the dividend forecast. If loan capital is offered, assets applicable should give a substantial cover and the profits should meet interest several times over. It is important to know the reason for a private business going public.

*Accounting policies* should be stated.

*Turnover* for at least the past five years (three year minimum for USM) should be detailed. Good reasons should be given for any setback in an upward trend. Inflation should be taken into account: at recent rates, sales should have been rising faster than inflation.

*Profit record* should be given for at least five years (three years for USM) and fluctuations should be explained. Again, the yearly increase should more than compensate for inflation.

*Profitability* should be measured by the percentage of pre-tax profits on turnover and in relation to net assets. The trend should be upwards.

*Future prospects* are more important than past results. There should be an indication that turnover is still expanding and a forecast given of the minimum profit expected for the current year.

*Dividend forecasts* should show the number of times the ordinary dividend expected to be paid will be covered by (a) anticipated profits and (b) recent profits. A forecast of earnings per share and the price–earnings ratio are equally essential.

*Dividend yield* should be calculated on the net payment plus the related tax credit to give the *gross* yield on the offer price.

*Asset make-up* should show the bases of valuation and when fixed assets were last professionally valued.

*Stock and work-in-progress* are particularly vulnerable items which should have been valued on consistent bases over the years. Any variations in the bases should be explained and have been accepted by the auditors. It is only too easy to under- or overstate profits by juggling, sometimes legitimately, with stock values.

*Patents, trade marks, franchises or concessions* should be valued realistically. They, like goodwill, are very vulnerable and can quickly become of little or no value. Accounting treatment of the purchase or capitalisation of future 'invisible' assets and writing off existing items should be stated. Special cases apart, the conservative — and financially wise — policy is to write off all such invisibles immediately or over a few years. Goodwill should also be dealt with similarly.

*Liabilities* need close examination. Bank and other short-term loans should be particularly looked at, especially noting repayment terms and whether they are secured on any of the assets or guaranteed by another company or individuals.

*Issue purpose.* The reason for issuing any new capital as part of the operation should be noted. Is new money needed for expansion, to repay loans or for the takeover of another business? The gross amount raised should be stated and its allocation for issue expenses and other purposes detailed.

*Source and application of funds* statements for at least five years will show how the company has dealt with its cash flow from undistributed profits, depreciation and other sources by way of financing expansion. The amount of self-financing is a useful indicator of the approach to expansion.

*Net assets* available to cover any loan capital and left for the equity are key factors. The net asset value per ordinary share should be compared with the offer or placing price.

*Goodwill* does not often appear as an asset in balance sheets. It may, however, be present in unwritten, paper form. Its amount depends on the relation of the offer or placing price to the *tangible* net assets. A newcomer may for example have an issued ordinary capital of 20 million 25p ordinary shares of which 5 million are offered for sale at 100p each, to make a total market capitalisation of £20 million. If the net equity assets are, however, only £6 million, or 30p a share, the concealed goodwill is £14 million (£20 million *less* £6 million) or 70p a share. The goodwill element becomes still greater if, as can easily happen if the offer is a runaway success, the opening price is, say, 125p. The equity capitalisation then becomes 20 million × 125p, or £25 million, and the paper goodwill has jumped to £19 million. Give a thought, therefore, to *all* that is being bought before applying for shares or, if unlucky in getting an allotment, rushing in to buy at the start of dealings.

The position would look very different if the offer had been 20 millions *£1* shares at par to show a balance sheet of:

Net tangible assets £  6,000,000
Goodwill              £14,000,000

instead of £6 million assets to cover £5 million *nominal* issued capital and no mention of the £14 million *premium* in the offer price. *All prospectuses should show the amount of the net tangible assets and their net asset value per share; there should be an extra big question mark over those that don't give the NAV.* Capitalisations of up to ten times or more net asset values can happen, particularly with a service company flotation.

*Vendors* of the shares are usually some or all of the people who have built up the businesses being marketed. Death duty problems may dictate that a fairly large proportion of the equity should be sold; or there may be other personal reasons for similar action. Founders are, however, sometimes reluctant to part with more than enough shares to make the operation feasible. Reasons for a sale are therefore important and should be stated. Caution may be necessary if a high proportion of the equity is on offer for no specific reason. Should a large proportion be retained, however, by a small number of vendors, the company may be classified for tax purposes as 'close'; which means amongst other things that it will not be subject to any dividend limitation in force.

*Contracts* such as service agreements, for capital spending, for the share marketing and any underwriting should be detailed. Service contracts may include commission or profit-sharing arrangements with some or all of the management.

*Offer costs* such as underwriting, professional fees, advertising, printing and other promotional outlays or commissions should be related to the (a) minimum amount to be raised from the shares offered; and (b) total capitalisation at the offer price. Depending naturally on individual circumstances and the proportion of the number of shares sold to the total issued, the ratio should be no more than, say, 5 per cent for (a) and 2 per cent for (b). A breakdown of typical underwriting costs is $\frac{1}{2}$ per cent to the underwriters (bank or broker sponsors); $1\frac{1}{4}$ per cent to the sub-underwriters (the 'insurers') and $\frac{1}{4}$ per cent to brokers submitting applications with their 'stamp' on — a total of 2 per cent. To these have to be added professional fees, advertising, printing and other promotion costs.

*Listing agreement.* Before the Stock Exchange will authorise listing it insists on the company signing a listing agreement which details the information to be given in future and its means of public dissemination. Specific action includes announcement in advance of board meetings which will decide dividends and announce profit figures, and the release of such important facts during market hours; publication of audited accounts, if practicable, within six months of the end of the financial period; inclusion in the accounts of sectional and geographical analyses of turnover and profits; statement in pence per share of earnings on the equity; disclosure of the interests of the directors and their families in the company's capital; and notification of the acquisition of 5 per cent or more of the voting capital by any particular holder, together with changes in directors' holdings.

The Stock Exchange also insists on publication of half-yearly reports, together with details of capital and other changes essential to a proper assessment of affairs. Directors and company personnel must not divulge price-sensitive information which would give privileges to individuals; developments which could affect the share price should be publicly announced. There are also strict guidelines about dealings in the company's shares prior to the announcement of price sensitive developments.

## HAVE A GO

An offer for sale or public issue is an opportunity for what the Stock Exchange calls *stagging*. In its bluntest sense this is simply a gamble that (a) an allotment of shares will be secured and (b) when dealings start they will be at a premium which will make a quick buck for the operator. The first difficulty is that the operation is unlikely to be a success unless the offer is oversubscribed at least three or four times. The second difficulty is that, if the offer is a success which justifies a premium, it will have been subscribed many times over and the possibility of getting an allotment is very chancy, or the allocation is a tiny 100 or 200 shares.

Oversubscription means that the issuing house has to decide on a fair way to make allotments, and it has various options: all applications below a certain amount can be eliminated; a ballot can be taken with proportionate allotment of, say, up to 200 shares in full; allotments can be of 200 shares up to a maximum application of 1,000 or some other total; a proportionate all-round scaling down; and various other permutations. The task is to ensure an equitable distribution and to eliminate the out-and-out stag. It is not eased by the fact that some offers are oversubscribed dozens of times and opening prices are at 25 per cent and upwards above the offer prices.

Stags operate in various ways. There may be one application for a large number of shares, or a number running into dozens or more for varying numbers of shares. Another method is a bunch of applications in various names, real or fictitious, for varying quantities. These or other permutations are practised. Multiple applications mean a lot of work obtaining and filling in application forms. And, as cheques have to be sent, committing a lot of money which may be far beyond actual resources. There have been instances where an offer has flopped and heavy stags have had to take all the shares they applied for and have been landed far out of their financial depths.

Issuing houses do their best to discourage stags. They refuse to accept multiple applications or announce that all cheques will be cashed. Or experience enables them to sort out the genuine applicants from the short-term speculators. Rightly, there have been some ruthless eliminations of multiple applications and promises of legal action against obvious concert parties.

Stagging may be fun — and sometimes profitable. But it can mean a lot of work, luck and tying up money for a week or more plus small reward — or loss — on a large commitment that could go wrong. Stags are very unlikely to be amongst the many dozens of millionaires created by the flotation of their companies on the USM! *Stagging, despite any excitement in it, can be a mug's game.*

Since the issues boom got going in 1981 most listed and USM offers have been oversubscribed from two or three times to up to 100 times or so, and there have been many spectacular market openings. A fixed price offer of 2,631,500 System Reliability shares at 270p drew 123,851 applications for 253,854,720 shares, with an opening price of 405p which later moved up to 500p. More recent examples include:

The offer at 135p of 46.5 million 5p shares of Laura Ashley, the fashion and design company, was more than 34 times oversubscribed and small investors lucky enough to get 300 shares in a ballot saw an opening price of 193p.

An Abbey Life offer of 135 million shares at 180p attracted 375,000 applications, of which only one-third got a chance of receiving a minimum 200 shares in a ballot for which the opening price was 235p.

Response to a marketing at 120p of 210.8 million shares of Wellcome, the international pharmaceutical group, was 430,000 applications totalling £4.5 billion and a 17 times oversubscription. The shares opened at 160p.

Speciality newcomers invariably attract extra interest, often the outcome of intense pre-promotion publicity; and produce spectacular results. An offer of 8.6 million shares of Tie Rack at 145p pulled in 315,000 applications totalling over £1,000 million and on the opening day the market price touched 202p. Sock Shop, a similar style retailer, made the headlines when its shares, offered at 125p, started dealings at 205p, soared to 290p and closed the day at 257p with a chance to go into the Guinness Book of Records as the highest ever opening premium. Pickwick Group, the record company, had a 50 times oversubscription for shares on offer at 125p and ended the opening day at 188p compared with a net tangible asset value of less than 8p.

But it's not all multi-oversubscriptions and mouth-watering opening premiums. One of the biggest ever crashes was the last sale of the Government's British Petroleum shares. Opening on 20 October 1987, the day after Black Monday, underwriters were left with almost all the 2,194 million shares priced at 330p, payable 120p cash down and two calls of 105p each in August 1988 and April 1989. Opening at 88p, the part-paids closed on the first day of dealings at 85p, an immediate loss of 35p; and later slipped away to around 70p, at which price the Bank of England and the Treasury put in a floor by offering to take all shares at 70p. Advertising costs of this privatisation tragedy were, as it happened, a staggering £23 million, or at least five times more than they would have been under a much less overplayed, but realistic, non-privatisation offer. Eurotunnel's flotation of 101 million units at 350p was another flop, with the opening price of 284p dropping during the first day to 250p on a wave of selling.

Other, smaller casualties were only 16 per cent of a 29,680,000 share offer of Mrs. Fields. Inc., a US-based cookie store operator, being taken up at 140p — the opening price for this, then the biggest USM newcomer, was only 128p. Another flop was a less than 51 per cent application for 3,150,000 shares of Lopex, a marketing services group. In both cases the underwriters had to take up the shares not applied for.

# 16

# Other issues

A notable feature of company finance in recent times has been the large amount of new capital raised direct from existing shareholders by means of the following.

## RIGHTS ISSUES

Rights issues are of ordinary shares, loan stocks, convertible loan stocks, and preference and convertible preference shares on terms which often give a 'bonus' or sweetener in income terms, and are mostly to provide new capital for expansion. The new shares are issued at a price below the market price of the existing shares.

A typical rights issue could be, say, one new 25p ordinary share at 60p for every three existing shares which stand at 100p. Shareholders can thus increase their stake by one-third. This means that they will have three old shares valued in the market at 300p plus one new share costing 60p, or a total of 360p for four shares. The average price then theoretically becomes 360p divided by 4, or 90p. As the rights are worth 10p an old share, the *ex-rights* price should be 90p, which would make the new shares worth a premium of 30p on the 60p issue price.

A rights issue does not have to be taken up, wholly or in part. As the rights will almost certainly open at a premium they can be sold. For instance, continuing the above example, a holder of 600 old shares would be provisionally allotted 200 new shares costing £120. If it was decided not to accept, the rights could be sold for 30p each or £60.

Also, if shortage of funds or other reasons debar taking up all the rights and there is a worthwhile premium, part can be sold and the proceeds applied towards the cost of the balance. Should the premium be substantial, enough rights can in fact be sold to pay entirely for the remainder.

It is, however, usually advisable to take up a rights issue, provided the market price is still comfortably above the rights price and provided that there is still faith in the company itself. One potent reason is that a well-run, prosperous company will put the new funds to profitable use. It can also be good policy to follow up a good investment: selling rights reduces the proportionate stake in the equity. And, as so often happens, prices of old and new shares improve after absorption of the issue and once the new capital is getting to work. (It is noteworthy that some rights issues, including quite large ones, fail to hold premiums on prices of the old shares and underwriters have to take up part of the offer, sometimes quite substantial.) *Action one way or another must, however, be taken before the offer closes.*

A rights issue can offer a chance to buy shares at a cut price. Sales by non-assenting holders can temporarily depress prices of both old and new shares. It is possible for a reasonably good opening premium to dribble away to almost nothing, but with the issue out of the way there can be a good price recovery.

There are, of course, rare cases where a rights offer is pitched for some special reason so much above the market price of the old shares that it should be ignored. An outstanding case was the British Leyland offer of 50p new shares at £1 when the old were standing at only 40p. The National Enterprise Board was following up its 78 per cent investment by providing the troubled car concern with a cash injection of £200 million.

The touch and go element in the success of rights issues was well exemplified by the then biggest to date — the June 1981 offer by British Petroleum to raise no less than £624 million. It was a two-way effort. One part was the basic offer of one new share for every seven old at 275p a share. The second part was the passing on to other shareholders at the higher price of 290p by the Government and Bank of England of their rights to take up 44.61 per cent of the issue. On the announcement, the old BP share price fell from 348p to 322p before closing that day at 330p, or comfortably above the two offer prices. Later, due to general market unease about a rise in interest rates and at the very size of the offering, the price of the old slipped away to 278p — 12p below the second tranche price — before recovering to over 290p. When applications were counted, shareholders had taken up 91.6 per cent of the basic entitlement but only 45.4 per cent of the secondary offer. But such can be the effectiveness and strength of the London market that the 65.8 million shares left with the underwriters were placed in strong hands in only some 45 minutes at a minuscule fraction above the issue price of the secondary offering! BP closed that day at 300p.

Rights offers naturally vary in size from a million pounds or so to hundreds of millions with, at the time of writing, British Petroleum holding the record at £1,515 million through the inclusion of new shares in the October 1987 privatisation sale of the Government holding. Next in size was a controversial money-raising effort of £921 million by Barclays Bank through a *deep discounted* rights offer of one new for two old shares at 250p compared with a market price of around 425p for the old. Other big-time money-raisers, all made before Black Monday 1987, were £837 million by Blue Arrow (again controversial and over half left with the underwriters), Midland Bank (£700 million) and Maxwell Communications Corporation (£630 million). And for 1987 as a whole, rights issues raising more than £1 million each were in the region of £9,000 million.

A long-standing UK principle is that, unlike usages in North American and other overseas markets, shareholders here have preemptive rights. Following the Big Bang invasion of US, Japanese and other overseas financial houses into London, erosion of this 'right' began. *Bought deals* were arranged under which whole issues were subscribed without any underwriting and sold on to all and sundry buyers at higher prices. Strong representations by pension funds and other institutions resulted, however, in the hammering out of guide-lines to restrict such deals so that, amongst other things, Listed companies may so issue no more than 5 per cent of their share capital in one year, and up to $7\frac{1}{2}$ per cent in up to three years. Discounts offered to outside investors must not exceed 5 per cent (including underwriting, typically 2 per cent) of the mid-market 'old' share price immediately prior to announcement of the issue. They apply to quasi-equities such as Euroconvertibles and warrants. Otherwise, it is expected that existing shareholders have the right to clawback a due proportion of the issue at the placing price.

Rights issues are made by means of *provisional allotment letters* sent to shareholders on the register at a previously announced date. A concentration of small-type details is somewhat off-putting, but is no excuse for not reading everything carefully and *acting in plenty of time so as not to lose out*. The working facts are:

*    Check that the correct number of new shares has been allotted.
*    If accepting, send a cheque for the full amount due in time to arrive at the latest by the closing date. Postal vagaries suggest posting three to four days before the deadline.
*    If all the rights are sold, sign form X on the back of the letter and send it immediately to the broker or bank who sold.
*    Do the same if part only of the new shares are sold. A 'split' letter will then be issued.

### 'LIFE-BOAT' ISSUES

These have been a feature since a number of companies, sometimes quite large ones, hit financial problems as a result of heavy trading losses, closedown of unprofitable activities, redundancy costs and other adverse effects of the UK's general economic lethargy. Rather than let them go into receivership or bankruptcy, with a loss of jobs and perhaps valuable export earnings, those with fair recovery chances are given a breather by the injection of cash capital or a rescheduling of their borrowings.

Banks are the first life-line with additional loans on realistic repayment terms, or — a radically new approach by British banks — the subscription of capital, usually redeemable or convertible/redeemable preference shares. The second line is the rallying round of the City institutions, particularly those with substantial equity or other stakes in the patient: they sponsor and/or underwrite cash-raising loan and share issues, with or without a reconstruction of the existing capital. Not unnaturally, such rescue efforts are banking on recovery by the troubled companies. It is, therefore, a brave individual shareholder who subscribes for issues which may mean pouring good money after bad. On the other hand, if the rescue succeeds the rewards could be good. 'Life-boat' issues may thus be worth looking into as speculations, particularly if they go to a discount after dealings begin. But don't forget that some of these bank/share operations have been wrong: the inevitable bankruptcy was only postponed.

### SCRIP ISSUES

These are the conversion of accumulated profits and reserves into new shares which are allocated 'free' to existing shareholders. They are paper operations which add nothing to the assets of a company: they do no more than bring the issued capital closer into line with net worth. There is a current tendency to describe such issues as 'bonus' shares. Until recently almost every issue was in ordinary shares. Now, however, a scrip issue may be in preference shares, sometimes redeemable and/or convertible. Some preference share issues are made partly to provide family and other interests with an income while ordinary dividends are being restricted in order to retain a substantial portion of profits for expansion or for some other reason.

An example shows what happens. A company with an issued equity capital of £5 million in 25p shares has accumulated reserves of £10 million: its net equity value is £15 million or 75p a share. A one-for-two (50 per cent) scrip issue is made with the effect that:

* Shareholders have three shares for their previous two.
* The issued equity is raised to £7.5 million in 30 million 25p shares.
* Though the net equity value stays at £15 million, reserves fall to £7.5 million.
* The net asset value per share falls from 75p to 50p. But in place of two shares with a NAV totalling 150p there are now three shares with the same aggregate value.

Providing future profits justify it, the dividend payout may be increased at the same time. If the last annual payment on the old shares was 4p, a merely maintained rate on the increased capital would be $2\frac{2}{3}$p. Instead of 8p from two shares, holders would get 8p from three shares. In practice, assuming continued prosperity and no need for dividend limitation, the new rate would probably be rounded up to at least 3p, which would make a total of 9p on three shares against only 8p on two old.

The market price of the old shares is also reduced. On a pre-scrip quote of, say, 90p the adjusted price for old and new would be 60p. Two old shares worth 180p would become three worth 60p each, or 180p. In fact, instead of moving sideways the price might rise on expectations that the scrip issue foreshadowed rising profits and dividend increases. The proportionate reduction in price might also attract more investors and motivate a rise.

## SHARE SPLITS

Another capital operation, these can benefit shareholders while adding nothing to the net value of the company. Some companies which have ploughed back big slices of annual profits have large reserves in relation to their issued equity capital. Their shares consequently stand at a good many times par value, which can be a deterrent to purchases by small investors. A £1 share may, for instance, be priced at £20. By splitting each £1 share into ten 10p shares there is no change in the total issued capital, but there are ten shares in the market against only one. Arithmetically, the price comes down to 200p. Increased demand might, in fact, put up the price to, say, 225p. A £1 share previously worth £20 would then become ten 10p shares worth £22.50. North American companies, incidentally, call scrip issues 'share splits'.

A contrary move is *consolidation*, which might be the conversion of five 10p shares into one 50p share. The effect might also be a relative improvement in price due to the better view taken of a company which, because it had been going through a bad time, decided to so improve its market image.

## CAPITAL LOSSES

A *capital reconstruction* is a very different operation. The par value of the shares is written down and may become necessary when a company has piled up losses but is still viable. Reconstruction writes off the losses and, provided profits can be earned, opens the way to resumption of dividends. The whole loss usually falls on the equity shares, which underlines the possible risks attaching to such interests.

Say that a company with an issued ordinary capital of £10 million in 40 million 25p shares has accumulated losses of £5 million which it decides to eliminate by writing down the shares by one-half to a par of $12\frac{1}{2}$p. Holders would still have the same proportionate interest in the equity, but in a more realistic form. The reduced shares would still be covered by net assets of £5 million or $12\frac{1}{2}$p each.

In practice, the par value might be restored to 25p by consolidating two of the reduced $12\frac{1}{2}$ shares into one share. Once more, though the issued capital would be halved to 20 million 25p shares, proportionate interests would stay unchanged. The need for reconstructions is an argument in favour of the American *no par value* (NPV) share, the book (or carrying) value of which can be relatively simply adjusted to look after accumulated losses. UK company law does not allow NPV shares, though the idea has not been without support and may come with a new Companies Act.

## SUNDRY ISSUES

These, taken in bulk over the years, add relatively little to the stock of listed securities. In some cases they actually reduce the total capital amount.

**Conversion offers** contribute little or nothing to overall listings: they simply replace one security with another and are mainly of gilt-edged and other fixed interest stocks. The simplest operation is the offer to holders of a maturing issue to exchange into a new stock instead of being paid out in cash. A sweetener may be added by way of an increase in interest to something above the going rate, or by a bonus of, say, £105 of new stock for £100 old. The offer is sometimes an exchange of stock or preference shares in a subsidiary company into an issue of a parent company wishing to streamline its capital structure. Such operations invariably have a sweetener big enough to make the conversion attractive to holders who wish to continue in a fixed interest investment. Reaction to conversion offers will depend on whether it is desired to continue to hold a fixed interest stock on current, or somewhat better, market terms, or to take any cash offer for investment elsewhere.

**Convertible issues** are a different proposition. Exercise of the conversion option means that a fixed interest stock disappears and an equity share takes its place.

**Shares in lieu of cash dividends** come as new listings.

**Warrants** change into shares only when they are exercised. A 'piece of paper' then becomes a listed share.

**Options** to subscribe for ordinary shares are given as incentives to executive directors and/or senior management by some companies. Terms are pitched at levels which it is hoped will give those who exercise them a bonus. Unhappily for recipients in high, wide and handsome days of booming profits which are followed by losses, executive options can turn from paper assets into liabilities with subscribers of part-paid shares having to be bailed out or having to face up to nasty losses. When fully paid, 'executive' shares become the same as the company's ordinary shares and are listed.

**Employee share option** schemes are a new way to give workers an equity participation in their company. Issue methods vary amongst the companies so far offering facilities. Two, however, are (a) direct subscription at a discount on the average market price over a specified period or at par, which ever is the greater, or (b) contractual savings plans where funds are accumulated to buy shares under a National Savings Pay-As-You-Earn contract or in an account with a designated building society. It will be interesting to see how such schemes develop amongst companies and amongst employees.

**Removals** from listings are made when dealings in small issues become very rare; a company goes into liquidation or is taken over completely; a company is dishonestly run or its shares are rigged; when a board of directors asks for cancellation; or, as already shown, through conversions or repayment.

**Suspension** of dealings usually happens when a listed company announces that news of a takeover or a deal, or some other price-sensitive change is imminent. It also takes place when the Stock Exchange is investigating unusual dealings in particular shares, or pending clarification of a company's affairs or financial position. The Stock Exchange incidentally monitors quite a lot of dealings and where necessary calls for information or suspends the listing. Boards of directors are expected to inform the Exchange immediately of any price-sensitive development. Suspension may be for only a few hours or it may last for several days, weeks or months, even years. Sometimes the outcome is adverse and the suspension becomes a cancellation. Mostly, however, especially when it is at a company's request, the outcome is favourable.

# 17

# Takeovers and mergers

Takeover bids and mergers are daily occurrences. They vary from small agreed cash purchases to spectacular battles involving hundreds of millions and billions of pounds and generating much heat, even ill-will. When one or both concerns involved are listed companies, investors must be given sufficient information on which to assess the merits of the offer. It does not automatically follow, however, that investors in the company being bid for should be the only judges. There are instances where a bidder company is ill-advised to make an offer — because it is offering too much; the merger would be irrational; it would take over a lame duck too sick to recover; or, it is the brainstorm whim of a whiz kid or a megalomania-struck entrepreneur.

The first intimation that something is in the wind should be a brief announcement by one or both parties that a bid is to be made or talks are on, or a request to the Stock Exchange to suspend quotations pending an announcement. In practice, an unexplained movement in the share price of the company to be bid for is often the first intimation that something is afoot. Another hint may be the publication (compulsory) of share acquisitions of over 5 per cent by a single buyer or a *concert party* of buyers acting in common. If a bid is on the cards, brief details of the terms may be given right away, may follow in a few days, or, if firm figures have not been worked out, may not be known for some weeks. Sometimes a bid comes out of the blue as a complete surprise to all but the bidder. Other times the bid-for company swiftly rejects the approach or promises a statement when there has been a chance to study the terms. Or there may be a joint announcement that the terms have been agreed by both parties and are recommended by the directors of the bid-for company. Not all agreed bids go through as recommended, however. Organised opposition can force retraction of the deal, bring an improvement in terms or produce a better offer from another bidder.

Few bids are agreed before their launch. The most usual reaction is, therefore, outright rejection and the start of a struggle, perhaps with the entry of a second bidder or several bidders. The horse-trading then begins and the propaganda wagons begin to roll. Circulars pour through shareholder's letter boxes, full page advertisements crowd into the newspapers, commercial television is recruited and big shareholders are contacted to reject or to accept the bid, all at great cost — sometimes extravagantly great cost — to all sides in the war. While the Takeover Panel strives to curb extravagant claims and the exploitation of dubious financial data, the language used can be impassioned, vitriolic and sometimes bordering on the libellous.

Reasons for bids or mergers vary. The most meritorious are, perhaps, when two companies in the same industry merge to make a stronger and more competitive unit in home and world markets. Others are the putting together of two or more companies in complementary businesses in anticipation of benefits from streamlining or working as one organisation. There are also takeovers of raw materials or component producers by pure manufacturers in order to get everything under one umbrella.

It can also be profitable for a business anxious to expand quickly to bid for a company with the productive resources, technical skills and other assets ready to hand in order to save time building new plants or developing new processes. Entrepreneurial skill is often, too, behind bids for sound but fuddy-duddy companies which are not making the best use of their assets or which are capable of expansion under new and thrusting management. Against this generally praiseworthy type are the bidders with the dubious intention of doing no more than sell off bits of the company, or the entire business, at a profit: these are the asset strippers.

Management buy outs (MBOs) are no longer seven day wonders. In 1987 their total value exceeded £3,000 million, some three times the 1986 tally. An MBO may be for an entire quoted or unquoted company, or for part of it; and be financed on borrowed money with or without the bank or other financial backer taking a share interest in convertible preference shares or loan stock and/or ordinary shares. Some of the earliest MBOs have come back to the market at considerably enhanced capitalisations on the original stakes!

The **offer document** will be the first, and perhaps the last document, sent by the bidder. It will set out the terms and conditions of the offer: information about both companies; the benefits anticipated from a merger; the effect on directors, management and employees; the financial effects of acceptance; the capital gains tax implications; and the way to accept. There will also be a letter from the bid-for company directors if they agree to the offer: this should state whether the terms have been approved by the company's merchant bankers or other advisers.

This general outline will be backed up by detailed information on the offer terms; financial facts about the two companies; particulars of any loan stock or preference shares offered; recent stock market quotations; share interests of the directors and their recent dealings in the shares of both companies; recent contracts of material interest; and details of any underwriting or placing arrangements. While the whole of an offer document should be studied, the key information should be found in the general details on the front page.

Terms are a major consideration. They take various forms, as under:
* Straight cash bid.
* Share offer.
* Mixture of shares and cash.
* Choice of shares or cash.
* Exchange of an equity for a convertible or other fixed interest stock.
* Mixture of shares and loan stock or other fixed interest security.
* Three-way mixture of shares, fixed interest stock and cash.

Offers in the form of shares or fixed interest stocks may be underwritten to give offerees the option of taking cash. Offers are generally subject (1) to a minimum acceptance level (usually anything from 51 per cent to 90 per cent); (2) to the offer not being referred to the Monopolies and Mergers Commission, or if it is, that it is not turned down as being against the public interest or for some other reason; (3) to any necessary increase in the capital of the bidder being approved by its shareholders; and (4) to the Stock Exchange granting a listing for the new securities to be issued. In other words, hurdles may lie ahead of offers.

***Benefits*** of the takeover or merger are naturally painted in their brightest colours: they should be carefully studied. Some get-togethers fail to live up to hopes and occasionally go sadly adrift. Euphoria easily creeps into agreed bids, particularly if the subject of the bid is doing badly. Equally, there are deals which are natural money-spinners and the wonder is that it takes so long for them to come about. On the other hand, if the offer is entirely in cash, the prospects of the merged group are no concern of an accepting shareholder who simply takes the money and gets out.

While it may not be vital that an existing board is absorbed intact or that no more than the key directors are taken over, it is important in these days of trade union watchfulness that the position of employees is safeguarded so far as is practicable. Organised opposition from employees and trade unions has blocked several controversial takeovers.

***Financial impacts*** of a takeover bid on capital values and income of the bid-for company's shareholders are such that improvements are the invariable rule. The market value of the existing shares will be compared with the value of the offer; and will show the projected gross income for accepting shareholders (except in the case of a cash offer) compared with the current figure.

***Capital gains tax*** liability, which is discussed in more detail in chapter 23, must enter into the calculations. A straight exchange into shares and/or loan stock is not a problem: the new holding is a continuation of an existing investment and tax does not come into the picture until the securities are sold. An out-and-out cash offer counts, however, as a sale by accepting shareholders and the proceeds must be set off against the cost of the original shares to establish profit — or loss — coming into gains tax calculations. Liability has also to be considered when the terms are part cash and part shares.

Bidders naturally hope for early ***acceptance*** of their offer. It is unwise, however, to act quickly, for the simple reason that, as happens frequently, the bid may have to be improved or a better offer turns up. Action should therefore be delayed until the last seventy-two to forty-eight hours. But even if the deadline is missed, a successful offer will be declared unconditional and late acceptances will be invited.

**Procedure** is, however, simple when the times come to act. All that is required is the signing of an acceptance and transfer form and sending it off with the share certificate as directed. If the investment is in more than one name *all* holders must sign the transfer.

*******

Some takeover battles are short and sharp. Others drag on for weeks or months to a conclusive or inconclusive end. A record for the course must surely be Herbert Morris which, after four separate bids and two Monopolies Commission reports, finally fell after seventeen months to Davy International for £9.3 million.

A hectic and much publicised example of two determined bidders battling it out with leap-frogging offers was the BAT Industries/Allianz Versicherung scrap for Eagle Star Insurance. A feature was that Allianz, a big German insurance group, had acquired almost 30 per cent of Eagle Star in a dawn raid in June 1981, but that the Eagle board strongly resisted all German attempts to take any part in the management. So when BAT, the worldwide tobacco conglomerate, rode in as a white knight with a bid of 575p a share it was welcomed. Bidding and counter bidding then went on apace until BAT's final offer of 700p settled the issue at the then UK record bid cost of £968 million. And a profit to Allianz on the sale of its Eagle shares to BAT of no less than £163 million!

The billionaire line was crossed with an agreed merger of British Home Stores and Mothercare Habitat into Storehouse worth £1,520 million at the market prices of these two well-known retailers. It wasn't too long, however, before there were murmurs of top management disagreements which indicated that while big may be glamourous it is not always harmonious. Dramatic is perhaps a mild description of the battle for Imperial Group, the tobacco, brewer and food giant. After Imps had agreed a £1,220 million merger with United Biscuits, Hanson Trust, the aggressive conglomerate, stepped in and in a very acrimonious scrap secured Imps at a cost approaching the two billion mark — and then set to work to sell off parts of the victim's empire!

Verbal denigration and self-praise were outstandingly strident and worrying in the bitter battle between Argyle Group, the supermarket chain, and Guinness, the brewers, for Distillers, the whisky/gin combine. Guinness, as the Courts later heard in detail, further muddied the waters by very definite non-U share buying tactics. Bringing home the costly nature of such warfare, Argyll later disclosed that if it had been successful the bid bill would have been £116 million, including £70.7 million underwriting commission; and an *actual* outlay as a loser of £34 million after crediting a £13.9 million profit on the sale of the Distillers shares accumulated as part of its bid tactics.

Another spectacular and more recent failure was the £1,800 million bid by Dixons, the camera and electrical shops group, for Woolworths, a contest in which four large institutions voted their 25.8 per cent holdings in favour of the victim against a *total* support of only 35.6 per cent for Dixons.

Though agreed bids are usually much smaller in money terms, there are exceptions such as a £686 million sale by Associated British Foods of its Fine Fare and Shoppers Paradise supermarkets to Dee Corporation, to make Dee the UK's third largest food retailer. Part of the purchase price, which aroused City controversy, was a vendor placing of £350 millions worth of Dee ordinary shares.

Takeover forays are no longer the prescriptive right of UK-based bidders. Predators in all shapes and sizes from all over the free world are now in the game, with Australians and New Zealanders amongst the most aggressive and persistent, and the French and Swiss (*vide* the Nestle/Suchard scrap for Rowntrees) joining in as late starters. Some of the Antipodean forays are by no means full bid ploys but are blatant 'arbitrage' deals to make a turn in a takeover battle or to be bought out as nuisances just as the 'arbs' are hopefully dealt with in America.

Conversely British companies have been going bald-headedly on buying sprees in the US, with multi-billion dollar and bitterly fought bids no longer rarities. Europe has also become an active area in anticipation of the 1992 Common Market changes which, amongst other things it is argued, call for bigger and ever bigger groupings in a new boundary-less EEC. While the normal takeover rules and investor tactics apply when UK companies are the targets, there is a definite difference when they are the bidders. About the only say — usually a mere whisper or whimper — shareholders have is to approve a capital increase to help foot the bill or for some legal reason.

During the time from launch of an offer to closure one outside influence can come to bear. The bid may be referred to the Monopolies and Mergers Commission on the grounds that: it is detrimental to competition by merging two units in one industry; it is lacking in industrial logic by attempting to link up disparate businesses; it would create a monopoly or near-monopoly; or for some other reason it would not be in the public interest. The Commission has to report within six months, which means that this length of time may pass before an OK or a refusal is given.

Some bidders choose to withdraw before the Commission reports or soon after a reference to it. Bids may also be dropped on clearance by the Commission.

Another, more closely concerned watchdog is the Panel on Takeovers and Mergers which administers the City Code on Takeovers and Mergers. Drawing on vast experience and ever ready to amend its rules, the Panel is a voluntary organisation whose members include all bodies concerned with investment and finance, though day-to-day operations are undertaken by a full-time executive. Offers have to follow the Code and, though it has no legal powers, the Panel comes down heavily on transgressors, who risk City ostracism if they do not fall into line. Deterrents to bucking the rules are powers to ask the Stock Exchange to suspend quotations during a bid battle and to refuse listings for new securities proposed to be issued.

The Panel insists on full information being given in offer documents and on the time the bid must stay open. It also insists that (a) profit forecasts must be prepared with the greatest care and be reported on by qualified accountants; (b) assets valuations must be made by independent professional experts on stated bases; and (c) there must be responsible and independent confirmation that resources are available to cover any cash offer.

Other rules cover the secret building up of large shareholdings by what is called 'warehousing' by companies and individuals working in concert. Another most important rule is that if any one party acquires more than thirty per cent of a company's voting capital it must, except in very special circumstances, make a public bid for the balance. This explains announcements that, say, XJA company now holds 29.89 per cent, and not a bigger proportion, of GIZ company's ordinary shares. There are also rules covering dealings in the bidder company's shares during the currency of the offer. A tough new code laid down in March 1986 seeks to control the unfair use of statistics and derogatory and aggressive tones in advertisements; not before time in view of the tactics of some bidders and bidees.

Investors who do not accept a bid may have a problem. The answer depends on its success. If holders of a minimum of 90 per cent of the capital that is bid for accept, the bidder can within four months notify the remainder that within two months he will compulsorily acquire outstanding holdings on the same terms. The only way to defeat such a compulsory purchase is to take the case to the Courts to settle, an action which rarely happens. As offers usually stipulate a minimum acceptance level, they are likely to be declared unconditional once that level is passed and then all further offers will be accepted. The path for acceptance thus stays open for late-comers. On the other hand, if the bidder does not receive sufficient acceptances to declare the offer unconditional, those who have accepted will get back their share certificates.

A sometimes serious problem can arise when a bidder accepts less than 90 per cent and cannot exercise the 'compulsion' rule. If acceptances are more than, say, 75/80 per cent but below the magic 90 per cent, the market in the outstanding shares may become restricted to 'one-way' business, particularly if the number of outstanding shares is small. Dissenters are thus left with shares which it may be hard to sell at fair prices. Their situation will become still harder if the merged company does badly or fails to achieve targets. The price will fall, leaving the majority interests with the chance to dictate a price below the original bid. Dissenters may, of course, see the other side of the coin. Their shares may improve in price and be subject to a higher bid if the new concern prospers. But the general rule must be: accept if a bid is more than 75/80 per cent successful.

**Dawn raids** hit the headlines in early 1980 as something not quite 'City U' in the acquisition of substantial shareholdings. The most spectacular raid was the joint building up of a 25 per cent holding in Consolidated Gold Fields by the closely associated companies, De Beers and Anglo American Corporation of South Africa. Following a secret, and much discussed, accumulation of 14 per cent of Cons. Gold by different parties, De Beers' brokers early on the morning of 12 February contacted large holders and then, on the opening of the market, stood there bidding until the total holding had been raised to 25 per cent. The bid price was 616p against only 525p the night before. By 10 a.m., 16.5 million shares had been picked up, of which 13.5 million were sold by 87 of the 191 institutions approached and the remainder through the market. Not surprisingly, this move was strongly criticised, particularly by holders who had had no possible chance of selling at the premium shut-out price.

A few more dawn raids had to follow before the urgency of laying down effective ground rules was translated into action. In the result, the Council for the Securities Industry made recommendations which make it possible for all shareholders to be able to participate. Broadly, this means that a dawn-raider can openly bid in the market for up to just under 15 per cent of the voting shares of the company and can then go on to buy up to a further 15 per cent from shareholders at large. In the latter event, an offer has to be advertised in at least two newspapers inviting tenders at up to a maximum price and with a seven-day closing date. Conditions will provide that the open offer is cancellable if less than one per cent of the shares bid for are not tendered and that the striking price will be the lowest price at which bids are accepted. An example, already mentioned, was the raid by the German insurance group, Allianz Vesicherung, for an under-30 per cent holding in Eagle Star. After acquiring a

14.9 per cent stake in the raid, a tender offer was then made for up to a further 15 per cent at a maximum price of 290p.

Subsequently, in September 1981, the 'dawn raid' rules were amended with the object of slowing down the rate at which a dominating holding can be bought by a bidder. Now, any party announcing a takeover bid must wait seven days before making significant purchases in the market. This gives the target company, and its shareholders, an opportunity to consider the position and to mount a defence or to take urgent steps to state why the bid should be resisted.

One situation which is not a bid but which means a change is the transfer of a UK company to another country. It happens to companies whose operations are abroad and in which a substantial local holding has been built up. The domicile is moved and UK shareholders become investors in a foreign company. A number of Malaysian tin, rubber and trading companies have featured in such transfers of domicile.

**Demergers** are a relatively new development which generally take two forms. One is the sale of a subsidiary or subsidiaries to employees who may go it alone or get backing and/or participation from banks and/or financial institutions. The other is the hiving off of part of the business into a separate company and the distribution of part or all of its shares to the parent company's shareholders, who may also be asked to put up cash capital by means of a rights issue.

### TAKEOVER STRATEGY

Bids and mergers must be taken very seriously. Few, if any, are altruistic. Most are hard-headed, commercial propositions which have a chance to live up to expectations. Some must, however, be looked on with suspicion about the motives or as the pipe-dreams of megalomaniac empire-builders. A check list should help to decide on the best action:
* What are the reasons for and logic of the bid?
* Does it make sense?
* Will the merged companies be viable as money-makers?
* What is the bidder's business and financial standing?
* Are the merchant bankers and/or stockbrokers backing the offer well-known and well regarded?
* How will acceptance affect share values and income?
* Is there any guarantee that the bidders will be able to complete their offer, particularly any cash part of it?
* In the case of a share or loan stock offer is a cash alternative assured by underwriting?
* If the offer does not look like succeeding, should the shares of the bid-for company be sold in the market while the price is buoyed up by the bid?
* Has the City Code been observed? Is the bid likely to run into trouble with the Takeover Panel?
* What are the chances of a reference to the Monopolies and Mergers Commission? And the risks of a thumbs-down?
* Defer action until the last 72 or 48 hours.
* But do not get shut in as one of a small minority of dissenters.

*Finally a note for speculators.* Money can be made buying the bid-for shares on the initial approach. Horse-trading or arrival of a second bidder usually boosts the offer price. At the worst there can be little or no loss should the first bid go through unchallenged.

And a P.S. Consider very carefully the implications and the promised benefits to come when asked to approve capital increases to pay for highly priced bid acquisitions. It sometimes pays to cut and run before the debacle.

****

The takeover world is creating its own vocabulary. White knights and white squires are hoped for rescuers from an unwanted bid. Concert parties, fan clubs and warehousing are operators hoping to avoid disclosure of single holders of over 5 per cent. Arbs and greenmailers are operators buying big stakes in the hope of being bought out at a profit by the victim. Poison pills are legal and other tactics to denigrate or obstruct bidders.

# 18

# Some specialised markets

There cannot be one, uniform set of rules for the assessment of *all* shares. Yardsticks suitable for industrial and commercial companies are not entirely of use for other sectors, as the following notes will show.

## BANKS AND MONEY HOUSES

Banks divide into two distinct categories — clearing (or 'High Street') and merchant. A saying succinctly describes the basic difference as 'A clearing banker lives on his deposits; a merchant banker on his wits'.

**A clearing bank** draws in money from a large and vastly varied number of customers which, after keeping enough in the till to meet cash withdrawals, it lends to other customers and invests in short-term securities. Its profits come from the difference between interest paid on deposit accounts, as distinct from current accounts on which no interest is usually paid, and the interest earned on its loans and investments plus commissions on foreign-exchange dealing, trust management, insurance and other services.

Although a clearing bank owns extensive and valuable premises, and perhaps has investments in other financial enterprises, its 'working capital' is its current and other deposits, its skill in deploying them, and a management which can keep risk-taking to a minimum while seeking the most lucrative business. Some banks have set up their own merchant banking organisations and are well entrenched in hire purchase, leasing and other credit finance. And, as noted in an earlier chapter, an historic break with age-long tradition, is the move into 'capital' investment in loan stock, preference shares and even equity in customer companies which, because of heavy losses or other troubles, have had to be reorganised to give fair hopes of recovery. Other moves which reflect the hectic competition within the money market are Stock Exchange membership through acquisition of established broking and jobbing firms; house mortgage lending; insurance; and estate agency.

For generations clearing banks published their profits after undisclosed, and often very substantial, transfers to hidden reserves and provisions for actual and potential bad debts. Now, there is much more disclosure about such key facts. Published profits are truer reflections of a year's operations; which makes it easier to compare individual progress and bank by bank. The basic tests are the profit earned on net assets — and their percentage relation to the total of current and deposit accounts. Price–earnings ratios and their comparison with other banks are also essential indicators of progress. The 'Big Four'

— Barclays, Lloyds, Midland and National Westminster — and some other banks have, incidentally, broadened their capital bases through issues of subordinated convertible or other loan stocks. An increasing amount of 'capital' financing towards the purchase of US and other foreign banking interests is being met by US and Euro-dollar loan issues or placings. The latest innovation is a hybrid, some would say a gimmick — a perpetual Eurobond which pays floating rate interest but which, like an equity share, is never redeemable. An unhappy feature of the move into American banking is that some acquisitions have so far not lived up to best expectations; have been losing money; need costly reorganisation or have to be sold at crippling loss.

Another, and more worrying, development has been the heavy and continuing need to write off and to provide against bad debts. While part of these provisions is against losses on UK business, the greater part is in respect of loans made in more euphoric times to republics in South and Central America; third world nations like Nigeria; Poland and other countries which have defaulted, or are in danger of defaulting, on the hundreds of billions of pounds and other currencies lent to them. Advanced by most of the world's banks, many of the loans are being 'rescheduled' in efforts to avert the complete collapse of the borrowers' economies and to give the bankers some chance to recover their money. It must be questioned, however, whether 'rescheduled' is a euphemism for 're-heated pie in the sky'. Rightly in such circumstances, the banks are acting together to stave off crashes. Their interdependence is accentuated by the fact that they hold a lot of each others Euro and other paper and that severe slumps in oil, agricultural and Californian real estate are forcing the closure, or need for rescue operations, of a growing number of smaller US banks, with a chain reaction which could blow up into a global crisis if some major banks have to be helped or be forced to close their doors.

At home, the burgeoning of banking and other services by building societies plus the entry of other institutions into the money services industry means increasing competition which will have to be met by taking on more risky business, cuts in profit margins or — hardly likely to happen — a standstill on expansion. Looming, too, is a plastic card crisis as personal borrowing mounts by the billions and the bad debt ratio rises. Also on the doorstep is the default risk on thinly covered home mortgages on properties whose value would slump sharply in the event of an industrial recession and its inevitable crop of redundancies. All of which reduces bank shares from blue chips to bingo markers.

**Merchant banks,** the bigger ones of which are members of the Accepting Houses Committee, have considerably broadened their activities in recent years. They still actively carry on their basic business of financing trade by accepting (in effect guaranteeing) bills of exchange drawn by their customers and by loans. In addition they are now very much concerned in the arrangement of Eurobond and other finance for large-scale overseas construction contracts, trade promotion, purchases of overseas assets, and loans for UK and foreign governments, local authorities, nationalised industries and a variety of businesses. Foreign exchange, and in some cases bullion dealing, together with investment management for pension funds and other clients are amongst other important services.

It is, however, in the field of corporate finance and advice that merchant banks come most into public prominence. Hardly a takeover or merger of any size takes place without their giving advice to each party and, as happens at times, getting locked into hectic and acrimonious battles. Such specialised work is apart from new issues, offers for sale, placings and rights issues for new or existing company clients and continuing financial advice. While the bread and butter comes from the acceptance and normal lending business, the jam has been coming in increasing dollops from the corporate side, where takeover activities have been providing handsome fees and underwriting commissions; and it is this side which will be worst affected by the slowing down in capital raising and takeover business which is inevitable, even if some way off.

An age-long practice has been to put substantial sums to hidden reserves before striking disclosed profits, thus leaving published price – earnings ratios as the best available data for share assessment. The flotation in June 1986 of Morgan Grenfell, one of the largest merchant banks and most successful of the takeover wizards, brought a break with tradition: the prospectus gave the *full, actual profits* for recent years. Still, merchant bank shares may have had their best days and have little long-term attraction.

There are also some listed deposit-taking institutions, which may not qualify as 'banks', that take deposits from the public and carry on hire purchase and credit finance business. Some of these concerns got into serious difficulties in 1973 and 1974 through over-lending on property. Some went to the wall, but those with chances of eventual recovery were helped by a 'life-boat' fund organised by the Bank of England — at the peak such loans totalled £1.18 billion. A few got free of the life-boat fairly quickly. But others needed more time to get back onto their own unaided feet. There is no doubt that, but for the life-boat, there would have been a very much worse and wider-spread crisis. Lessons were then learned which brought some much needed and tighter supervision of 'fringe' financial activities.

**Discount houses** are a relatively simple form of financial organisation which specialises in short-term money. They deal in bills of exchange and, by far the largest sector, in the Treasury Bills which the government sells each week. They also take positions in short-dated gilt-edged stocks on which they get interest and make a profit (or loss) on realisation, and buy local authority bonds. Their operations call for great skill and judgement in foreseeing movements in interest rates: fractional variations can mean the difference between profit and loss. Good profits can be made on gilt-edged dealing when interest rates are falling but it comes much harder when they are rising; and it is easy to slip into losses if the forecasting is wrong. Apart from their relatively small share capital and reserves, discount houses get their funds from commercial and other banks on what is termed 'call money' which is repayable on demand, often on 'overnight' terms. If call money is in short supply, they may be 'forced into the Bank' (the Bank of England) which is the 'lender of last resort', and have to pay a higher interest rate for the facility. The number of houses is being reduced through takeovers and mergers, and it is being questioned as to how long the survivors will remain independent; in fact, about the only attraction in the shares of the listed companies is an eventual takeover profit.

**Money-broking houses** cover a much wider field than the discount houses. Their activities include bond trading on an international scale with some making aggressive, and so far profitable, entries into the enormous US markets.

## INSURANCE/ASSURANCE

There are three types of insurance companies — life assurance, general insurance, and composite which transact both life assurance and general business.

While 'life' primarily means financial provision against death, it includes endowment, pensions and educational assurance, and annuities. Mortality studies over many generations enable a life company to estimate its liabilities pretty closely and to set its premiums at rates which ensure a surplus. A large proportion of the surpluses is allocated to the so-called with-profit assurances and a much smaller proportion to shareholders' funds. Shareholders' share of actuarial surpluses should increase as business grows.

**Life assurance** shares should be assessed on the growth in new business, premium income, investment income, earnings and dividend payments, and the expense ratio. The percentage earned on life fund investments and the ratio of expenses to total income are also important as indicators of successful investment policies and prudent management. The abolition in the March 1984 Budget of tax relief on the premiums of new assurances brought a pause in the continuing growth in business; but such is the industry's ability to produce new schemes and to market its wares that the upward trend is back, or is getting back, to its old and impressive pace.

**General insurance** ranges over a multiplicity of risks from household and car cover to ships, aeroplanes and accidents. Inflation has played havoc with much of this business, with premium rates generally lagging behind the soaring cost of claims. Underwriting losses rather than profits have therefore been all too common in recent years, offsetting part of the income received from invested funds. Premium increases and elimination of high risk business, particularly in North America, are now, however, tending to get general accounts into better balance with an encouraging reduction in losses or return to profits. Assessment of composite shares is thus bedevilled by the less certain results of general business. Fair guides are, however, the profit and dividend record over five to ten years; the return on investments, which include substantial holdings representing shareholders' funds; and the steps taken to eliminate general fund losses.

Until the BAT/Eagle Star takeover, insurance shares were fairly pedestrian performers. Now, however, and already reflected in share prices, every one of the quoted companies is a possible target. After the BAT move it can no longer be argued that it would cost far too much to buy up the biggest companies like the Prudential, Guardian Royal Exchange, Commercial Union or General Accident. Otherwise, the sector offers investment opportunities, with the pure life companies certain of steady profit progress despite the hiccup caused by the abolition of the 15 per cent tax relief on premiums.

**Insurance brokers** usually combine the two activities of agency business on behalf of clients and actual insurance of risks through membership or control of Lloyd's underwriting syndicates (a side of their business they might have to sell off following changes in Lloyd's rules). Inflation has certainly boosted the broking side as premiums have been driven up by the need for greater and greater cover by their clients and useful profits have been earned on short-term investment of funds passing through their hands. Broking should continue to expand but, as some difficulties and competition overseas have shown, the Lloyd's side has been having some bumpy and loss-making rides. Uncovering, to put it mildly, of some extraordinary re-insurance transactions gave an unpleasant taste to Lloyd's as a whole and in particular to shares of the few quoted members. These falls by the wayside are, however, being dealt with and, with a possible resumption of takeover bids by US and other foreign counterparts, broker shares have speculative possibilities.


## PROPERTY PROBLEMS

Theoretically, property shares are the almost perfect investment in an inflationary period. The land on which buildings stand cannot disappear and in view of its shortage should grow in value. Buildings should also appreciate as replacement costs zoom up. In fact, the middle 1970s were a traumatic and nerve-searing period for the industry. Easy money and the eagerness of fringe banks (with a helping hand from the clearing banks) to lend on almost anything fired a boom in which speculation swept away realities. When the crash came many big and small operators went to the wall. Long, tedious and involved bailing-out operations were begun to save those with a chance, often very thin, of survival. Even the biggest, most soundly based companies had to face sharp drops in values and difficulties in raising finance on reasonable terms to complete developments in hand. Compared with heady revaluations which had been claimed and sometimes written into balance sheets, downward revisions reduced paper castles to realities.

Despite the thousands of millions of actual and paper losses, the crash did some good. Property shares can again be assessed on traditional bases of real values, financial structures, prospects and earnings. Assets have recovered in a firm market with well-established companies reporting worthwhile yearly movements in market values.

Property company financing is different from that of most other companies. Because of inherent faith in property as a solid asset, anything up to 50/60 per cent, sometimes more, of the capital structure is in debentures, loan stocks, mortgages, bank and other borrowings. Which means that a relatively small equity does well if affairs prosper but badly when things go wrong. Unhappily for a few companies, large sums were borrowed at high interest rates in the boom days. There was also some money-raising in foreign currencies which subsequently rose sharply against the pound and added to the debt burden.

Profits (or losses) come from two sources — letting of investment properties (which may or may not have been developed by the company itself) and sale of development projects. A few companies are entirely, or almost entirely, investment concerns which do little or no dealing. Others are largely development-for-sale experts and a number are a mixture of both types. The simple aim of the investment companies is to produce a surplus of rental income over operational costs and loan interest. The developers are at the mercy of the market and much depends on their astuteness in anticipating demand in the right places at the right times.

Whether investment or development, properties under construction produce no income. In fact, they cost money by way of interest on capital outlay until let or sold. The treatment of such interest is debatable. One argument is that it is part of the construction cost and should be capitalised by addition to the cost of the property. The opposite, conservative, view is that the interest is part of the running costs and should be charged against normal profits. Companies using the capitalisation formula may charge the interest to profit and loss account and offset the cost by a credit from reserves. But for this expedient, companies with costly development projects would show little profit — or actual losses. A company charging all interest against revenue and still able to pay dividends is, however, the safest.

A revival after 66 years is the listing of single property companies by which, unlike the rest of the sector with portfolios of dozens or hundreds of separate properties, only one large unit is owned and operated. Clearly this means greater risks and makes SAPCOs somewhat speculative.

Investment in property shares should not be willy-nilly simply because property is believed to be a good long-term holding. *Points to watch* are:
* Type — investment, development or mixture.
* Spread of holdings geographically and kind — factory, shop, office, commercial, residential ...
* Suspension of exchange control in October 1979 has led to increasing investment in US and other overseas property, which may or may not be profitable — there are a lot of sharks in the US real-estate sphere.
* Financial structure — ratio of *all* loan capital and borrowings to equity.
* Repayment dates of borrowings and amounts in foreign currencies. Bunching up at early dates can mean refinancing headaches with the threat of forced sales of the most marketable properties.
* Valuation policy — annually, other period or roll-over method of partial valuation each year — and if by independent valuers or by the directors.
* Reversion prospects are important to future profits. How much of the property let at currently low rentals comes up for review, and when?
* Management record. Some soundly run companies came through the slump with little or no permanent scarring.
* Measure of support by large institutional lenders and shareholders to ease the unwinding of overbought situations. Some institutions have had to help in order to safeguard their investments.
* The revenue and profit record.
* The option to adopt March 1982 values as the base for capital gains imposts will cut tax bills and stimulate sales of older properties whose original cost could be very much lower than the current market values.
* Companies with a concentration of properties in the City of London will be hit if the present rush for prestige offices dries up or reverses, or if high hopes of money-making out of the Big Bang lead tenants to mass withdrawals from financial markets.
* Generally, in fact, it is possible that in the face of the extensive construction of new office and business premises, and soaring building and

development costs, another share market peak is close at hand, or already reached – and a slump is inevitable.

* Finally, a comparative exercise. There is a fundamental difference between major groups like Land Securities and MEPC, which have a large part of their funds in a relatively small number of massive offices and other developments, and smaller companies which own a much greater number of houses and flats. The downside risk on the latter is obviously less than on the former — a few vacancies are hardly noticeable. So it is worth looking at companies like Bradford Property Trust which pays its dividends out of net rentals from some 7,500 dwellings and investment income; and ploughs back surpluses on property sales (averaging over £2 million a year after tax in recent years) into expansion, and buying in its shares.

# 19

# Natural resources — a basic investment

There is no doubt that, even if only slowly, living standards of a large proportion of the world's population are rising, and for the better-off are steadily moving ahead. Translated into hard, material fact this means that demand for food, clothing, other essentials, and consumer durables and non-durables will inexorably expand. More food will have to be produced. More natural resources will have to be turned into more manufactures and services.

The corollary is that one of the best investment media is in companies which exploit natural resources, the demand for which cannot help but expand over the years despite economic recessions which, as history has shown, inevitably correct themselves.

There are two categories of natural resource companies — foodstuffs and raw materials. Growing food is a repeatable process. Extraction of raw materials is totally different. Once raw materials are dug or pumped out of the ground the sources of supply are finished and the value of what remains must rise. It is, therefore, logical that, despite the increasing capital cost of exploiting new sources of supply, one of the best long-term investment should be natural resources.

In stating this fact it is well in mind that some metal industries have been going through very tough, even rough, times, and full recovery will take a little time. But 'downs' are not unusual. There have been many booms and slumps over the generations. But each time, particularly in the slumps, corrective measures have eventually got to work to restore the balance of supply and demand. Over-production correctives, all seen at work in recent years, include closure of uneconomic mines; voluntary curtailment of production; restriction schemes for a whole industry or by one or more producing countries; postponement of the commissioning of new plants; and putting development plans on ice. Though time is needed for such steps to reverse the trend, the cumulative effect is slowly seen in the rise in prices which accompanies the fall in unsold stock levels.

Boom or slump, other factors have for some time been at work on the supply side. Governments have imposed restrictions on development, have tried to control markets, have curbed production, nationalised properties and, often most damaging of all efforts, put onerous taxes on output and profits. Some governments like British Columbia and Australia have seen the folly of their ways and have reduced taxation to bearable levels or have lifted strangling restrictions on development, capital investment, foreign participation, environmental and sales policies.

Environmentalists, preservationists and ecologists have thrust their ideological views on existing and potential producers through demands, all too often unrealistic in hard commercial terms, for safeguards and shutdowns. Added to never-ending rises in production costs, the extremist views of these do-gooders will, if allowed to continue, hamper existing and new production to the extent of creating serious shortages of natural resources as the world needs increasing supplies to meet rising living standards, particularly in the third-world countries. All these factors will tend to increase the values of existing producing properties.

Wars are another restraining factor. The armed raid into Zaire in May 1978 brought a temporary closure of some of that country's copper mines. Though it has not happened up to the time of writing, the current, drawn-out Iran/Iraq war gave periodical rise to rumours that oil supplies through the Gulf will be cut off.

A feature of the natural resources industries is that it is not always all downs and all ups. Over-production of copper, nickel, and iron ore in recent times has, for instance, been offset by bursts of demand for zinc, lead and some of the rare earths. Gold, silver and platinum are no longer rare metals used mainly for hoarding and jewellery: they are in steadily rising use in many forms of industrial production. Diamonds, though also in increasing demand by industry, keep their age-old attractions as ornaments and a hedge against inflation.

Oil, after a lengthy period of high and very profitable prices for producers, became a dirty word when the OPEC countries failed to agree cuts sufficient to bring output into line with consumption, and the price of crude fell to less than one-third of its previous levels of $30 and upwards. Small producers were forced to plug their wells and exploration outfits went bust or partially or wholly curtailed their drilling activities. On the other hand, the big integrated groups with their spread of interests ranging from production to retailing, chemicals and ancillary activities have so far come through the crisis with little or no damage to their overall profits and strong enough to live through further production upsets; like the best metal miners their shares are very far from being write-offs.

In the metal industries finance for expansion of existing mines and development of new ventures is now arranged in well-tried ways. A common practice is to raise a large part of capital costs by loans which, whether linked to sales contracts or other arrangements, are in effect repayable out of profits. In fact, once South African gold mines reach the production stage they pay for all but major future development out of profits, with or without the help of short-term loans.

An example of successful loan financing is provided by Lornex Mining, the British Columbia opencast copper/molybdenum mine, of which Rio Algom, the Canadian end of the Rio Tinto-Zinc group, owns over 68 per cent and Teck Corporation some 22 per cent of the equity. Total costs of developing the mine (one of the largest in Canada) was some $193 million, of which $131 million was provided by loans and barely $11.5 million by equity capital. Less than seven years later the loan debt had been paid off out of profits, an operation helped by booming copper prices in 1973 and 1974. Since then substantial increases in the mining area have been brought into production, with the outlay again financed out of accumulated profits.

The risks involved are brought home by the financial problems of a big nickel/copper project in Botswana. Largely due to initial technical difficulties and to a slump in nickel and copper prices, substantial losses have piled up. The future profitability of this mine depends, therefore, on substantial increases in the prices of its metals, of which there have recently been promising trends.

Two morals are to be drawn from these examples. First, the best mining speculations are those which were established producers before capital costs started zooming; which have long lives; and which can earn some sort of a profit even when their products are a glut on the market. Second, it can pay to buy into 'on-the-floor' ventures without friends but which have reasonable survival chances.

Investment in mining can be restricted to a single metal or two or more products. Producers of single metals are, as it happens, mostly in the rare category — gold, platinum and diamonds, though many tin companies are 'one-metal' ventures. It is common, however, to have a mix of products such as gold and uranium; copper and nickel or silver; lead, zinc and silver; copper and molybdenum; and copper and gold. The advantage of mixed producers is that if one metal is in over-supply another may be in demand. Gold/uranium mines proved this when depression in one metal was countered by strength in the other.

An example of the benefits of mixed output is Bougainville Copper, the Papua New Guinea project which, through CRA, is another important part of the Rio Tinto-Zinc group. Although the main metal is copper with a useful addition of silver, a large *by-production* of gold makes it one of the world's biggest gold mines. No wonder that Bougainville was able to ride a copper slump when gold was trading at up to peak prices and in 1988 has been benefiting from good copper prices.

Single metal producers can certainly come off best when their product is booming. They can, however, be the biggest losers in a slump. Dual producers can ride storms when one metal is up and the other down, and do well when both are on the up and up. The safest spread is, however, provided by the mining finance houses whose interests usually stretch over a number of products and, political risks in mind, over a number of countries.

Some 'houses' such as Anglo American Corporation and General Mining Union Corporation (in South Africa), Cominco, Teck and Noranda Mines (in Canada) and Broken Hill Proprietary, CRA and Western Mining (in Australia) are overseas companies. Others are, however, UK-based. Rio Tinto-Zinc is a good example. Its spread takes in copper, gold, iron ore, uranium, lead, zinc, silver, borax, aluminium, steel, tin, coal, oil, natural gas and other products in Australia, Canada, Papua New Guinea, Namibia, the USA, South Africa, Europe, the UK and other countries; and it is an active prospector.

An intriguing new holding company with a promising spread of interests in established, developing and exploratory plays is Metall Mining, a Canadian-based corporation floated in 1987 to hold substantially all the mining interests of the West German group Metallgesellschaft, a world leader in the non-ferrous metals, smelting and refining, trading and fabrication industry. Metall's stakes include shareholdings in established producers, Teck Corporation and Cominco in Canada and MIM Holdings in Australia; and amongst exploration and development projects the giant Ok Tedi gold/copper producer in Papua-New Guinea, the two Canadian copper miners Afton and Highmont, the Callion gold venture in Australia and the Cayelli Bakir copper/zinc/silver play in Turkey.

Amongst interests mainly centred in Africa, the UK, North America and Australia, Consolidated Gold Fields, another successful UK company, spreads its net over gold, tin, energy materials, iron ore, lead, zinc, silver, ilmenite and other beach metals, copper, construction materials, finance and exploration.

A valuable, but far from appreciated, feature of mining finance house shares is that they invariably sell at below their net asset value; sometimes the discount can be anything up to 50 per cent or more. This valuable discount is increased, moreover, when one company holds shares in another finance house whose shares are also selling at a discount. The cost of indirect buying into mining ventures can thus be extremely cheap.

Still wider 'cushions' are provided by investment type holding companies whose large or majority holdings are in a spread of operating companies. Brascan, a Canadian company built up by members of the Bronfman family, is a useful example. Its interests range widely over base and precious metals; oil, gas and coal; brewing; packaged foods; agricultural products; the world's largest sanitary tissue makers; paper products; life assurances and other financial services; and hydroelectric production. Through its holding of over 46 per cent in Noranda Mines, Brascan is involved in the development of the recently discovered Hemlo field which could become one of Canada's greatest ever gold producers.

In the case of gold itself, it is not widely enough appreciated that geographic selection is not confined to South Africa, where apartheid and sanctions have disturbed investment confidence. There is a good range of established, new and profitable gold mines in Canada, Australia and the USA well worth consideration.

Trends in metal prices are obviously a factor in share investment assessment. Over the past ten years or so there have been wide, and at times wild, fluctuations. After touching $850 an ounce in 1980 on heavy speculation, gold had a price range of $390–503 in 1987 and has since (up to mid-1988) bobbed mostly around the $450 level. Base metals have, however, gained in overall strength from early 1987, with some trading at the best prices for some years. *The Economist* commodity indicators spell this out. Starting 1987 at 99.3, the dollar metal index finished the year at a high of 183.8, while the sterling equivalent moved from 86.2 to 126.6. By August 1988 the dollar index had gone over the 200 mark.

Though many of the biggest oil companies are based overseas, there is a useful UK sector. British Petroleum and Shell give wide global and production diversification, with Ultramar playing a much smaller but active part in narrower fields. There are also companies such as London & Scottish Marine Oil which give direct participation in North Sea and Celtic Sea operations. A number of investment trusts, especially some of the Scottish companies, have interests in North Sea explorers and producers, while Viking Resources concentrates on oil and gas holdings.

Investment in tea, rubber, palm oil and cocoa can be direct through a number of producing companies, some of which are, however, a restricted share market because of their small issued capitals. The easier and safer way is through the large management companies which not only give a spread over two or more commodities but add extensive interests in industrial, merchanting, insurance, finance and other activities in the UK and abroad. Go-ahead companies with wide and varied activities are James Finlay & Company and Harrisons Malaysia.

Surprisingly, the choice of actual food producers is relatively small compared with the number of wholesalers, retailers and processors. Associated Fisheries and Tate & Lyle are amongst the direct producers. Dalgety has a wide spread of interests in food and agricultural production, processing and marketing in Australia, New Zealand, the UK and North America; and is active in milling, malting, commodity trading, timber, chemicals and engineering. Unilever is even bigger and with a greater spread of world-wide interests.

## RESOURCES GUIDE

An intriguing feature of many mining companies is diversification away from their main products. This, as already shown, may come from by-products; from further exploration of existing properties; from new exploration; from partnership arrangements with other companies; or from farm-outs with other developers.

It is common for large and small mining houses and/or producers to form joint exploration or development ventures from scratch or on the properties of sometimes relatively small existing companies. Risks and costs are thereby spread amongst a number of venturers, of which some of the bigger ones appropriate large sums every year for exploration. Many efforts come to nothing and fade out of existence, as the big Australian mining booms have shown. But good and profitable winners do turn up to compensate for the losers.

A significant development has been the move of some of the world's oil majors into the metals and coal fields through bids for outright takeovers or for majority share interests in producing companies and mining houses. There has also been some swapping or takeover action in the oil sector, mostly amongst Canadian and US companies. A UK example of oil-to-minerals was British Petroleum's £410 million takeover of Selection Trust at a big premium on the latter's market price. In the US, takeover and share purchase operations by oil companies — and others — soared far into the multi-billion dollar sphere with some titanic battles between two or more contenders for one mining victim. The mining industry's recent troubles curbed such activity. The 1987/88 recovery in base metal prices makes possible, however, a return of takeover — and merger — activity; which adds spice to the shares of producers that are again making worthwhile profits, helped by improved productivity and a streamlining of activity.

While certainly not literally applicable to most dead and buried hopes, it is worth recalling what is purported to have been Mark Twain's definition of a gold mine as 'a hole in the ground owned by a liar'. Such a definition pinpoints a realistic and often harsh market fact: wide and exaggerated swings in the prices of shares of new mining and oil ventures often take place when the only information is from bore hole results from which extravagant dreams and hopes can be built up. Realism doesn't come until actual values begin coming out of the ground; share prices may then fall if dreams are not realised, or rise if actual metal grades or oil flows are above the most optimistic forecasts. But for the speculator, as for the mining houses, one good winner can pay for several losses.

And one secret of success is knowing, and remembering, the ramifications of individual mining and oil companies and the 'houses' such as Consolidated Gold Fields and RTZ, the UK-based groups.

# 20

# Going foreign parts

An increasingly major proportion by market value of the company securities officially listed on the Stock Exchange are the stocks and shares of non-UK registered concerns. Over the 500 mark, they include a variety of companies based in 37 countries, including the USA, Canada, South Africa, Australia, Malaysia, Hong Kong, Japan, France, Holland, Germany and other European territories. Shares listed range from those of multi-billion American giants like International Business Machines and General Motors to small, expiring South African gold mines.

The gamut of dealing facilities does not end, however, at the listed stocks. It is possible to buy and sell readily-marketable securities listed on any other recognised stock exchange throughout the free world; this gives a very big choice. Jobbers and market makers have arbitrage arrangements with their equivalents in all active overseas markets. Some brokers also have branches in the leading centres. In particular, there is a substantial two-way trade with New York, Montreal and Toronto, Sydney, Melbourne and Perth, Tokyo, Johannesburg, Hong Kong, Kuala Lumpur, Singapore and, nearer home, with Paris, Amsterdam and Brussels.

Big Bang has greatly expanded turnover in London as well as boosting its trading with other markets, and with dealings going on up to 24 hours a day. Market makers with overseas offices or associates do business round the clock simply by 'handing on the book' to New York as London closes for the day with New York then handing it on to Hong Kong or Tokyo as Wall Street closes – and the Far East passing it back to London as the new dealing day starts around 7 a.m.

## DEALING FACTORS

For a little over forty years from August 1939 exchange controls sharply restricted portfolio investment in foreign securities. This meant that unlike the single consideration of price which entered into dealings in home-based securities, three factors eventually affected overseas transactions. They were:
* Local market price.
* Sterling exchange rate.
* Investment currency (or dollar) premium.

Because foreign currencies could not be freely bought at normal exchange rates, funds for new purchases had to be found elsewhere. They came from an investment (dollar) pool which was made up of currencies realised from sales of overseas securities. The availability of funds depended on the flow into and out of the pool. Supply and demand thus dictated the cost of such dollars. As buyers generally tended to dominate on balance, a premium (which depended on the buyer/seller position at any one time) usually had to be paid over the free-market rate for the investment dollars.

Not surprisingly, particularly in periods of heavy buying of Australian, American, Japanese, Hong Kong and other foreign shares, the premium shot up at times to around the 90 per cent range — one dollar cost up to $1.90 or more. On the other hand, in slack buying times or through heavy selling, the premium traded down to single figures, a position which developed in 1979 in anticipation of the abolition of exchange controls.

*On 24 October 1979 all controls were suspended.* The dollar pool expired. Dollar and other foreign currencies became freely available at normal market rates. Apart from Rhodesia/Zimbabwe having to wait until the ending of UDI, the whole free world became an investment oyster. Local share prices apart, this left only exchange rates as the 'x' factor in overseas investment.

**Sterling exchange** rates can, and do, fluctuate sharply and widely. In February 1975, for instance, £1 bought over 2.40 US dollars. By October 1976 the rate had dropped to under $1.60. After a recovery to over $1.95 in January 1978, the rate fell away within about four months to around $1.80, only to start climbing again towards the $2 mark. By the summer of 1979 it was ranging up to, and sometimes above, the $2.30 figure. The first half of 1981 saw one of the most dramatic drops from over a $2.40 level to under $1.80. A slump to below $1.30 in 1984 and to a record low of $1.05 in early 1985 resulted from high US interest rates and the UK's economic and labour problems. Recovery followed, however, to around the $1.50 level by mid-1986; and by mid-1988 the rate was was in the $1.90 region as fear was engendered by continuing deficits on the US budget and balance of payments.

An example shows how exchange rate movements can affect the sterling cost and value of overseas shares. Suppose 100 American shares were bought at $30 when the £ stood at $2.00, the cost would be:

$$\frac{100 \times 30}{2.00} = \pounds1,500$$

Again suppose that the share price does not move but the £ falls to $1.50, the sterling value would become:

$$\frac{100 \times 30}{1.50} = \pounds2,000$$

There has been a sterling gain of £500 without a movement in the local share price. On the other hand, if the shares had been bought at the $1.50 rate and sold at the $2.00 rate, the loss would be £500. *UK buyers gain from a strong pound; sellers benefit from a weak pound.*

Keeping the two market factors well in mind, it is worthwhile taking a look at some of the main overseas stock markets with their particular attractions and peculiarities.

## AMERICAN ANIMATION

Despite the monitory, and admonitory, efforts of the Securities and Exchange Commission, which polices stock market, financial and company activities, US stock markets are subject to sharp, even frightening, swings. Just as the 1929 Crash is well recorded and still argued over, the Crash of 19 October 1987 will be analysed all ways up and down over the years to come. That Black Monday saw the greatest 'meltdown' in panic selling which drove the Dow Jones Industrial average down by a record 22½ per cent to 1738 and sent stock markets all round the world clattering after with heavy, and sometimes record, one-day slumps. But that was America — over-optimistic or over-pessimistic — and in the calmer aftermath it was seen as an overdue correction of an over-priced equity market. Two specific reasons for blasting prices were the belated recognition that deficits in both US budget and balance of payments were far, far too huge; to which the bears added talk of a coming recession. Fuel was added by the programme trading operations of the market 'bosses', the pension funds and other financial institutions in whose hands increasing proportions of stocks are accumulating. Until the budget and BOP deficits are whittled down to manageable levels, Wall Street will have its up and downs, but with the latter unlikely to be as cataclysmic as the Black Monday crash.

Ironically, despite the bear-inspired talk of a recession, the US economy at mid-1988 was in good shape and improving. Unemployment has been falling; inflation is being held at 4–5 per cent; exports are growing and imports slowing down; and personal spending and capital investment show little to worry over. Add the fact that Black Monday squeezed out a lot of the water and Wall Street remains a promising long-term investment area for those ready to ride the bumps. Spice is added by the non-stop takeover operations of US, British, Japanese and other overseas groups and entrepreneurs seeking out huge and small targets, and with spending money soaring into multi-billions of dollars.

A cautionary factor is, however, the dollar which lost lots of its former glory in 1987 and early 1988; and which will continue to bob up and down. But if the budget and BOP shortfalls are slashed to nil or to manageable figures, the dollar will recover sharply, which will mean that, as shown earlier, a currency profit will be added to any stock price gain. Though many individual stocks with promising prospects are currently to be found, the cautious way in is through investment or unit trusts with a large part, or all, of their money in US stocks.

## CANADA LONG-TERM

It is only slowly being realised that Canada could be one of the most promising and profitable investment areas of the 1990s. Below the surface it is one of the world's richest areas of gold, silver, most base metals, coal, oil and natural gas. Above ground it has vast forest areas and is a leading wheat producer. It has problems such as unemployment, racial differences and a depreciated dollar. Yet, though it has been enjoying a stock market reappraisal, there are still many shares which are under-valued on medium- to long-term prospects, a fact which is being appreciated by the growth in takeover bids for the most promising enterprises.

While banks and leading industrial companies will be the safety-first way in, mining and other natural resources stocks should produce the fireworks and give the best chance of gains. But a warning: an increasing number of relatively small Canadian mining stocks are always being actively promoted. Some of these ventures, especially those sponsored by responsible and well-known promoters, have bonanza chances, but others may in the end produce nothing but empty holes in the ground. This means that the safest way in is through established companies with widespread interests and proven track records. Mining and oil 'houses' such as Cominco, Metall Mining, Noranda, Rio Algom and Teck Corporation are straightforward choices. But, if a wider spread taking in forest products, industrial and transport activities is wanted, a natural front runner is Canadian Pacific, with Brascan a useful follow up. Development of the rich and extensive Hemlo field in Ontario, which is likely to become one of Canada's biggest gold producers, should continue to stimulate interest in mining shares such as Teck and Noranda which have large stakes in the eventual producers. Inco, the large nickel producer with some diversified interests, is a recovery stock which has lost popularity following extensive losses resulting from a drop in demand for its main product; but which got back on the buy-list on a sharp rise in nickel prices.

## AUSSIE CAPERS

Australia has for many generations attracted UK investment and some of its leading companies — banks, agricultural, commercial and mining — were launched with the help of British capital. It was not, however, until the mining boom of the 1960s that it drew large-scale attention, mostly speculative. A flood of new, and often very specious, exploration companies began to jostle the old, well-established metal producers for stock market attention — and blatant gambling. Prices soared, all too often on nothing more than the issue of a prospecting licence; talk of nickel (then a magic word), iron ore, lead, zinc, copper, gold, oil and natural gas finds; and dubious, unconfirmed assays of spectacular mineral strikes. A lot of easy money was made. A lot more was lost. And, as happened after October 1987's Black Monday on Wall Street, the Australian follow through was crucifying, with 50 per cent plus falls all too many, even amongst some of the best shares.

Many of the newcomers have gone the bankrupt way of large numbers of other mining hopefuls. Some struggle on, however, to meagre success, to prospecting or development deals with well-heeled, solid companies, or in the Micawber-like hope that something will turn up before the money runs out. Helped by tough stock exchange requirements, the Australian market has lost some of its worst casino habits. Yet, such is the speculative appetite of Australians, it does not take much to start off new boomlets.

There is little doubt that extensive reserves of metals, coal, oil, gold and diamonds remain to be exploited. But there are investment snags. Conservationists, in particular, are striving to prevent development of large, thinly populated areas with promising uranium, diamond and nickel reserves which could become profitable mines, adding to Australia's growing prosperity and overseas currency earnings.

The least speculative way in which to invest 'down under' is through the shares of broadly-based groups like Broken Hill Proprietary, CRA, Peko Wallsend and Western Mining; old-established mines such as MIM Holdings and North Broken Hill; and the enterprisingly-run Australian banks. Queensland Coal provides a direct way to participate in any improvement in demand for 'black gold' which could result from a reversion to steam plant production of electricity if the anti-nuclear lobbyists have their way.

There are also UK-registered groups like Rio Tinto-Zinc, Consolidated Gold Fields and Dalgety, all of which have Australian interests. A US way into MIM, which operates one of the world's richest base metal mines, is through the American company Asarco, which owns a major interest in MIM.

Some Australian exploration, mining and oil companies have a 'no-liability' type of share which is only partly paid-up. A 50c share may, for example, have had only 20c called up on it, to leave a balance of 30c to be called when new capital is needed. The advantage of 'NL' shares is that if it is decided to call it a day the call can be ignored, the shares forfeited and the loss confined to their cost to date. The disadvantage in buying such shares is that the buyer has to be prepared to put up more cash in order to follow up his speculation.


## SOUTH AFRICAN HEADACHES

South Africa is a natural for investment. It is far and away the largest free world producer of gold. It is rich in diamonds, uranium and coal. It has huge stores of other minerals beneath its large surface. Mineral sales alone are worth billions of Rands a year, and there is a large agricultural output plus expanding industrial activities. But, and it is a daunting but ... the country is political dynamite. Smouldering for years, apartheid has boiled up to a major international issue, with sanctions being imposed — or demanded — by a variety of nations. In the result, the Union has been forced to impose foreign exchange controls which have sharply reduced, or held in check, share prices and dividend income when converted into pounds, dollars and other overseas currencies — and not surprisingly heavily dented the confidence of existing and potential shareholders. Equally unsurprisingly, the slump in exchange rates has boosted turnover and profits of the mines and other businesses on translation of their export earnings into depreciated Rands, to the benefit of local investors but loss or only small gain to overseas shareholders. South African shares are thus currently much of a gamble on (a) settlement of the apartheid imbroglio, withdrawal of sanctions and a restoration of reasonable political and economic relations with the outside world; and (b) with this, a very sharp improvement in the Rand. A favourable outcome could double or treble share prices and produce handsome uplifts in dividend income when converted into pounds or dollars. There is a good choice of worthwhile mining, financial and industrial companies to include in a diversified portfolio.

For many years the South African ('Kaffir') market in London was dominated by gold shares, with diamonds joining in. Few industrials were traded. Then came uranium as a by-product of gold. Gold–uranium producers boomed until, with over-production and under-demand, the uranium price fell to much less profitable levels. This, coupled with a low fixed gold price and rising production costs, sharply cut down UK interest in Kaffirs. It was not until the gold price was freed to find its own level that there was any revival. Much of the recent impetus has, however, come from the US where there has been an expanding interest in gold. America can, in fact, be to the fore as a market-maker and London quotations are now in dollars as well as pounds.

A major part in South African development has been played by the *mining houses* which, in the earliest days, were set up by the fabulous Barnatos, Joels, Beit, Rhodes, Robinson, Wernher, Bailey and other opportunists to finance gold and diamond ventures and to open up enormous land concessions. Years later, their ranks were joined by other shrewd entrepreneurs, amongst whom was the late Sir Ernest Oppenheimer, founder of what became the mightiest of all houses, the Anglo American Corporation of South Africa.

As their activities and wealth grew, the mining houses began to spread their interests into industry, property, banking and other enterprises while continuing to deploy their exploration expertise in the African continent and, later, in Australia, North America and other territories. Amalgamations have reduced the number of houses, but the creations of the pioneers continue in the influential Consolidated Gold Fields, a UK company; Gencor (an amalgamation of General Mining and Union Corporation) and Johannesburg Consolidated Investment, with Anglo American and Anglo-Transvaal Consolidated Investment the 'new boys'. De Beers Consolidated Mines, an Anglo American close associate, is also a mighty power in the land. In addition to its dominance in the diamond world, De Beers has extensive investments in other mining, industrial, commercial and financial enterprises, the market value of which can be a large part of its own share price, to leave the fabulous diamond interests in at a fraction of their market value.

Investors with courage to ride the political hazards and no strong views on apartheid have a good choice of South African shares, of which some one hundred are listed on our Stock Exchange. Participation can be direct into individual companies or into a diversified interest through the mining houses.


### FAR-EASTERN FERMENTATION

One effect of high speed communications has been to bring far-distant stock markets closer into an international orbit. Trading between London and the Far-Eastern exchanges in Hong Kong, Kuala Lumpur, Singapore and Tokyo is as much of the day's work as it has long been with Wall Street and European bourses. Which is not to say that picking profitable oriental investments is simple. It is, in fact, a job for the specialists, and they are not always right in their selections and timing.

**Hong Kong** is an outstanding example of spectacular booms and costly slumps. Only a few years ago almost everybody in the Colony with any sort of money was buying all kinds of shares. Prices doubled, redoubled, quadrupled and even the sky did not seem the limit. Suddenly it was realised that the boom was largely on paper. The crash was more hectic than the crazy uprush. The main market index, the Hang Seng, plummetted from a high of 1775 in 1973 to a mere 150 in the following year. But, as always happens in a slump, good, sound shares were dragged down below their realistic worth. By 1977 some of the poise was being regained and by 1978 overseas interest was re-attracted and recovery got under way, with the result that 1981 saw another spectacular boom, later followed by a big setback as fears developed as to what will happen when the Colony reverts to China in 1997; and then again more recently another recovery. Hong Kong is a specialist market still and one which should be entered with eyes wide open. Sentiment was not helped by the decision in March 1984 of Jardine Matheson, one of the leading Hongs, to transfer its ultimate holding company to Bermuda and by several huge scale financial scandals. But, as in the past and as after Black Monday '87, Hong Kong can recover its stock market poise very quickly.

**Kuala Lumpur** has been gaining in size since the Malaysianisation of tin and rubber companies previously registered in the UK began. Most of the leading tin and rubber companies are now locally domiciled and local investors are actively increasing their holdings in them. Concentration of small companies into bigger units has been another feature, and this process seems set to the point where a large part of each industry will be concentrated into a few large groups such as Malaysia Mining Corporation.

**Singapore** market deals in a number of Malaysian companies as well as the shares of local concerns. On-the-spot knowledge is particularly important and, as noted later, the best non-local way to participate is through the long-established trading and management companies, some of which are UK-concerns. Here again over-speculation and some financial scandals have emphasised the need for caution in entering a very volatile market.

**Taiwan, Korea and Thailand** have stock markets and in view of these countries' prospering economies efforts have been made to introduce UK and other investors to them through specialised trusts. While, on the theory that it can pay to get in on the ground floor, the risk is great and the appeal must be very much for sophisticated speculators ready to lose their shirts. Amongst the hazards are limited markets and company accounting procedures which, even at best, would not even begin to be acceptable for consideration of a quote on Western world stock exchanges.

**Tokyo** is a very active market in which there is a big overseas interest. While there have been some sharp ups and downs in recent years there is no doubt that a great deal of money has been made in Japanese shares. Japanese trade and exports have been booming for some time. Japan is, in fact, an example of prosperity overdoing itself. If world trade is to grow at a pace needed to get countries with adverse trade balances on a prosperous course, Japan will have to cut her exports and/or greatly increase her imports. A cautious view of the general industrial outlook may, therefore, be necessary.

Also never to be forgotten is that Japanese markets are laws unto themselves. Price earnings ratios are mostly far above Western levels with share prices ranging into the stratosphere at 100 times or more yearly earnings. Net asset values can be extravagantly high by occidental standards. Substantial parts of the profits of some companies come from stock market operations, not from normal trading! Accounts and reports can be obscure and give little worthwhile information. With fewer havens available, a sizeable proportion of the average Japanese's income goes into shares, of which the quantity of newcomers is less than the demand – efforts are being made by UK, US and other foreign brokers and banks to ease the pressure by the introduction of non-Japanese stocks to the Tokyo market. And finally, the market is dominated by three large investment houses who exercise considerable control over it.

*Taking a general investment view of the Far East,* the safety-first entry should be through diversified media. A number of unit trusts specialise in the whole area or parts of it and some investment trusts have substantial proportions of their funds so deployed. For the more direct way into Hong Kong, Malaysia and Singapore there are two banks, Hongkong and Shanghai and Standard Chartered, plus the long-established trading and management companies such as Harrisons & Crosfield, Inchcape, Sime Darby and Jardine Matheson. The large-scale rubber units include Consolidated Plantations and Harrisons Malaysian Estates, while Malaysia Mining is the largest tin miner with Australian diamond engineering and other interests.

### EUROPEAN ELIGIBLES

Shares of around 80 Danish, Dutch, Finnish, French, German, Luxembourg, Norwegian, Spanish, Swedish and other European companies are officially listed on the Stock Exchange. They include Royal Dutch Petroleum, Unilever N.V. (the associate of Unilever Limited) and Philips Lamps from the Netherlands; Bayer (the chemical group), Commerzbank and Deutsche Bank from Germany; Total – Compagnie Française des Petroles from France; and Swedish Match.

This is, however, far from the end of the European tally. A substantial arbitrage goes on with Amsterdam, Paris, Brussels and Swiss, German and other continental bourses in both local and UK-listed securities. British investors thus have a very wide choice. Once more, however, it is wise to rely on specialist knowledge outside the field of well-known internationals such as Royal Dutch, Unilever and Philips.

As with other foreign investment, a territorial and company spread is obtainable through unit and investment trusts which concentrate wholly or substantially on European shares. Belated realisation of the good profits being earned by German and other European companies has in fact stimulated the launch of a diversity of specialist unit trusts and other investment media, to the extent that some care is necessary in making selections.

### PAPER WORK

During the forty-year exchange control period UK investors were entirely, or largely, cushioned against paper work in the buying and selling of overseas stocks and shares. All holdings had to be kept in the hands of authorised depositaries such as brokers, jobbers and banks. If registered, they went (with the exception of foreign companies with UK registers) into 'marking names' acceptable to the market. Dividends and interest on marking name securities were passed on to investors after deduction of income tax and, usually, at a small collection cost. Now, buyers can go straight on to overseas registers and personally hold certificates and bearer stocks, if they so wish. But, as explained below, it is not always expedient to do this. Investment life can be simplified by sticking to registration in marking names, and made safer by leaving bearer stocks in the safe custody of banks or brokers, for these reasons:

* Transfers do not have to be signed. Nor, when selling, do certificates and bearer stocks have to be personally delivered.
* There is no problem of delivery of sales in the 'shapes' such as 100 lots of American and Canadian shares which the market expects for 'good delivery'. Odd lots not in marking names or holdings in personal names may, however, be 'bad delivery' and sellers may have to take a somewhat lower price to allow for the cost of normal market delivery.
* Dividends and interest paid in foreign currencies are automatically collected and the net proceeds passed on to the holder.

In fact, in the case of registered securities, about the only good reason for personal registration is that annual and other reports, and dividends, are received automatically, and some investors like to have such direct contact. Generally, however, the problem of reports can be solved by asking the company registrar to be put on a mailing list as a shareholder whose shares are registered in a marking name. Many American and Canadian companies pay particular attention to shareholder relations.

Other factors of note are the nature of overseas securities and registration costs, if any. Such considerations for the main countries in which UK investors are interested are as follows:

**America and Canada:** Though North American companies keep share (stock) registers, certificates are virtually bearer in form. All a seller has to do is to sign on the back in front of a witness and hand over the certificate. This is a safety-first reason for registration in a marking name or, otherwise, deposit of the certificate with a bank or broker for safe custody. The market likes delivery in 'shapes' of 100 shares and can pay less or charge more for 'odd lots'.

**Australia:** Both buyer and seller have to sign transfer forms to go on to company registers which, in the case of the larger concerns, may be kept in more than one centre — CRA, for instance, has registers in Melbourne, Sydney, Brisbane, Perth and Canberra. It is thus important if shares are accumulated over a period that all go on to the same register where there are dual facilities. Dealings in Australian shares are subject to minimum market-able quantities such as 100 or more depending on the price range. A few Australian companies maintain UK registers.

**Europe:** EEC companies have their shares in bearer form, which therefore pass simply by hand from seller to buyer. Again for safety, these should be left with a broker or a bank, who will 'cut' the coupons to collect, and then pass on dividends as they fall due for payment through UK agents or a foreign bank.

**Hong Kong:** Like Australia, both buyer and seller have to sign transfers and foreign holders have to pay costs which currently come to about 1 per cent.

Dealings are in minimum market numbers which depend on price. Lengthy delays can take place in the receipt of transfers and still longer delays before buyers' share certificates come to hand — which is one good reason for a speedy extension of TALISMAN to this very volatile market.

**Japan:** As securities are not allowed to leave the country everything is in the hands of local agents who carry out transfers, and collect and remit dividends and interest.

**South Africa:** Most companies in which British investors are interested have UK registrars. Transfers are, therefore, the same as for UK securities. Buyers pay UK transfer duty and only sellers have to sign transfers.

**Dealing note:** As some of the leading American, Canadian, South African and Australian brokerage houses have London offices it is possible to deal direct through them on their markets.

# 21

# Investment and unit trusts

A lot of people choose to leave the management of their investments to the professionals. If the capital is fairly substantial they hand it over to a stock-broker, merchant or commercial bank, or investment consultancy, with or without giving the manager discretion to do what is thought best. Alternatively, with large or small amounts, they do some of the selection themselves through investment trusts or the relatively newer medium, unit trusts, through either of which ways they spread their money and risks.

**INVESTMENT TRUSTS**

Investment trusts began life more than 100 years ago as media for spreading funds over foreign and colonial government stocks, American railroad bonds, water stocks and other fixed interest securities. They were followed by land mortgage companies which lent money to Middle-West US farmers. In the 1890s the trusts began spreading into equities, though, as happened for many years, they kept a substantial part of their funds in fixed interest stocks and preference shares. For some time now the emphasis has, however, been very much the other way. Equities now dominate portfolios, with few or no fixed interest stocks included and then usually as short-term investments to take advantage of changing interest rates.

While the basic principles of providing a flexible spread of investment applies to both investment trusts and unit trusts, there are important differences in their make-up and operation. The notable features of investment trusts are:

* They are limited companies whose own shares can usually only be bought and sold through the Stock Exchange. The normal market law of supply and demand influences prices.
* Their share capital is fixed and can only be increased with the approval of shareholders. They are 'closed end', as the Americans would say.
* They can 'gear up', however, by issuing prior charge capital or borrowing money in other ways, such as by dollar or Euro currency loans and by foreign exchange forward transactions.
* Investment policies are flexible, to give wide freedom of action. Many have holdings in unlisted investments such as technology, health care, oil and gas exploration, mining, property, farms and other ventures. Some concentrate on one sector such as technology, oil or small companies.
* Otherwise, there are broad categories of investment policy — capital and

income growth; capital growth; income growth: smaller companies; and special features.
* Managements are alive to the longer-term benefits of 'anti-marketwise' operations: of buying when all is gloom and selling when a boom looks like bursting.
* Managements are also far from averse to turning over holdings as opportunity dictates.
* Most companies follow the early tradition of international-mindedness and on average have some 30/50 per cent or more invested in overseas securities.
* A few concentrate entirely or largely on geographic areas such as North America, Japan, Australia or the Far East.
* Size varies from a few millions of pounds of assets to over £1,000 million.
* Because of the 'closed' nature of investment trusts, new investments can only be acquired out of the proceeds of selling existing holdings, or by borrowing.
* To enjoy tax benefits they must retain not more than 15 per cent of the income they receive from shares and securities.

Some 200 investment trusts are currently traded on the Stock Exchange or USM. Some are individual companies run by their directors, with or without the cooperation of investment management advisers. Others are members of groups of from two to ten or more trusts, run by the directors and by management companies which may or may not be owned by the trusts in the group. A particular feature is that running expenses average only about 50p per £100 of assets — a very cheap price for expertise!

Two special features calling for detailed comment are (a) gearing and (b) the discount at which investment trust shares can be bought on their net asset values.

**Gearing** is a double benefit — or disadvantage if things are on the down trail. First is the capital aspect. Most investment trusts have some 'old' fixed interest prior charge capital in the form of debentures, loan stocks or preference shares at interest rates ranging from as little as $3\frac{1}{2}$ per cent to around 7 per cent, and mostly averaging only some 5 per cent. A few also have low coupon convertible stocks. While the preference issues are permanent capital, it should be borne in mind that most loan capital issues are repayable and that a fair number of low interest stocks are due for redemption in the near future. On the other hand, as noted later, there has been a move to issue debenture stocks, but at higher rates in the region of 10 per cent or more. The proportion of fixed interest to equity capital may also be relatively low, particularly with companies which have made equity scrip issues in good times.

Further capital gearing is provided by overseas borrowings to finance purchases of foreign securities. The suspension of exchange controls from 24 October 1979 facilitated, and encouraged, the raising of such loans, which can be in various forms, the most common being:
(1) Straight dollar or other foreign currency loan borrowed specifically to buy overseas investments.
(2) Back-to-back loan which means matching a loan of sterling and the borrowing of an overseas currency with an overseas company or other

party wanting to borrow sterling, usually for investment in the UK, and to lend the foreign currency.

(3) Currency swap, which is somewhat similar to (2), as the two parties exchange currencies and agree to re-exchange them at the same exchange rates at a fixed future date.

(4) Multi-currency loan in a mixture of currencies with the mixture changeable at a fixed date. This gives the borrower flexibility in international investment without having to take a cross-currency risk between the loan and the portfolio financed by it.

The effect of these methods is to provide three borrowing options: market and local currency; market and borrowed currency; or a mixture of markets and currencies.

Example 1 shows the effect on equity values of the two types of capital gearing.

There are in fact two methods of calculating net asset values. One, as used in the following examples, is to take the prior charge capital at par when deducting it from the gross net assets. The other is to compute the figure after deduction of loan and preference capital at market values. The latter normally produces a higher NAV. Despite this accretion, the first method is preferable and, as NAVs are theoretically realisation values on the bases of repaying prior charges at redemption values, it should be used in all comparisons. Using the par replacement basis, example 1 shows the impact of two types of capital gearing on NAVs.

### Example 1

(1) Issued capital is £14 million in £4 million fixed interest stocks and shares and £10 million in 40 million 25p ordinary shares.

| | |
|---|---|
| Net assets are | £44,000,000 |
| Deduct fixed interest capital | 4,000,000 |
| Available for 40m ordinary | £40,000,000 |
| Net asset value per ordinary | 100p |
| If net assets rise by 20% to | £52,800,000 |
| Fixed interest still takes only | 4,000,000 |
| Available for ordinary rises to | £48,800,000 |
| Net asset value per ordinary share rises by 22% to | 122p |

(2) Issued capital remains at £14 million and £5 million loans are raised. Net assets rise to £49 million less £9 million (£4 million fixed interest capital + £5 million loans) or still 100p a share. *But if:*

| | |
|---|---|
| Net assets rise to | £59,000,000 |
| Fixed interest will still equal only | 9,000,000 |
| Leaving for ordinary | £50,000,000 |
| Making net asset value of ordinary 25% more at | 125p |

The second aspect of gearing is its effect on net revenue available for equity dividends, as example 2 shows.

**Example 2**

| | |
|---|---|
| Net revenue | £2,200,000 |
| *Less:* Prior charge interest and dividends | 200,000 |
| Available for 40m ordinary | £2,000,000 |
| Net earnings per ordinary are | 5p |
| Net revenue rises by 13.6% to | £2,500,000 |
| *Less:* Prior charges (same) | 200,000 |
| Available for 40m ordinary | £2,300,000 |
| Net earnings rise by 15% to | $5\frac{3}{4}$p |

The general reduction in interest rates of recent times has encouraged trusts to return to the debenture market. Some issues are normal fixed rate stocks yielding a point or so above comparable gilts and with longish lives. Others offset lower interest coupons with the titbit of warrants to subscribe for shares over a period of years. There are also convertible stocks. And, though few, *stepped interest* debentures where interest increases, say, from 8 per cent for the first year by 1 per cent a year to 14 per cent with final redemption anything up to thirty years ahead. The move to exempt from gains tax profits on the sale of new fixed interest stocks should encourage the issue of low coupon stocks at discounts to attract high rate income tax payers. Such issues could become even cheaper and more popular if warrants were added. Temple Bar Investment Trust struck a novel note through an issue at par to its shareholders of a 6 per cent convertible stock 2002 which holders can call for redemption at £1.17 per £1 nominal of stock at the earlier date of 1992.

On the share side, some trusts are stimulating shareholder activity by the issue to them of free share warrants with a cashing-in price equal to the market price at the issue date. Also, thanks to abolition of the 15 per cent investment income surcharge there has been a revival in the option to reinvest dividends.

Another potentially promising innovation has been the joining of forces of a life assurance office with an investment trust to provide self-employed and other life insurance pensions facilities. Marketed by Sun Life, pensions savings are invested directly into the shares of Scottish American Investment Trust. A second scheme, Commercial Union Prime Investment Trusts Fund, spreads savings over ten trusts which at the launch in early 1984 had combined assets of around £2.6 billion.

An outstanding feature of investment trust equities, disturbing to old holders but good for new investors, has been the discount at which they have been selling compared with net asset values in recent years. Naturally varying trust by trust, the discount has been as high as some fifty per cent, was for a time around the forty mark and more recently has been in the 20/25 per cent area, with the trend continuing downwards. Several reasons account for this state of affairs and the change in sentiment.

Unlike unit trusts, investment trusts cannot advertise their shares: publicity

is limited to details of half-yearly and annual results and chairmen's statements. A narrow share market has been partly corrected by increased supplies
through scrip issues and splitting of high par value shares into 25p or other
small units. The number of shares in issue by smaller companies has been
increased by mergers into bigger units.

Though some stockbrokers tend to promote their own share recommendations rather than recommend the ready-to-hand spread offered by an investment trust, other firms are active in the investment trust market and offer
highly specialised services. Press comment has directed attention to the
advantages of this way of buying a share portfolio at a useful discount. The
Association of Investment Trust Companies, which speaks for about 99 per
cent of the industry, has also done good work through practical efforts to
explain the functions of trusts, and, as dealt with below, the production of a
year book and useful statistics.

The most dramatic impact has, however, been takeover bids by pension
funds searching around for ready-made portfolios without having to pick up
bits and pieces through a stock market which often cannot supply largish lines
of shares. Some financial and industrial companies have also taken the
takeover way of raising capital for their expansion plans by acquiring an
investment trust and then liquidating its portfolio. With capital gains tax no
longer payable, there is no excuse for a bid not being very close to net asset
value. Trust managers claim, in fact, that as takeovers can be a cheap way to
buy blocks of underlying shares and successful management, a premium is
justified. There is no doubt that investment-hungry pension funds with big cash
flows will continue to mop up the larger investment trust companies. Mergers
are also possibilities. In a recent case British Assets Trust produced an
ingenuious scheme to resolve an opposed outright bid for Investor Capital
Trust by limiting its holding to 51 per cent and giving ICT shareholders an
option to exchange into a BAT 6 per cent loan stock convertible into existing
common shares of GBC Capital, a successful Canadian investment company
and partially owned subsidiary of BAT.

In the meantime prospects of a useful narrowing of the discount gap have
been encouraged by an awakening of American interest in this bargain
basement way to get a ready-made spread of investment in UK and other
shares. A start was the setting up by Lazards, the merchant bankers, and their
New York associate, and Wood Mackenzie, the UK stockbroker trust specialists, of a 'club' of two dozen American investors to buy shares in UK and other
investment trusts and funds. If the 'club' idea grows it could be followed by
arrangements for leading investment trust shares to be dealt in over-the-
counter in the USA.

Some smaller trusts have dealt with the discount problem by liquidation and
distribution of the proceeds to shareholders, who have then had to find new
homes for their cash and, perhaps, to pay capital gains tax. Others have
changed their status by unitisation: as unit trusts they have, as will be seen
later, put their share price on to a net asset basis.

A much newer trend amongst established trusts is to get shareholders'
approval to take powers to (a) wind up or unitise at the end of a stated period
such as seven or ten years; and/or to (b) consider one or other of such steps
annually at specially called extraordinary general meetings. Similar powers are
a specific part of some recently floated new trusts. A further development

designed to cope with the discount problem is to register the trust in Panama or some other country which gives companies powers to buy their own shares in the market.

An extra attraction of many companies is a double discount through their holdings in other trusts also standing at below net asset values. Some managements have, in fact, a declared policy of buying other trust shares to take advantage of the discounts. Several go all out on this policy by concentrating completely or largely on investment trusts.

**Some notable changes** in the past few years have increased the attractions of investment trust shares and widened the field in which they can operate.

*First,* and of greatest value, was the ending of exchange controls in October 1979. This threw world stock markets wide open to dealings without dollar premium or other hampering brakes. The old-time complete geographic freedom was regained, and prompt advantage was taken of this new-found flexibility, particularly in the promising American, and Japanese and other Far-Eastern markets. While, because of the lower yields generally offered on overseas stocks, this widening of portfolios may mean some curtailment of income growth (perhaps even a short-term reduction) it widens the prospects of capital growth by reason of the much greater investment opportunities.

*Second,* and not before time, a capital gains tax annoyance was eliminated in the 1980 budget. From its inception in 1965 CGT produced complicated and fiddly problems for both trusts and shareholders, and various expedients were used over the years to mitigate a double charge. Investment trusts now no longer pay gains tax on their capital gains. This means that, as detailed in the taxation chapter, investors only are now liable to the tax, and then only on gains on sales of their investment trust shares.

*Third,* in April 1981, the Stock Exchange made changes in listing requirements which encourage greater investment in unquoted and small companies, and in non-corporate activities such as joint ventures, partnerships and participations. Investment trusts can now have up to 25 per cent of their gross assets in Unlisted Securities Market and unquoted holdings compared to a previous 15 per cent limit. Also, US over-the-counter (unlisted) securities qualify as quoted holdings. There has thus been a welcome addition to one of the original objectives of encouraging the financing of new ventures.

*Fourth,* new investment trusts without a track record can apply for an official listing or to enter the Unlisted Securities Market. This has led to the flotation of new ventures concentrating on investment in small companies, recovery situations, new technology, Japan, Mexico or some other specific industry or overseas market.

*Fifth,* some managements and investment trusts are now providing facilities for (a) reinvestment of dividends; (b) regular savings plans for monthly investments of £20/£25 upwards; and (c) occasional lump investments of £250 plus, with the two latter facilities open to non-shareholders. Pooled funds are invested once a month in market purchases of existing shares of the designated trusts and apportioned out to participants. This gives small investors the benefit of bulk buying and if the schemes grow, of share prices creeping up closer to net asset values with a reduction in discounts on NAV.

*Another change* which could help, even if only in a small way, or just psychologically, to cope with the discount problem are powers given in the 1981 Companies Act for companies, including investment trusts, to buy back their own shares. Not all managements favour the idea — at least at this stage.

Measurement of investment trust progress overall and by individual companies is helped by ample statistics. Overall comparison with other mutual investment media is seen, for instance, in the following data compiled by 'Money Management', Opal Statistics and the Association of Investment Trust Companies for one to seven years to 1 November 1987, a date, be it noted, *after* the Black Monday crash. The table shows the average growth of £1,000 invested in the various media, and the Retail Price Index (RPI):

### INVESTMENT TRUSTS v. OTHER MEDIA

|                  | 1 Yr. £ | 3 Yrs. £ | 5 Yrs. £ | 7 Yrs. £ |
|------------------|---------|----------|----------|----------|
| Building Society | 1,056   | 1,208    | 1,383    | 1,649    |
| Insurance Bond   | 1,016   | 1,318    | 1,721    | 2,034    |
| Unit Trust*      | 955     | 1,579    | 2,593    | 3,268    |
| Investment Trust*| 1,059   | 1,635    | 2,949    | 3,654    |
| R.P.I            | 1,042   | 1,136    | 1,251    | 1,495    |

* Net asset value plus re-investment of dividends = total return.

Performance by individual trusts naturally depends on the investment policy, objectives and expertise of their management and whether portfolios are general in geographic and industry spread or are concentrated on a particular sector. Sticking to the £1,000 original investment the seven-year total return and geographic spread of a random selection at March 1988 shows the variations in performance:

| Company | Return £ | Geographic Spread % | | | |
|---------|----------|-------|--------|-------|-------|
|         |          | U.K.  | N. AM. | Japan | Other |
| Alliance | 3,514 | 50 | 36 | 9 | 4 |
| Bankers | 4,291 | 54 | 29 | 3 | 14 |
| City of Oxford | 3,847 | 100 | – | – | – |
| Crescent Japan | 4,805 | – | – | 100 | – |
| Fleming American | 2,207 | 5 | 95 | – | – |
| Fleming Far Eastern | 5,100 | 1 | – | 72 | 27 |
| Globe | 3,224 | 70 | 19 | 9 | 2 |
| Kleinwort Small Cos. | 4,559 | 99 | – | – | 1 |
| Lowland | 7,287 | 89 | 3 | – | 8 |
| Romney | 2,995 | 19 | 31 | 32 | 18 |
| T R Industral + Gen. | 3,170 | 60 | 19 | 10 | 11 |
| Witan | 3,216 | 59 | 19 | 10 | 12 |

Investment trusts are well to the fore in the financial and statistical data given in their annual reports. Data ranges from financial performances over ten years or longer (or from launch for the 'under-tens') to the geographic and sector spread of their investments, plus details of major holdings or even a complete schedule of the portfolio. A good example of the main data comes from the 1987 report of The Scottish American Investment Co. which records an increase of 82 times in its dividend and 84 times in its share price between 1945 and 1987; and whose management had the foresight to offload part of its portfolio before the Black Monday crash of October 1987. Key facts are:

| SCOTTISH AMERICAN INVESTMENT | | | | | | |
|---|---|---|---|---|---|---|
| Year ended 31 Dec | Gross income £'000 | Ordinary (Gross) | | Investment valuation £'000 | Net asset value p | Share Price p |
| | | Earned £ | Paid £ | | | |
| 1955 | 942 | 0.30 | 0.21 | 16,623 | 6.0 | 4.5 |
| 1960 | 1,429 | 0.48 | 0.39 | 25,663 | 9.3 | 9.8 |
| 1965 | 1,955 | 0.69 | 0.57 | 34,724 | 13.1 | 11.6 |
| 1970 | 2,238 | 0.59 | 0.58 | 49,281 | 17.4 | 16.0 |
| 1975 | 2,751 | 0.71 | 0.69 | 47,916 | 17.1 | 14.5 |
| 1978 | 4,453 | 1.14 | 1.10 | 69,423 | 27.0 | 20.0 |
| 1979 | 4,624 | 1.27 | 1.25 | 72,740 | 29.7 | 21.8 |
| 1980 | 5,238 | 1.48 | 1.43 | 97,146 | 40.7 | 32.5 |
| 1981 | 5,202 | 1.59 | 1.57 | 101,559 | 44.9 | 33.0 |
| 1982 | 5,723 | 1.70 | 1.65 | 137,617 | 52.3 | 38.8 |
| 1983 | 7,221 | 1.63 | 1.73 | 184,439 | 65.0 | 48.0 |
| 1984 | 6,376 | 2.03 | 2.00 | 160,048 | 74.2 | 53.3 |
| 1985 | 6,935 | 2.55 | 2.34 | 187,256 | 85.4 | 69.8 |
| 1986 | 7,052 | 2.50 | 2.57 | 235,821 | 101.5 | 87.0 |
| 1987 | 8,818 | 2.95 | 2.86 | 227,045 | 102.2 | 80.0 |

Of Saints shareholders' funds of £228,434 at end-1987, the total equity holdings of £206,658 were divided by sector and geographically as under:

| Sector | % | Geographic | % |
|---|---|---|---|
| Capital goods | 21.4 | U.K. | 49.1 |
| Consumer goods | 32.8 | N. America | 22.7 |
| Other groups | 15.5 | Europe | 8.0 |
| Oil and Gas | 3.4 | Japan | 5.3 |
| Financial | 13.6 | Australasia | 1.7 |
| Commodities | 3.0 | Hong Kong | 1.7 |
| Subsidiary Co. | 0.8 | Other areas | 2.0 |

Equities, it will be seen, were 90.5 per cent of shareholders funds and the balance of 9.5 per cent was made up mainly of U.K. gilts (£16,174,000), short term corporate notes and net current assets.

**Split trusts** are an intriguing variation of the traditional company. There are around forty, and their make-up, as the description implies, is to divide their share capital into two classes — income and capital. With or without the addition of loan capital, the income shares take all or most of the net revenue and the capital shares get all or most of the appreciation in net asset values.

Investors wanting income can, therefore, look for increasing dividends but in most cases little or no increase in capital. Investors concerned mostly with growth can hope for it through the capital shares which, depending on the constitution of the company, will not get dividends — tax liability will thus be limited to capital gains tax on any profit on sale. A worthy conception, typical of the industry's inventiveness, is the *charitable split trust* where the trustees of the charity subscribe the 'income' capital and the investing public the capital shares. The charity thus gets all the income and the public the capital gains on winding up. A fresh spurt in new 'split' trusts in 1986 included variations in redeemable income and capital shares of new investment companies, UK-based and off-shore.

Winding-up dates are fixed for most of the split trusts. Buyers of income shares are on to a fairly safe bet that dividends will keep pace with, or outpace, inflation but that, unless repayable at a premium, their capital will be eroded. Buyers of capital shares take on the ups and downs of changes in portfolio values. If values rise they benefit, if they fall they stand the loss. Capital shares thus move much more widely. In bear markets they can have a nil value, while doubling, trebling or even quadrupling in bullish times.

As with any investment, it is axiomatic that the performance of individual companies over varying periods helps to make choices of shares. Fortunately, the Association of Investment Trust Companies provides ample material. Its *Investment Trust Year Book*, gives comment on performance and new developments, together with explanatory articles on the nature of trusts, taxation and other pertinent matters. Key facts from the latest annual reports and ten-year records of earnings, dividends, net asset values and share prices provide a financial picture of each company. These data are backed up by the performance of individual trusts in the different management groups over one, five and ten years for net asset value; total return on assets; share price; and total return to shareholders; and percentage increase in dividends over five and ten years. Such figures, particularly the total return to shareholders, help to put investment trust performances on a similar, if only theoretical, basis to unit trusts which measure their success by their growth including reinvestment of dividends. Other tables show the grouping of investment trusts by size of assets; percentage of overseas investments in various areas; yields; and proportion of unlisted holdings.

Another helpful publication covering a great deal of ground in non-technical style is the *Financial Times Guide to Investment Trusts*. Particular features include performance tables covering individual companies; an easy to follow tabulation of geographic, industry and sectionalised interests of each; and details of the management groups.

## UNIT TRUSTS

Unit trusts differ in several fundamental ways from investment trusts. They are regulated by the Department of Trade and Industry; are governed by a trust deed; unit holders' rights are protected by a trustee; and meetings are only held to make important changes in the trust deed or to merge with another trust. Other major features are:
*    The capital is variable. Units are created or cancelled in accordance with demand. They are 'open-ended'.

* Selling (offer) and buying (bid) prices are based on net asset values calculated at daily or other intervals.
* There is no discount, unlike investment trusts.
* Subject to approval by the trustees on behalf of the Department of Trade, new and existing trusts can advertise as widely as the managers choose.
* Purchases and sales are largely direct through the managers. They can, however, be made through stockbrokers, insurance brokers, banks, solicitors and other professional advisers.
* Prices allow for all dealing costs. The offer price includes an initial charge, now fairly generally up to 5 per cent.
* Management expenses are discretionary, but, with the exception of some specialised or offshore funds, are in the region of 1 per cent per annum with a tendency to rise to 1½ per cent or more.

Otherwise, unit trusts follow the investment trust pattern of spreading their funds over a range of securities under the expert guidance of management companies which may have up to 20 or more funds, plus bond schemes, in their stables. All shapes and sizes are to be found amongst the 1,200 or so trusts currently operating. High yield ... low yield ... general ... fixed interest ... capital growth ... 'small' company ... property shares ... recovery ... natural resources ... technology ... gilt-edged ... American, Australian, Japanese, Far Eastern or European ... offshore funds ... there is something for almost every investment taste. Decontrol of sterling in October 1979 gave an impetus to overseas investment by already established trusts and the formation of new ones to invest entirely in foreign shares. Since August 1981 they can invest up to 25 per cent of their assets in Unlisted Securities Market companies, while newer powers allow investment in traded options.

Two methods of investment in unit trusts are usually available. One is a block purchase with a minimum investment to start with of, say, between £250 and £1,000, but with no upper or lower limits on additional purchases. The other is regular monthly investment of a minimum of, say, £20. Facilities are generally available for the reinvestment of dividends, so increasing the accumulation of capital. Some managements offer discounts for large lump sum investments of from, say, £2,000 to £5,000 upwards. There are also exchange arrangements whereby shares in approved companies will be accepted instead of cash subscriptions, with savings in brokerage and other expenses.

Another attraction of monthly investment is 'pound averaging', which means that more units are bought when prices are low and fewer when they are higher. The average cost is thus evened out over the investment period and decisions on the best buying times are largely solved.

On the reverse side, some managements provide an annuity type facility. A regular income at the rate of five per cent, six per cent or more per annum is paid half-yearly out of a fixed sum investment. This can be a good proposition so long as unit prices are rising: any income shortfall in the trust is wholly or partly made good by a rise in the value of the units remaining after sales needed to make up the half-yearly payments. But it is not a good idea when prices are falling: capital is then used up too fast. Participants must, therefore, take account of market trends and, if they can do without the inflow, switch off withdrawals until unit prices recover. Managers of such schemes will probably warn participants when they think it wise to switch off.

A further facility offered by managers with at least six different trusts in their stable is a planned spread of investment in their funds to produce a monthly income.

Unit trust investors have two dividend payment options. They can have them paid out in the usual way. Or they can reinvest them automatically in the purchase of additional units and so, like National Savings Certificates, compound their investment; a feature which some managers encourage by allotting the new units at a discount of up to 2 per cent on the offer price.

Two methods of reinvestment are used, though not by all trusts. The net amount of each dividend is invested in extra units and fractions of a unit. For example, a net dividend of £11.66 on 4,050.63 units buys a further 27.13 units and raises the holding to 4,077.76. Alternatively, the amount of the net dividend is added to the original cost of the holding and the number of units remains unchanged. For instance, if £15 dividend is due on 2,000 units bought for £1,000 the holding stays at 2,000 but the cost goes up to £1,015, a change reflected in the quoted prices of the units.

Gearing is a major difference between unit and investment trusts. The latter, as already shown, can gain capital and income benefits by having part of their capital in fixed interest stocks and by borrowing. While some unit trusts borrow on what are called 'back-to-back' loans for overseas investment, the great majority have only one class of capital — their units, which are the equity. Some managers of trusts invested overseas do however 'hedge' dollar and other foreign currencies by forward purchases or sales, to get protection against fluctuations in rates.

In addition to UK-based unit trusts there is a growing number of *off-shore funds* operating from the Channel Isles, Bahamas, Bermuda and other overseas territories. These offer a wide choice from the general fund to specialised types including investment in actual metals as well as natural resources producers. As they are not subject to UK 'rules' and customs they generally have higher front load and annual charges. Most are under responsible and experienced management, including a number of UK groups.

Rivalry amongst management groups is keen. Performance is rightly a key factor in claims to success and in the sale of units. It is, as to be expected from the wide variety of trusts and the expertise level of managements, extensive, varied and downright erratic in some cases. The general aim is, however, to out-perform rivals and to beat the applicable share indices. One plus of the City policing efforts imposed by the new Financial Services Act is classification of some of the unit trust dealing and pricing practices which had been causing concern. Now managements have to follow clear-cut rules on unit pricing and commissions paid to intermediaries.

There is also active competition between old and new managements to market new ideas such as switching within a small group of their funds, and to spread portfolios over a wide geographical field. Two recent launches exemplify the search for new ideas (some would say gimmicks). First is a *fund of funds* which invests in other unit trusts and is open to the criticism that two initial charges are thus involved. Second is the linking of instant borrowing and a cash dispenser service with investment in one or both of two UK trusts. On the other hand, there can be a follow-my-leader trend in the promotion of specific type funds such as Japanese or any other investment field scooping the limelight. In fact, if there has to be criticism of the industry, it is that the choice is too wide and a bewilderment to many potential investors. True, there are many unit trust advisory organisations; but as they live on commissions, often including extra incentives to promote particular trusts, care is needed in using those who are firmly established and do not 'churn' portfolios to boost their commission income. Advisors should be asked to disclose their sources of remuneration before handing over unit trust portfolios for their management.

Performance over short and, more importantly, long periods is obviously essential. One source is reports issued by individual trusts. These can be yearly or, more usually, half yearly. They can vary in financial content from bare details of current valuation, portfolio content and distribution declared to much fuller statements. A really informative report will give a detailed list of investments divided into appropriate sectors and its valuation; portfolio changes — new holdings, increased holdings, and total and partial disposals — during the period; income account and current distribution; capital account, especially showing realised and unrealised gains and losses; and a note of the principal holdings. Also added will be a review of investment conditions over the past months; performance compared with appropriate market indices; and income distributions over a period of up to, say, ten years.

Ample data are also obtainable over a wide spectrum of trusts. Most comprehensive is the *Unit Trust Year Book* compiled by Financial Times Business Information in conjunction with the Unit Trust Association. In addition to explanatory articles on the functions and workings of unit trusts, a major feature is the percentage capital growth (income included) and 'league-table' position of individual trusts in various sectors such as UK general, equity income, UK growth, international, North American, Far East, commodity ... over periods of up to ten years. Detail is added with basic facts on individual trusts with price and income records for up to ten years. Other tables show trusts in order of size, their dividend yields and facts about the various management groups.

Up-to-date performance figures for all unit trusts are given monthly in *Money Management* magazine which follows the same categories as the *Year Book* and which shows the results of £1,000 (income reinvested) over one, two, three, five and seven years. Stockbrokers and investment advisory specialists specialising in this field also produce factual material on progress and advice on purchases and sales. Newspapers add to the fund of fact by publishing 'league tables' of performance.

Though it is instructive to chart the changing positions of the 'runners', it is imperative to bear in mind that activity in individual market sectors can exert a substantial influence on particular trusts such as specialist ones. Bursts of glory can be short-lived. What is today's front runner can quickly become an also-ran for a lengthy time. Equally, the laggard can put up a good show, given time.

Short-term operations apart, it is the long-term trend which matters for most investors. It is in this field that many of the general funds which go for both capital growth and rising dividend income show up well over the years. A goodly number of general trusts have increased dividend distributions by twice or more over the past ten years, while a few of the oldest-established funds can show multiplications of up to six times or more on a life of 25 years upwards.

Capital growth for many trusts has also been good, though the caveat must be entered that some of the newer specialist funds have at times fallen behind the general ones. The record of M & G Dividend Fund since its launch in May

1964 to end-1987 shows how a representative general trust can perform. The following table sets out the highest and lowest offered prices of income and accumulation units, and gross annual distributions per cent on the initial price of 50p:

| Year | Income | | Accumulation | | Distributions % per annum |
|------|--------|--------|--------------|--------|----------------------------|
| | High & Low p per unit | | | | |
| 1965 | 54.6 | 48.5 | 57.5 | 50.4 | 6.63 |
| 1966 | 58.5 | 46.9 | 63.1 | 50.6 | 6.92 |
| 1967 | 58.8 | 48.3 | 66.5 | 53.5 | 7.28 |
| 1968 | 74.4 | 54.0 | 87.1 | 62.3 | 7.28 |
| 1969 | 76.9 | 55.4 | 91.7 | 67.3 | 7.50 |
| 1970 | 62.5 | 49.6 | 77.5 | 62.7 | 7.87 |
| 1971 | 81.5 | 52.7 | 110.0 | 68.5 | 8.14 |
| 1972 | 100.3 | 81.8 | 139.4 | 110.4 | 8.54 |
| 1973 | 101.0 | 66.0 | 142.2 | 95.5 | 9.28 |
| 1974 | 72.2 | 39.3 | 104.5 | 61.5 | 10.66 |
| 1975 | 87.5 | 38.8 | 144.7 | 60.8 | 12.53 |
| 1976 | 97.5 | 67.0 | 161.2 | 113.3 | 13.94 |
| 1977 | 126.4 | 78.8 | 227.3 | 138.6 | 15.66 |
| 1978 | 142.0 | 111.9 | 269.3 | 207.4 | 18.07 |
| 1979 | 152.7 | 116.3 | 298.8 | 242.1 | 20.45 |
| 1980 | 147.5 | 121.4 | 316.2 | 252.8 | 23.71 |
| 1981 | 161.7 | 124.3 | 360.0 | 279.4 | 26.29 |
| 1982 | 168.7 | 141.5 | 412.7 | 336.6 | 26.57 |
| 1983 | 221.4 | 161.2 | 589.4 | 408.4 | 27.14 |
| 1984 | 287.8 | 221.7 | 799.5 | 590.4 | 28.83 |
| 1985 | 358.1 | 284.1 | 1027.1 | 789.2 | 32.55 |
| 1986 | 454.8 | 340.3 | 1339.4 | 983.2 | 38.03 |
| 1987 | 690.4 | 450.6 | 2096.1 | 1349.0 | 44.48 |

These figures underline the benefits of reinvesting distributions in accumulation units. They also give an indication of the way in which pound-averaging through monthly investment would have worked.

Unit trusts are treated for *capital gains tax* in the same way as investment trusts. They no longer pay it on their own gains and the investor is liable only on any profit on the sale of his or her units.

## INVESTMENT INDICATORS

* Investment and unit trusts are good ways to spread the risks inherent in share buying. They are particularly suitable for small and first-time investors.
* The market discount makes investment trusts the better choice for lump sum investment of, say, £1,000 or £250 in a savings scheme.
* The monthly and lump sum schemes mentioned earlier have opened the door for the small investor to put savings into investment trusts at a low cost and put I.T.'s on a very competitive basis with unit trusts.
* Some investment and unit trusts which have stuck entirely or largely to UK investments have done well and should continue on the up-track. But it is good policy to look for geographical diversification of up to 30 per cent or more in overseas stocks.

* Forward-looking investment trusts ready to bank on the recovery chances should have up to 10 per cent of their funds in oil, metals, commodity and other natural resources shares.

* Investment in specialised trusts, particularly specialised unit trusts, calls for good timing. Europe-orientated funds, after a pedestrian performance, took off in 1985, did well for a while and then dribbled off. Australia, though having good patches, has not lived up to some high hopes. Far Eastern funds have a mixed record, but bought at the right time can be good money-makers on a two to three years' view. Japan has provided some good investments, but, because of a possible flattening out of the economy, should be carefully watched. High risk, even dangerous, areas are Thailand, Korea and other Far Eastern emerging countries, plus China.

* North America, despite some ups and downs, is a promising overseas market. The USA has vast natural resources and the ability to work through economic depressions. Though largely overlooked, Canada is an equally promising area which has so far been largely untapped, by unit trusts in particular.

* Natural resources, or commodity, unit trusts should have good prospects of capital gain as world trade continues to pick up.

* While it can be profitable to switch unit trust holdings, account should be taken of the costs involved in moving from one trust to another, particularly if they are not in the same management group.

* Sales of unit trust units can be costly because of the spread between bid and offer prices quoted by the managers. While the spread for leading and active trusts may be no more than 7-8 per cent, it can be as much as 13 per cent — a unit bought at 100p might have to rise in price to 113p bid before breaking even.

* Consider the size of an established unit trust before investing in it. If below, say, £2 million, particularly after a few years in business, it may be too small to pay its way in management expertise and to carry on as a viable venture.

* All other things being equal, if the choice is between an investment trust and a unit trust, go for the I. T.; discount on net asset value alone is in its favour.

* Investment and unit trust savings plans automatically provide pound cost averaging. Each monthly subscription buys shares or units at current market price which is almost certain to vary and the accumulating total then stands in the average cost to date.

# 22

# Good watch prevents misfortune

Application of the above old proverb to investment is no guarantee against loss. But it does ram home that study and watchfulness are essential to success in picking likely winners, and then of keeping an eye on their running. There are plenty of tools to help with the job.

Newspapers are a natural, handy way to keep in touch with the investment world — and to get ideas. National and provincial dailies give City reports which may range from a 'column' to several pages of company and other news; comment and share recommendations; closing prices for leading stocks and shares; unit trust prices; and commodity, money market and foreign exchange data. Many evening papers give City reports and a selection of prices. Sunday newspapers add to the list with a column or page of comment and recommendations; or, as with the 'heavies' — *The Observer, The Sunday Telegraph* and *The Sunday Times* — wide coverage of financial and business affairs. Getting on to the track of a good investment is not confined, however, to the City pages. General news items about new inventions and other developments can be the start of looking into particular companies.

The widest coverage, as would be expected, is provided by *The Financial Times*. One particularly useful tool is the columns of closing prices for leading securities stretching from gilt-edged to mining shares and taking in many small to medium-sized companies. Price changes on the day are backed up by details of net dividend paid, dividend cover, gross yield, price–earnings ratio, and current year high and low prices. Other helpful information includes the Financial Times and FT–Actuaries indices mentioned in chapter 13 and the list of markings in the Saturday issues. The latter gives a 'Leaders and Laggards' table showing the percentage rises and falls in the different groups of the FT–Actuaries indices.

The leading weekly publication is the *Investors Chronicle* which gives a wealth of information on company affairs, stock markets, commodities, the money market, and economic and industrial trends. The *IC* analyses and comments on the profits and accounts of many hundreds of companies in all fields of enterprise, and has special features on particular companies or groups of companies. Quarterly indices give investors who file their copies a ready-to-hand reference medium on a variety of companies and their progress. *The Economist*, though not so prolific on company news, is invaluable for its wide-ranging coverage of world economic, business and political affairs which can have a pertinent impact on stock markets. Monthly publications such as *Money Management, Money Observer* and *What Investment* — cover a range of investment media and provide up-to-date records of unit trust performance.

**Company reports** can, though not always, add usable information to the financial accounts discussed in chapter 9. They should be read from cover to cover: the gem may be hidden in small type. It is not necessary to be a shareholder to get a copy. Many companies which advertise their results actually invite non-shareholders to write for the full report. Particular points to note are:

*   The *chairman's statement* should comment on the highlights of the financial year and explain rises or falls in turnover, profits, assets and liabilities; deal with major or new developments in hand or projected; explain changes in senior personnel; and so far as possible in these uncertain times, make a forecast or give an indication of future prospects. Many companies, particularly those with varied activities, report on trading experiences and prospects in a *review of operations,* which may highlight any specially new and interesting developments.

*   *The directors' report* gives details of capital changes; analyses of divisional and geographical sales (and sometimes profits); the share interests of directors; and the names of owners of more than 5 per cent of the voting capital. The latter, especially if comparisons can be made with previous years, can be a hint that someone is building up for a takeover bid or that astute investors think well of the company. Reductions in share stakes may, on the other hand, be a warning that big backers are doubtful about the future. Unexplained changes in directors' shareholdings may also be significant.

*   An *analysis of shareholdings,* which more and more companies now give, shows the strength of institutional investment. Here again, comparisons over several years are helpful in showing the views of investment experts. Despite the stimulus to growth given by the British Telecom and other denationalisation issues, the general tendency is a decline in total holdings of individual share owners and an increase in institutional stakes — amongst the leading and largest companies, anyhow. Investment trusts are amongst the rare exceptions recording increases.

*   Additional comments made by the chairman at the *annual general meeting* are also worth listening to or reading if reported in the Press. It is an unhappy fact of company life that too few shareholders bother to attend meetings. The best attendances are usually when things are going wrong. Meetings are occasions when questions can be asked and, if lucky, additional information winkled out by judicious and persistent probing. Tactics which produce the best results are to prepare questions and comments in advance; to be precise and lucid; and not to ramble on as some inquisitors do to the detriment of their efforts. A clever chairman can make mincemeat of wafflers.

*   *Proxy cards* sent out with the accounts give 'absentee' shareholders the chance to let the chairman or another director vote for them on motions before the meeting. Cards set out the various resolutions to be voted on, such as approval of the directors' report and accounts and the election of directors; and provide spaces to be ticked 'for' or 'against' each item on the agenda. Separate cards will be available if there is also an extraordinary general meeting to increase the authorised capital or borrowing powers, or for some other special matter. It is safe to fill in and return proxies when things are going well. But it is a very different matter if trouble is around

and the board is fighting off justified opposition or criticism. Careful thought must then be given to the way to vote — for or against the motions set out, or for a non-board individual who is taking up the cudgels.

**Interim reports** are useful indicators of progress and should be studied. While a few companies such as British Petroleum, Shell, Imperial Chemical Industries, Unilever and some other large groups issue quarterly figures, the great bulk of companies report half-yearly. These statements invariably give turnover and profits for the period with comparative data for the corresponding period of the previous year, and, perhaps, figures for the preceding half-year or quarter and also for the whole of the previous year. A key feature can be detailed or brief comment on trading for the period, any major development and prospects for the rest of the year. It is also not unusual to add forecasts of minimum profits for the whole year and the total dividend to be expected.

Such interim reports are worthwhile guides to the immediate future. But in some cases not too much should be read into them. This particularly applies to companies in seasonal trades such as retail stores which generally do their peak trade prior to Christmas and hotels and caterers which may rely on summer business for a substantial part of their yearly profits. More important is to look at the figures over a series of half-years, not just the corresponding periods. Such an exercise gives a more realistic picture of the long-term trend.

**Extel Statistical Services** provide detailed information about UK-listed, USM and Third Market companies. Annual cards give details of the business, subsidiary and associated companies; capitalisation and changes in recent years; loan debt; directors' and other interests of 5 per cent or over in the share capital; analysis of profits for ten years or more; dividends, and when announced and paid; share earnings and priority percentages; balance sheets for two years; equity net asset value; high and low share prices over a period of years; gross yields and price–earnings ratios at a range of prices; and a summary of the chairman's statement, including the important prospects item. News cards cover interim reports and other developments between year-ends. A new Listing service covers prospectuses and placings of UK companies. Entire services, sections or groups of companies can be subscribed for, or individual cards can be bought from Extel or obtained from stockbrokers.

Other Extel services of value to investors cover the larger North American, Australian, European, Singapore and Malaysian, and Middle East companies, and new and existing international bond issues. Monthly analyses of UK and Irish new issues and placings include full details of scrip issues, options, acquisitions, conversions, consolidations and liquidation distributions. A taxation service, used by the Inland Revenue, provides the basic data for calculating adjusted prices of securities held on 6 April 1965 (starting date for capital gains tax): a newer publication gives prices of all relevant listed securities, unit trusts and other issues at 31 March 1982, the base date for CGT indexation. There is also a twice-yearly publication listing securities declared by the Inland Revenue to be valueless or of negligible value.

**Datastream** provide a highly sophisticated, computerised service to stockbrokers, banks, investment trusts, insurance companies, pension funds and other big investors. Data banks, up-dated daily, provide programmes which cover UK,

American, European, Japanese and Hong Kong companies and securities. Daily prices are stored together with latest dividend and earnings facts, profit and loss accounts and balance sheets, and current and historical stock market ratios for each company. Extensive information is provided for all major industrial sectors in the various countries. Screening facilities enable clients to find stocks meeting their criteria. Annual account data is also available so that companies can be compared and contrasted. Key details of many thousands of international bonds are another part of the service which includes Euromarket and traded options systems information. Visual and print-out valuation facilities enable stockbrokers and other subscribers to know the up-to-the-minute position of large and small portfolios.

**McCarthy Information Services** provide what is in effect a press cuttings facility. News and comment on all companies with ordinary listings on the Stock Exchange in the leading daily, evening and Sunday newspapers, the *Investors Chronicle* and *The Economist* are reproduced on individual sheets. Other services cover Australian, European and North American companies.

**Handbooks,** which can be useful research tools, published annually and half-yearly are: *Extel Handbook of Market Leaders* and *The Stock Exchange Press Company Handbook*. Each gives data on most UK companies of any size, the range extending from company profile, activities and capitalisation to five year (or more) profits, earnings and dividend record, latest balance sheet data, share price graphs and statistical ratios. A more selective effort is *Hambro Performance Ranking Guide* which concentrates on profitability, growth, productivity, liquidity gearing and so on. *Investors' Companion to the Top 100 UK Companies* is in effect, a professional analysts' profile of the Footsie 100 constituents. It shows how each company works, what is does, how its performance can be analysed, and which are the key figures and variables.

**Telephone price services,** the newest source of one-off information, are provided by *The Daily Telegraph Teleshare Price Service* and the *Financial Times Cityline*. Of course, there is always the stockbroker with his SEAQ and Topic screens, and perhaps the local bank or building society with a limited screen service.

**Share stake** announcements can give hints of coming developments and potentially profitable lines of enquiry can come from watching these announcements. Shareholdings of five per cent or more have to be reported. Directors have also to notify increases or decreases in their holdings. A sudden purchase of a large block of shares or the building up of a stake by one investor or a group of 'related' buyers can, though far from always, foreshadow a takeover bid. Sale of a large holding or the persistent reduction in a stake may, on the other hand, indicate loss of confidence in a company and be a selling signal. *The Financial Times* reports details of share stakes.

**Professional advice.** Original research is not, of course, everyone's idea of the best or most practicable way to pick investments. Many investors do not have the necessary expertise, time or facilities: they have to rely on others for guidance. There are various sources of professional advice.

Stockbrokers are a natural first choice; it is an important part of their work to advise and to arrange portfolios to meet particular needs. Most firms will actually take over the management of portfolios, with or without discretion to buy and sell without reference to their clients. Part of the service will be reports on holdings at quarterly, half-yearly or other intervals. Such management services are, however, subject to a minimum size of portfolio, which may be as little as £10,000/£20,000 or as much as £50,000/£100,000. Equally, while some firms have facilities to handle small normal business, others tend to concentrate on larger accounts.

The leading stockbroking firms produce general market reports, economic and trade commentaries and detailed studies of individual companies and industries. A number of stockbrokers add to their general service by specialisation in particular markets such as oils, chemicals, textiles, insurance, banks, investment trusts, mines and so on. Others have branch offices in a few overseas countries and specialise in Australian, North American, Japanese and other Far Eastern, European and other markets.

A broker should also be ready to encourage the individual researches of clients by the supply of Extel cards and Datastream print-outs about dividend and interest dates, yield, conversion terms for appropriate stocks and other facts which help in the selection of suitable investments or to make comparisons amongst different groups of securities.

Clearing banks have advisory and management services similar to those of stockbrokers and, like them, have minimum limits to the capital they will take under their management wings.

Merchant banks offer skilled management, but with few exceptions will handle only large portfolios of, say, £100,000 or upwards. There are, however, a number of non-banking management organisations which will take on funds of a much smaller amount. In view of some recent scandals care is essential in putting one's investments in the hands of the latter, particularly if they are given full discretion to act without reference to clients. They should have sound foundations, a good and easily checkable track record and be reliably recommended.

Most investment trusts and larger unit trust management companies also provide services for individuals as well as for pension funds and other institutional or corporate investors.

Though far from the least valuable, some newspapers and weekly publications run advisory services on individual securities and portfolios, and will recommend purchases. Some of these services are free but limited in the number of queries which will be covered. Others charge fees related to the work involved. One widely read and well-informed advisory publication is the *IC News Letter* which is mailed to reach subscribers each Wednesday. This 'mid-week special', as it is popularly called, has a long-running record of successful comment on particular shares and industries, and other groups of investments.

Booming stock markets have brought a spate of other advisory 'letters' and share tipping sheets, some emanating from America and the Continent. Some are the products of sound and reputable analysts and publishers who offer well-researched and impartial advice. Others are, however, the emanation of unknown so-called experts who tout for subscribers on a few short-term successes, probably USM shares with a limited market. Agreed, some of the newcomers may eventually have consistently good money-making crystal balls. But, the canny approach is to check well on credentials before parting with a hefty subscription.

Finally, a thought about investment analysts and tipsters. None can be right all the time; if they were they would soon retire with millions in the bank. However expert and impartially conscientious, they are subject, like all of us, to human misjudgement. It could therefore be unkind to a highly respected Canadian brokerage house to mention that one of its New Year forecasting efforts suggested that eight mining shares were poor starters; yet little more than a month later all were up in price, by as much as 50 per cent in one case. Again, research by *Forbes,* the respected US financial journal, showed that *actual* earnings of twenty companies were 73 per cent lower than analysts' *forecasts.*

Finally, to end on a sample of terminology produced by a brokerage house: 'Momentum indicators are in a moderately overbought position and are showing less upside force on a rate-of-change basis than was the case between late January and mid-February. That condition is to be expected in view of the duration of the market's advance from its early December testing low. Such lengthy uplegs, even within dynamic bull markets, have usually led to at least a few weeks of hesitation or minor pullback. Few, if any, serious divergences or non-confirmations now exist among the averages and other trend measures. Until divergences or non-confirmations appear, we think that a reasonable course is to remain constructive about prospects.' Or: Keep on hoping now you know!

# 23

# Those dratted taxes

Two taxes — income and capital gains — directly concern investors. Neither is particularly simple or straightforward. In fact, however correct they may be officially, they frequently seem incongruous, even inequitable. It is, therefore, vital to a minimisation of liability to understand the seemingly weird and wonderful ways of the taxmen.

## INCOME IMPOST

The 1988 Budget yielded some simplification and an overall reduction in income tax rates. Compared with six bands previously, there are only two rates, for 1988/89. Basic rate is now 25%, with a single top slice band of 40 per cent payable on *taxable incomes* over £19,300, against a 1987/88 range of 40 per cent to 60 per cent. This means that 40% is not payable until *pre-allowance incomes* exceed £23,395 for married men and £21,905 for single persons. The allowances are: married men £4,095 and single people £2,605.

Income tax at the basic rate is paid or deemed to have been paid on most interest and dividends before investors receive payment. Two methods which sharply distinguish between interest and dividends operate:

(1) Tax is *deducted* from interest.
£100 gross interest will be shown as:

| | |
|---|---:|
| Gross interest | £100 |
| Less income tax @ 25% | 25 |
| Net payment | £75 |

(2) Tax is *credited* on dividends.
A net dividend of £75 will be shown as:

| | |
|---|---:|
| Dividend payment | £75 |
| Tax credit @ 25% | £25 |

True, the end results are the same. Each payment is £75 and £25 tax has been paid on behalf of the investor. And, as seen later, when it comes to individual assessments it is £100 which counts as income. The tiresome fact is that a tax return has to show:

| Interest | £100 | Tax deducted | £25 |
|---|---|---|---|
| Dividend | £75 | Tax credit | £25 |

There are some exceptions to the deduction rule when payment is made gross. And some variations in its application. Such income is not, however, exempt from tax. It must be entered in tax returns in the normal way. Three categories of investment income are concerned:

First, *interest paid gross* without deduction of tax: the main investments in this category are:

$3\frac{1}{2}$% War Loan

Government stocks on the National Savings Stock Register

Other deposits the interest on which is not on an annual basis.

Second, *building societies* and *banks* pay a reduced (composite) rate of tax based on what it is estimated the average investor would pay. Interest is then distributed to investors on a 'tax paid' basis to which two conditions apply. First, investors who are not liable to income tax cannot reclaim anything; this can be an important factor when considering building society investment. Secondly, it is taken into reckoning on a *grossed-up basic rate* basis where there is liability; this means that £75 of net interest received in 1988/89 is counted as a gross receipt of £100. The grossing impact is most strongly noticeable when higher rate tax is payable.

Third, *overseas investment income;* though two lots of tax are deducted, the net outcome is the same. First is a local non-resident or withholding tax at a rate which the UK has mutually agreed with many countries. Second is the balance to make up the basic UK tax. Payment of the net distribution is made direct if the company or other body has paying agents such as registrars in this country, or the holder is on the local (main) register. Otherwise, if the securities are held in 'marking names', banks or stockbrokers will collect and credit customers. There may also be direct payment in local currency, in which case the bank draft or cheque will have to be endorsed and sent to the investor's bank for collection in sterling — again with the bank deducting the appropriate UK tax.

When UK registrars make payments the foreign currency is converted into sterling at a rate ruling on a specific date and this is shown on the voucher. Methods of setting out the essential details vary, but the essence for a gross dividend of £100 from, say, a Canadian company would be:

| | | |
|---|---:|---:|
| Gross dividend | | £100.00 |
| *Less:* Canadian non-resident | | |
| shareholders' tax @ 15% | £15.00 | |
| UK income tax @ 10% | £10.00 | 25.00 |
| Net amount | | £75.00 |

Figures to enter in the tax return are gross dividend £100 and tax deducted £25. This is the same treatment as for interest. Overseas dividends do not go into the tax credit section.

Some investment income is exempt from income tax and capital gains tax. The exemptions are interest on Savings Certificates, Index-Linked Bonds, and Save-As-You-Earn contracts and Premium Savings Bond prizes. Also exempt is the first £70 interest on *ordinary accounts* with the National Savings Bank; but note: *all interest on investment accounts* is liable to tax.

Income tax liability may not end with deductions from investment income. On the one hand, total taxable income from all sources may not be enough to absorb all tax allowances and reliefs and a repayment is due from the tax authorities. On the other hand, total income may attract extra tax above the basic rate.

Taxpayers with substantial investment incomes have to face higher rates if their total income from all sources exceeds certain limits. The stage at which higher rates begin to bite first depends on the personal and other allowances due. For *1987/88* the tax-free zones were £2,425 single person and £3,795 married man, with higher rate bands of:

| £ | % |
|---|---|
| 17,901–20,400 | 40 |
| 20,401–25,400 | 45 |
| 25,401–33,300 | 50 |
| 33,301–41,200 | 55 |
| Over 41,200 | 60 |

For 1988/89 the move up to 40 per cent is, as already mentioned, when pre-allowance incomes go over £23,395 for married men and £21,905 for single persons. What is actually payable, however, partly depends on the income make-up — if wholly investment, repayments are likely; if a mixture of earned income or pension subjected to PAYE and investment, probably nothing either way; and if over the basic rate limit, something extra to pay. Some 1988/89 examples may help:

*Example one:* A single person aged 56 with no earned income receives UK company dividends of £4,500 with tax credits of £1,500; other interest and dividends of £2,000 with tax deductions of £500; building society interest of £375 tax paid; and $3\frac{1}{2}$% War Loan interest of £300 paid gross. The tax position is shown overleaf.

*Example two:* A retired married man aged 67 has pensions of £12,000 from which PAYE of £1,976 has been deducted; gross investment income of £6,000 with £1,500 tax credited or deducted; £750 net building society interest; and £1,000 $3\frac{1}{2}$% War Loan interest paid gross. His tax liability is shown overleaf.

*Example three:* A married man of 60 paying tax in full at the top slice rate of 40 per cent on his earned income has a gross investment income of £8,000 against which tax of £2,000 has been credited or deducted. As only 25 per cent has been paid on the investment income liable at top slice 40 per cent, additional tax of £1,200 (£3,200–£2,000) is due.

Points about income tax on investment income to bear in mind are:
* Repayment claims can be made half-yearly in October and April.
* Assessments to higher rate tax are made after the 5 April tax year-end, normally around May/June.
* Completion of tax returns can be simplified by keeping two running lists of taxed investment income. Each with two columns, one will record UK company dividends — column one: cheque received, column two: tax credit. The second will list *other* taxed dividends and interest — column one: gross amount, column two: tax deducted.

*Example one*

|                                          | Income £ | Tax £ |
|------------------------------------------|---------:|------:|
| UK dividends                     £4,500  |          |       |
| *Add:* Tax credits                1,500  |          |       |
|                                          |    6,000 | 1,500 |
| Other interest and dividends (gross)     |    2,000 |   500 |
| Building society interest          £395  |          |       |
| *Add* Tax at 25/75ths              125   |          |       |
|                                          |      500 |   125 |
| War loan interest                        |      300 |   nil |
| Totals                                   |   £8,800 | £2,125 |

Tax is payable on £8,800 *less* the personal allowance of £2,605:

|                    |           |
|--------------------|----------:|
| Gross income       |    £8,800 |
| *Less:* Allowance  |     2,605 |
| Taxable            |    £6,195 |
| Tax @ 25%          | £1,548.75 |

As £2,125 is deemed to have been paid, a repayment of £576.25 is due.

*Example two*

|                                        | Income £ | Tax £ |
|----------------------------------------|---------:|------:|
| Pensions                               |   12,000 | 1,976 |
| Dividends and taxed interest           |    6,000 | 1,500 |
| Building society interest        £750  |          |       |
| *Add:* Tax @ 25/75ths            250   |          |       |
|                                        |    1,000 |   250 |
| Untaxed interest                       |    1,000 |   nil |
| Totals                                 |  £20,000 | £3,726 |

Tax due on £20,000 (less the £4,095 personal allowance) at 25 per cent is £3,976 (to the nearest £). As only £3,726 is deemed to have been paid, the balance of £250 (in respect of the untaxed interest) has to by paid.

\*   Provision for payment of extra income tax should be made by transfers to a building society share account, a bank deposit account or, if the amount will be large, by purchases of certificates of tax deposit, which earn a good rate of interest.

\*   And the moral. High-rate taxpayers not relying on investment income should opt for capital appreciation for all or most of their money. They benefit from the CGT exemption limit (£5,000 for 1988/89) which is tax free.

## COPING WITH CAPITAL GAINS TAX

Changes in the Capital Gains Tax computation rules during the first seventeen years from its inception on 6 April 1965 were mainly new exemptions; in the matching of sales with purchases; and increases in the exemption limits, with the tax rate staying at 30 per cent, as it did up to 1987/88.

A major, and overdue, change come in 1982. From 6 April 1982 inflation was taken into account by indexation in line with rises in the Retail Prices Index (RPI) from March 1982, by an uplift in the cost of stocks and shares disposed of *more than one year* after acquisition. Three years on, the 1985 Budget brought three worthwhile changes:

* The one year 'waiting' period was abolished. Indexation started from 31 March 1982 or actual acquisition date if later.
* If the pre-indexation cost of a holding was less than the 31 March 1982 value, the latter could be used to calculate the indexation uplift.
* Losses could be indexed like gains.

The *indexation formula* is $\dfrac{RD - RI}{RI}$ with RD being the month of disposal and RI the March 1982 RPI or the RPI in the month of acquisition if later.

This was followed in the 1988 Budget by another major, and much needed, cost price valuation option. From 6 April 1988 the market value on 31 March 1982 (G-day) can now be substituted as the CGT cost if it is greater than actual cost. The *market value base* replaces, and moves on, the original base which gave the option of cost or market value at 5 April 1965.

Examples show the pre- and the new, 1988/89, indexation at work:

One: Shares bought in May 1983 for £2,000 were sold for £4,000 in January 1988 when the index had risen 22 per cent to 1.220. The CGT cost was thus £2,000 plus £440 to become £2,440 (£2,000 × 1.220) and the *taxable* gain was £1,560 (£4,000 − £2,440) as against the *actual* gain of £2,000.

Two: If the same shares had been bought in May 1981 the uplift — from March 1982 be it noted — would have been 30 per cent to make the CGT cost £2,600 (£2,000 × 1.300) and the taxable gain would have been reduced to £1,400 (£4,000 − £2,600).

Three: If the May 1983 purchase at £2,000 had been sold in January 1988 for only £1,500 the CGT loss would have been £940 (£2,440 − £1,500) compared with an actual loss of £500 and a saving of tax on an extra £440.

Four: If the January 1988 sale of the May 1983 purchase at £2,000 had realised only £2,100 there would have been a *tax loss* of £340 (£2,440 − £2,100) against an actual profit of £100.

That was the situation for realisations during the indexation tax years up to 5 April 1988.

A key factor in valuing securities held before the new G-day is that they will be deemed to have been acquired at their market value at 31 March 1982; and that the rebasing does not increase a gain or a loss compared with what it would have been under the rules up to 1987/88 and with account being taken, where appropriate, of the pre-6 April 1965 rules. This means that if there is a gain since 31 March 1982 and a loss under the indexation regime, or vice versa, there will be a no gain no loss situation and rebasing will not alter similar cases for assets held on 6 April 1965. Under this rule:

If a 'basic' gain of £12,000 compares with a March 1982 market value gain of £17,000 the chargeable gain is limited to £12,000.

If a 'basic' loss of £8,000 goes against a March 1982 valuation loss of £19,000, the allowable loss is limited to £8,000.

If a 'basic' gain of £23,000 compares with a March 1982 value loss of £13,000 there is no gain/no loss.

Prior to indexation, matching sales with acquisitions was, as it has since turned out, relatively simple. The gain on an outright sale for £3,000 of a single purchase holding of £2,000 was, for instance, £1,000 — or if the proceeds were only £1,000, a loss of £1,000. Partial sales out of single purchase or accumulated holdings were matched at the pool (average) cost or, depending on the rules at the time of sale, a first in first out (FIFO) basis or a last in first out (LIFO) basis.

Indexation has increased, and to many investors it has complicated, the arithmetic of calculating cost. The simplest working is a single sale of a singly acquired holding — the cost has only to be increased by addition of the indexation factor; such as:

Sale of 10,000 shares bought at 60p in September 1984 for 120p in November 1987 with the respective indices being 1.000 and 1.130, to give an uplift of 13 per cent:

| | | |
|---|---:|---:|
| Sale proceeds | | £12,000 |
| Cost | £,6,000 | |
| + Index .130 | 780 | 6,780* |
| Assessable gain | | £5,220 |

compared with actual gain of £6,000.
*Cost: £6,000 × 1.130

*Note:* Some publications such as the *Investors Chronicle* and *The Daily Telegraph* produce monthly indices from March 1982, from which changes between acquisition and sales dates can easily be derived.

Computing assessable gains, or losses, on sales from holdings accumulated over a period of time at varying prices is a more detailed and painstaking exercise. Indexation has to be accumulated on balances each time there is an addition or a sale. For example, these share transactions:

| | | |
|---|---|---|
| June 1983 | Bought | 10,000 @ 40p |
| Sept. 1984 | Bought | 10,000 @ 60p |
| Dec. 1984 | Rights issue 1 for 2 | 10,000 @ 50p |
| Dec. 1985 | Sold | 15,000 @ 100p |
| May 1986 | Bought | 5,000 @ 80p |
| Nov 1987 | Sold | 10,000 @ 120p |

The indexation factors being respectively .070; .010; .060; .020; and .040. and the sale proceeds £15,000 and £12,000.

| Date | No. Sh. | CGT − Cost − | Actual |
|------|---------|--------------|--------|
| June '83 Bought | 10,000 | £4,000 | £4,000 |
| Index. .070 | | 280 | |
| | | 4,280 | |
| Sept. '84 Bought | 10,000 | 6,000 | 6,000 |
| | | 10,280 | |
| Index .010 | | 103 | |
| Dec. '84 Rights 1:2 | 10,000 | 5,000 | 5,000 |
| | 30,000 | 15,383 | 15,000 |
| Dec. '85 Sold | 15,000 | | |
| Index .060 | | 923 | |
| | | 16,306 | |
| | | −8,153 | −7,500 |
| | 15,000 | 8,153 | 7,500 |
| May '86 Bought | 5,000 | | |
| Index .020 | | 163 | |
| | | 4,000 | 4,000 |
| | 20,000 | 12,316 | 11,500 |
| Nov. '87 Sold | 10,000 | | |
| Index .040 | | 493 | |
| | | 12,809 | |
| | | −6,405 | −5,750 |
| Nov. '87 Balance | 10,000 | £6,404 | £5,750 |

Indexed gains on the two sales were respectively £6,847 and £5,595, a total of £12,442 or £1,308 less than actual gains of £13,750 (£7,500 + £6,250).

Indexation is not applicable to some gains or losses such as sales within ten working days of purchases designed to benefit from RPI rises from one month to the next.

Otherwise, indexation or not, basic rules to keep in mind are:

* Losses can be set off against gains, with any unused balance in one year being carried forward.
* Prices take into account incidental costs. The all-in buying figure is the price *plus* brokerage, VAT and transfer duty. The net selling figure is the price *less* brokerage and VAT. Both figures are normally the final amounts shown on contract notes.
* Bank and other holding charges and subsequent expenses on bearer and other securities should be added to cost prices.
* National Savings Certificates, Savings Bonds, Save-as-you-Earn plans and Premium Savings Bond prizes are exempt from CGT.
* Gains on British Government and other gilt-edged stocks sold after 2 July 1986 are also exempt. Equally, losses are not allowable.
* From 2 July 1986 gains and losses on UK company debentures and loan

stocks which do not have any element of equity, such as convertibility, are also outside the net.
* Gains and losses on Business Expansion and Private Equity Plans are likewise excluded.
* Losses can be set off against profits with any unused balance in one year being carried forward.

Computation of gains and losses can be eased by keeping records of acquisitions and sales in one or all of three sections, or pools:

* Pre-1 April 1982 holdings, the market value of which must be compared with actual cost. If cost is lower consider writing up the book figure to market value.
* Post-31 March 1982.
* Short-term.

*     *     *     *     *     *     *     *     *

Tax actually payable takes account of exemption limits and current tax rates, both of which were changed in the 1988 Budget. After annual increases broadly in line with inflation to £6,600 for 1987/88, the *exemption limit* was cut to £5,000 for 1988/89. Simultaneously, the flat rate tax of 30 per cent which had ruled since 1965 was scrapped.

Again from 1988/89, the impost is now, in effect, an extension of income tax with net capital gains dealt with as the top slice of income. This means liability in 1988/89 at (1) 25 per cent on an assessable total up to the basic rate limit of £19,300; and (2) at 40 per cent on any excess. For example, if income before allowances is £15,000 and net gains £10,000 CGT payable by a married man will be:

| | | |
|---|---:|---:|
| Income | | £15,000 |
| Gains | | 10,000 |
| | | 25,000 |
| *Less:* Allowances | | |
| Personal | £4,095 | |
| Gains | 5,000 | |
| | | 9,095 |
| Net taxable | | £15,905 |

As the net is below £19,300, gains tax is 25 per cent on £5,000, or £1,250. A single person with the lower personal allowance of £2,605 would be liable on a net total of £17,395, also below the £19,300 limit, and would likewise pay £1,250 CGT at the 25 per cent rate.

If the income was £30,000 and the gains still £10,000, the total of £40,000 less the married man's personal allowance of £4,095 and CGT exemption of £5,000 leaves a taxable total of £30,905 which is above the £19,300 basic rate limit. CGT is thus payable at 40 per cent on £5,000 (£10,000 − £5,000 exemption).

When gains, after the £5,000 exemption, partially push the taxable total above the £19,300 basic limit, the position for a married man with £20,000 income and £10,000 net gains would be:

| | |
|---|---:|
| Income | £20,000 |
| Gains | 10,000 |
| | £30,000 |
| *Less:* Allowances | 9,095 |
| Net taxable | £20,905 |

Basic rate would be payable on £15,905 (£20,000 − £4,095 personal allowance) of the income; and gains tax would be 25 per cent on £3,395 (£19,300 − £15,905) and 40 per cent on £1,605, a total bill of £1,490.75. On the old basis and 1987/88 exemption limit, the gains tax would have been only £10,000 less £6,600 equals £3,400 at 30 per cent, or £1,020.

*Losses* not set off against net gains can be carried forward year by year until used up. Which means that when net gains come into the picture the full benefit of the exemption limit should be taken as per this example:

| | | |
|---|---:|---:|
| Accumulated losses in hand | | £5,500 |
| Net gains 1987/88 | | £7,800 |
| Net gains 1988/89 | | £12,300 |
| The tax positions are: | | |
| 1987/88 | | |
| Net gains | | £7,800 |
| Losses brought forward | £5,500 | |
| Loss to reduce gains to £6,600 | 1,200 | 1,200 |
| Balance of loss/net gains | £4,300 | £6,600 |
| Tax on £6,600 less £6,600 | | nil |
| exemption 1988/89: | | |
| Net gains | | £12,300 |
| *Less* losses brought forward | | 4,300 |
| Assessable net gains | | £8,000 |

Tax is payable on £3,000 (£8,000 less exemption £5,000) at 25 per cent or 40 per cent, or part and part.

*Husband and wife* are entitled to only one exemption limit between them; tax is payable on their combined gains in excess of the zero limit, £5,000 for 1988/89. Each can however get up to full exemption if they have not been married for the whole of a tax year beginning 6 April. Transfers of holdings between spouses are not taken into account: they pass to the new holder at their original cost, to show neither gain nor loss, and coming into the picture only when the new owner sells. If forecasts fructify, husband and wife will each have their own exemption from 1990, by when each will be assessed individually in their own right.

*Children* who are minors are due their own exemption limit on net gains on realisations of their individually owned investments.

*Investment and unit trusts* have been exempt from gains tax since April 1980. Share and unit holders are, however, assessable in the normal way on realisations.

Consideration so far has been on what can be called the ground rules for calculating the cost factor. Other rules apply to rights issues, takeovers and other operations, as follows:

**A scrip issue,** as noted in Chapter 16, adds nothing to the value of a shareholding. It is, therefore, not liable to gains tax. All that is necessary is to alter the number of shares held and the new, effective cost price. For example: 1,000 25p shares are held at a cost of £1,500, or 150p a share. A scrip issue of one new share for each two held is made. The holding becomes 1,500 shares, still at a cost of £1,500, but an average price of 100p. Records have to be amended to 1,500 at 100p and £1,500 cost. If the original shares were bought before 6 April 1982, the G-day price is adjusted accordingly, say, from 90p to 60p.

The position is not so simple when the scrip issue is in preference shares, or in loan stock. The original cost remains the same but has to be apportioned between the original ordinary and the scrip allocation. This is done on the basis of the market prices on the opening day of dealings in the new securities. For example:

> 1,000 25p ordinary shares are held at a cost of 150p or £1,500.
> A scrip issue of one 8% (net) preference share is distributed for each two ordinary.
> Opening prices are: ordinary 210p and preference 80p, to give respective values of £2,100 (1,000 × 210p) and £400 (500 × 80p).
> The £1,500 purchase price is apportioned:

$$1,000 \text{ ordinary } \frac{£2,100 \times £1,500}{£2,100 + £400} = £1,260$$

$$500 \text{ preference } \frac{£400 \times £1,500}{£2,100 + £400} = £240$$

**Rights issues** of similar class shares are treated as additions to existing holdings. For example, if there is an issue of one new share for two old at 100p, a holding of 2,000 shares bought in 1984 for £3,000 (150p a share) becomes 3,000 at a cost of £4,000 (£3,000+£1,000), or $133\frac{1}{3}$p a share. On old holdings bought before G-day the new are averaged out and the G-day value adjusted accordingly.

Tax treatment of proceeds from *sales of rights* depends on the relation of the proceeds to the cost of the holding. If the proceeds are less than five per cent of the cost they will be treated as a small distribution which reduces the cost and defers payment of any tax until disposal of the holding. But if the proceeds are greater than five per cent they are treated as a part disposal with a possible CGT liability on any profit.

**Takeovers and mergers.** Original cost, or G-day value if applicable, is still the datum line for new securities or cash, or a combination of the two, received on a takeover or merger. The simplest case is a straight *exchange of shares* such as:

> 1,000 Company A shares, bought in 1985 at 150p at a cost of £1,500, are taken over by Company B on the basis of two of its shares for one A. The holding then becomes 2,000 Company B shares at the original cost of £1,500 or 75p each.

**An outright** *cash takeover* is a sale. The gain or loss is the difference between its amount and the original cost or G-day value. For instance, if Company B had taken over the above Company A shares at 250p each, the cost of £1,500 would be deducted from the £2,500 cash proceeds to show a gain of £1,000.

Takeover terms are sometimes a mixture of *cash and shares*. Treatment of the cash portion depends on its relative size. If it is less than five per cent in relation to the value of the shares on the first day of dealings, it is dealt with as a reduction in the price of the new holding. But if the cash element is substantial, it is treated as a part disposal. If, for example, the terms for the 1,000 Company A shares were two Company B shares plus 50p cash per A share and the opening price of B shares was 100p, the position would be:

The 1,000 A shares which cost £1,500 have become 2,000 B shares with an opening market value of £2,000 plus £500 cash. The cash gain will be:

| | | |
|---|---|---:|
| Cash proceeds | | £500 |
| *Less:* Apportioned cost: | | |
| $£1,500 \times \dfrac{£500}{£500 + £2,000} =$ | | £300 |
| Gain | | £200 |

Which reduces the cost of the 2,000 B shares by £300 to £1,200 or 60p per share.

When takeover terms are a *mixture of loan or debenture stock and shares* values are also based on opening-day market prices. Say that, instead of cash as in the above example, £500 loan stock is allotted and the opening price is £90, with the shares opening at 100p. The position then is that the original holding of A shares, which cost £1,500, has become £500 loan stock worth £450 and 2,000 B shares worth £2,000, a total value of £2,450. The cost of the loan stock is thus £450 × £1,500 ÷ £2,450 or, say, £275. The cost of the 2,000 B shares then equals £2,000 × £1,500 ÷ £2,450 or, say, £1,225. The 'cost' prices of the new holdings are thus £55 for the loan stock and $61\frac{1}{4}$p for the shares.

**Capital reduction.** Another situation arises when a company gets into difficulties and faces up to its losses by a capital reduction, the impact of which invariably falls on the equity shares. It has, say, to write off £5 million against an issued ordinary capital of £10 million. The 50 per cent loss is met by reducing the £1 shares to 50p. A holder of 2,000 £1 shares which had cost £3,000 would then have 2,000 50p shares. The cost price would not, however, be affected. The 'reduced' shares would still stand in for tax purposes at £3,000, or £150p each.

Where a company is in liquidation or in serious difficulties and it is impossible to sell shares because the listing has been cancelled, it may be possible to claim a *notional loss*. This means proving to the Inland Revenue that there is little or no chance of recovering a large part of the purchase price or that all has been lost. The task is not easy, but where the outlook can be shown to be very bad it is worthwhile making the effort.

It is argued that investors fortunate enough to be making good profits should try to limit the yearly total to the exemption limit and so pay no tax. This is all very well if it does not mean missing a profit which can be run over into the next tax year. But a profit is always a profit and many a gain has slipped away by holding off a sale for tax or other reasons.

On the other hand, if a profit is looming close to the tax year-end of 5 April it might pay to gamble on not missing it by holding up a sale until the start of the new tax year. The current gains bill might then be less if the gamble comes off. In any event, the tax payment will be deferred for another twelve months.

Another popular idea is to take losses before the tax year-end as a set-off against profits. This can be profitable if there is a conviction that the losers will go on falling and sound investment policy dictates getting out while the going is good. But, and many speculative hearts are buoyed up by such a hope, there may be fair chances of recovery. In this event, thought should be given to a bed and breakfast operation described in chapter 4.

**Gains tax pointers.** The following points may help to reduce the toil of making gains tax returns and to keep tabs on the assessments:
* Make a list of all holdings showing acquisition dates and cost, divided into 'date' sections, as already mentioned.
* Keep all contract notes and probate lists.
* Don't make a loss merely to keep down tax bills.
* But consider bed and breakfasting heavily depreciated holdings.
* Holdings showing profits should also be considered as 'up' bed and breakfast operations.
* Losses not used up in one tax year can be carried forward until exhausted by future gains.
* Extel Statistical Services provide details of 31 March 1982 prices as adjusted for any scrip or rights issues. Stockbrokers can supply up-to-date information.
* Some companies already give the March 1982 prices in their annual reports, a lead which all companies should follow.
* Gains tax is normally due for payment on 1 December.

# Glossary

ACCOUNT: The period, usually two weeks and sometimes three weeks, into which Stock Exchange dealings are divided.

ACCOUNT DAY: The day for settlement of bargains done during the account, usually on a Monday, ten days after its end on a Friday.

ACTUAL: The price at which a market maker will deal as a buyer or as a seller.

AFTER-HOURS DEALINGS: Transactions done after the mandatory quote period of 9 am to 5 pm.

ALLOTMENT LETTER: An official notification that the recipient has been allotted a specific amount of stock or number of shares under a public issue, offer for sale or rights or other issue.

AMERICAN DEPOSIT RECEIPTS (ADRs): Certificates issued by American agents for shares of UK companies dealt in in the USA.

APPLICATION FORM: The form accompanying a prospectus, newspaper advertisement or other document offering stocks and shares for subscription, and which must be completed by the applicant.

APPLICATION MONEY: The amount per £100 of stock or per share payable on application for a new issue or offer for sale. This may be the whole amount or a percentage, to be followed by further instalments payable on allotment and/or by calls.

ARBITRAGE: The business of taking advantage of price differences for particular securities dealt in on two or more markets by buying in one and selling in another (or *vice versa*).

ASSOCIATED MEMBER: A Stock Exchange member in his own right who is not a partner of the firm with which he is associated.

AT BEST: An instruction to a broker to deal at the lowest possible price for a buying order and at the highest possible price for a selling order.

AUTHORISED CLERK: An employee who is not a member but who is empowered to deal on his member firm's behalf.

AUTHORISED DEPOSITARIES: Agencies such as banks, stockbrokers, market makers and professional people authorised by the Bank of England to hold foreign and bearer stocks on behalf of owners.

AVERAGING: The process of buying more securities on a fall or selling on a rise in order to level out the price of bull or bear transactions.

BACKWARDATION: A payment per share or unit of stock made by a bear (seller) to a bull (buyer) for the loan of securities for which the bear wishes to defer delivery.

BARGAIN: A purchase or sale deal done on the Stock Exchange.

BEAR: An individual who sells securities he does not own, or which he does not want to deliver, in the hope that they can be repurchased at a profit before delivery has to be made.

BEAR MARKET: A weak or falling market.

BEARER STOCKS: Securities which are not recorded on registers and which pass physically by hand from seller to buyer.

BED AND BREAKFAST: Selling securities and buying them back to establish (a) a loss or (b) a profit in order to benefit from the capital gains tax exemption limit.

BENEFICIAL OWNER: The ultimate owner of a security irrespective of the name in which it is legally registered.

BID: The price at which a market maker or investor is prepared to buy stocks or shares. When a price is quoted as 'bid' it generally means that there are more buyers than sellers.

BIG-BANG: 27 October 1986, the day the new regulations took effect.

BLUE CHIPS: Shares of companies, usually large, well-established and prosperous concerns, which have a high status as investments.

BONDS: In Stock Exchange terms, securities (usually fixed interest) issued by governments and other borrowers, and 'Euro' bonds, which are generally in bearer form and interest on which is collected by detachment of coupons.

BROKEN AMOUNT/NUMBER: An odd amount, such as sixty-nine shares, which is not a normal market quantity. As transfer costs may be proportionately higher than for round amounts, a seller may have to accept less than the normal market price and perhaps have to pay transfer stamp as well. This applies particularly to North American, Australian and Hong Kong shares.

BROKER/DEALER: A member firm providing advice and dealing services.

BULL: An individual who buys securities in the hope that they will rise in price, often before he has to pay for them. A 'stale bull' is one whose optimism is waning and who may be ready to cut any loss.

BULL MARKET: A rising market.

BUYERS ONLY: When a market maker qualifies a price in this way he is ready to buy but not to sell stock.

BUYING-IN: A means whereby over-due deliveries of securities are 'bought-in' through the market by the Buying-in Department of the Stock Exchange.

●

CALL OPTION: The option to buy a stated amount of securities at a specified price during a specified period.

CALLS: The amounts still payable after allotment in order to make part-paid securities fully-paid. There may be one, two or more calls spread over a specified period. Failure to meet calls may mean forfeiture of the security.

CAPITAL DISTRIBUTION: A special payment, say out of capital profits, differing from a normal dividend, or a payment by way of a reduction in capital.

CAPITAL REDUCTION: In effect a writing-down of the nominal value of shares in order to eliminate an accumulation of losses which almost always falls entirely on the equity capital.

CAPITALISATION ISSUE: A free allotment of shares made in proportion to existing shares out of accumulated reserves. Usually known as a 'scrip' or a 'bonus' issue. Such issues add nothing to the assets of a company.

CASH AND NEW: The sale of shares bought during one account and their immediate repurchase for the next account.

CASH BONUS: An extra dividend paid out of exceptional profits which is in addition to a normal dividend.

CASH SETTLEMENT: Payment for transactions on the day after dealing as distinct from fortnightly account settlement.

CERTIFICATE: The document showing the ownership of a security, which has to be handed over on a sale and which should be kept at a bank, stockbrokers or in another safe place.

CERTIFICATION: The marking on a transfer deed that the relevant share certificate has been lodged with a company's registrars or with the Stock Exchange. Certification is particularly necessary when part only of the shares in one certificate are to be transferred, or there is a transfer to more than one buyer.

CHEAP MONEY: When interest rates are low, money is described as 'cheap' for borrowers.

CHOICE: The position where a broker can buy from one market maker at the same price as he can sell to another market maker. For example, market maker A may be quoting 77p–79p while market maker B's price is 79p–81p.

CLOSE PRICE: A narrow margin between bid and offered prices.

CLOSING: Selling or buying to close a purchase or sale opened in the same account.

CLOSING PRICES: The prices ruling at the official close of the market. Business done afterwards is at 'after-hours' prices.

COMMON STOCKS/SHARES: A United States and Canadian term for equity, or ordinary, shares. They often are of 'no par value' (NPV).

COMPENSATION FUND: A Stock Exchange fund maintained to compensate investors if a member firm fails to meet its obligations and is 'hammered'.

CONSIDERATION: The cost of a purchase or the amount of a sale before charging brokerage, transfer expenses, VAT and other expenses.

CONSOLS: A market term for the two gilt-edged securities, $2\frac{1}{2}$ per cent Consolidated Stock and 4 per cent Consolidated Stock.

CONTANGO: Consideration, or rate of interest, paid for carrying-over a transaction from one account to the next account.

CONTINGENT: The carrying out of a buying order being contingent on the execution of a selling order, or *vice versa*. Also means the settlement of selling and buying transactions on the same day without the passing of money.

COUPON: A detachable warrant which has to be presented to paying agents in order to collect interest or dividends on bearer securities, which have sheets of coupons attached to them. New sheets of coupons are obtained by the exchange of a 'talon', which is part of the sheet.

COVER: The number of times interest and dividends are covered by available profits.

COVERED BEAR: A seller of securities he owns who hopes to repurchase later at a profit and who hopes to save repurchase expenses by not having to deliver.

CUM: Means 'with'. A price so quoted includes the right to any recently declared dividend, scrip issue, rights issue or other distribution.

CURRENT YIELD: Or 'flat' or 'running' yield, is the annual return on an investment at current price as based on the interest rate or dividend. It is arrived at by multiplying the annual rate per cent by the nominal value of the stock or share and dividing by the all-in price paid.

●

DEAL: A transaction or bargain which, in Stock Exchange terms, means a purchase or sale of securities.

DEALING FOR NEW TIME: Buying or selling securities in one account for the next account, which is permitted during the last two days of an account.

DEALING WITHIN THE ACCOUNT: Purchase and sale, or *vice versa*, within a Stock Exchange account. Commission is charged only on the opening transaction.

DEAR MONEY: Money is 'dear' when it is scarce and interest rates are high.

DEED OF TRANSFER: The legal form giving registrars of securities authority to transfer sales from one holder to another.

DIFFERENCE: The balance due to or by a client on transactions during a Stock Exchange account.

DISCOUNT: The amount by which a security is quoted below its par or paid-up value. For example, a 50p share which is 25p paid-up is at a discount of $2\frac{1}{2}$p if it is quoted at only $22\frac{1}{2}$p. Similarly, a fully-paid stock standing at £$97\frac{1}{2}$ is quoted at £$2\frac{1}{2}$ discount.

DISCOUNTED: An indication that some anticipated future event has been taken into account in the future price.

DIVIDEND COUNTERFOIL: The 'top' attached to dividend or interest cheques which gives details of the payment, including the rate and amount of income tax credited or deducted. Counterfoils must be carefully kept to assist with the preparation of income tax returns and repayment claims.

DIVIDEND COVER: The number of times that dividends are covered by available profits.

DIVIDEND/INTEREST WARRANT: The cheque for dividend and interest payments.

DIVIDEND MANDATE: A form completed by an investor authorising a company to pay dividends or interest direct to a bank, building society or to some other person.

DOLLAR STOCKS: A market term for American and Canadian stocks and shares.

DOUBLE OPTION: The right to buy or sell a security at an agreed price within an agreed period, usually not more than three months.

DRAWINGS: The process of selecting, usually by lottery, bonds for repayment under a sinking fund or other arrangement for redemption by 'instalments'.

●

EARNINGS: The amount of profits after meeting all interest and preferential dividend payments available for the equity capital expressed as so many pence per ordinary share.

EARNINGS COVER: The amount, or the times by which, an ordinary dividend is covered by earnings. For example, earnings of 6p per share cover a 2p dividend three times.

EQUITY: Another name for ordinary shares, which usually take all the risks and are entitled to the balance of profits after meeting prior charges. Equity-holders are also entitled to what is left of the net assets after meeting the demands of any other classes of capital.

EX: Means without. A price so quoted excludes any recently declared dividend, scrip or rights issue, or other distribution.

EXCESS SHARES: Shares remaining from a rights issue after existing shareholders have taken up the number to which they are entitled. The excess may be sold in the market, or are 'sold' on a *pro rata* basis at the issue price to existing shareholders who apply for extra shares.

●

FINAL DIVIDEND: The last distribution for a company's trading period, usually a year. Some companies pay only one dividend a year. But most also pay interim, or half-yearly, distributions. Others, like many North American companies, pay quarterly dividends.

FIXED CHARGES: In the investment sense these are interest on debenture and loan stocks and dividends on preference shares, each ranking in front of ordinary shares for their service.

FLAT YIELD: Another term for current (q.v.) or running yield.

'FOOTSIE': The FT-SE 100 Share Index covering 100 leading UK shares, started from 3 January 1984 with a base of 1000 and updated minute by minute.

FRANKED INVESTMENT INCOME: Dividends received by one company from another which has borne corporation tax on its profits. Such income is not again liable to corporation tax. It is particularly important to investment trusts.

FREE MARKET: A situation where it is possible to readily buy or sell large amounts of securities.

FT30: The *Financial Times* index of 30 leading industrial and commercial shares, started in 1935 and calculated hourly with a closing index at 5 p.m.

FUNDS, THE: Another name for UK Government stocks, which was at one time widely used.

●

GEARING: The relationship between debenture and loan capital, preference capital, and equity capital. High gearing means that prior charge capital is large in relation to the equity (ordinary) capital. Low gearing means the reverse.

GILTS/GILT-EDGED: Market names for UK Government and similar stocks.

GROSS: In investment terms, the interest payable before deduction of income tax or the 'gross' amount of UK dividends after adding the tax credit to the actual distribution. In other words, the gross amount of any distribution before income tax deduction or credits.

GROWTH STOCKS: The shares of companies believed, or expected, to have possibilities of profit and other expansion. Immediate dividend yields are usually low, the hope being that distributions will grow and share prices will rise.

●

HIGH COUPON: Fixed interest stocks carrying a high rate of interest. 'High' naturally varies in line with interest rates generally, but may be taken to be several points above the norm.

HOUSE: Colloquial name for the floor of the Stock Exchange, London.

●

INCOME BONDS/DEBENTURES: Securities, the interest on which is payable only out of profits.

INDEX-LINKED GILT: A Government stock, the interest and capital value of which change with the Retail Price Index.

INSTALMENT: Payment for new issues is sometimes made up of application and allotment monies followed by one or more instalments (calls), thus spreading payment over a period of time.

INSTITUTIONS: A term covering pension funds, insurance offices, banks, investment and unit trusts, building societies and other 'professional' investment bodies.

INTERIM DIVIDEND: Many companies spread dividend payments over the financial year by distribution of an interim, or interims, followed by a final distribution after the year-end.

IRREDEEMABLES: Gilt-edged, debenture and loan stocks which have no fixed redemption dates, or are 'undated'. They are, therefore, generally repayable only at the option of the borrower or, as with companies, on a liquidation or in special circumstances such as a takeover.

ISSUING HOUSE: A merchant bank, stockbroking firm or other institution which arranges and sponsors new issues of capital and arranges their underwriting.

●

JOBBERS: The original name for dealers in securities on the Stock Exchange. They had no direct contact with the public the deals being done between them and stockbrokers. Under the new Stock Exchange system, there are firms which can act as dealers ('market makers') and also as brokers. This is called 'dual capacity'.

●

KAFFIRS: A name given to South African gold mining and related shares.

KANGAROOS: A name sometimes given to Australian shares.

●

LETTER OF INDEMNITY: Request to a registrar to issue a new stock or share certificate in place of an original which has been lost, destroyed or stolen, with the holder undertaking to indemnify the company for any loss resulting from the issue of the duplicate.

LETTER OF RENUNCIATION: Completion of a form by the holder of an allotment of shares or stock wishing to pass the entitlement to someone else.

LICENSED DEALER: A dealer in securities *not* a Stock Exchange Member who is licensed to trade by the Department of Trade and Industry.

LIMIT: A broker may be limited to buying at a stated maximum price or to selling at a stated minimum price.

LIMITED MARKET: Individual securities or groups are so described, when, because of shortage of stock or for some other reason, it is difficult to buy or sell.

LINE: An above-normal or large amount of stock or number of shares available for sale.

LISTED COMPANY: A company whose shares are officially quoted as opposed to those dealt in the Unlisted Securities Market (USM), or Third Market.

LISTS CLOSED: Public issues and offers for sale have their application lists open for a specified time. Lists are closed when the time expires or the offer is fully subscribed. Lists for popular offers may open at 10 a.m. and close at 10.01 a.m. on the same day.

LONDON PARITY: The sterling equivalent of a North American or other overseas stock price.

LONG: A bull position or description of a holder of a particular stock or share.

LONGS: Government and similar stocks with repayment dates (lives) of more than fifteen years.

LOW COUPON: In contradistinction to 'high' coupon issues a fixed interest stock carrying a low rate of interest.

LUMP: A market term for a large or largish amount of stock or number of shares.

●

MAKE-UP PRICES: Prices fixed by the Stock Exchange Council to facilitate settlement of bargains, particularly at the end of an account.

MAKING A PRICE: When a market maker quotes, or 'makes', a price he is usually ready to deal in a reasonable market quantity of the security, buying at the lower price and selling at the higher one.

MARKET MAKER: The term used under the Stock Exchange rules after October 1986 for the function previously known as 'jobber'. The difference is that jobbing firms were previously clearly defined as separate from broking firms. Now, if they wish, firms may both make prices of shares and also deal directly with investors in them.

MARKETABLE AMOUNT: The amount of stock or number of shares in which a market maker quoting a price would reasonably be expected to deal. As circumstances differ considerably between active and inactive securities the amounts vary.

MARKETABLE SECURITY: A stock or share capable of being sold on any market.

MARKING NAMES: Description of banks, stockbrokers, market makers and others who are authorised by the Bank of England to hold overseas securities on behalf of UK residents.

MARRYING: The linking by a broker of a selling order with a simultaneous buying order. An alternative is a 'put-through' (q.v.).

MEDIUMS: Government and similar stocks with repayment dates of five to fifteen years.

MIDDLE PRICE: The half-way level between buying and selling prices, such as 78p if the quotation is 77p–79p. Newspapers and other publications quote middle prices.

MINIMUM PRICE: The price below which the Government and water and other companies offering issues of stock or shares by tender will not accept applications.

MONEY STOCK: A very short-dated gilt-edged or other security which is due for repayment a short time ahead.

MORE ONE-WAY: When mentioned by a broker or market maker it is an indication that bigger business could be done either buying or selling.

●

NAME TICKET: The form giving details for registration of the purchase of securities, which the buying broker passes to the seller.

NEGOTIATION: The putting together of buyer and seller outside the normal price-making mechanism.

NET ASSET VALUE (NAV): The amount by which the assets of a company exceed all liabilities, including loan and preference capital, divided by the number of equity shares in issue. For example, if the net amount available is £20m and there are 40m 25p ordinary shares the NAV is 50p.

NEW TIME/NEW-GO: Purchases or sales in one account for settlement in the next account. Such transactions can take place during the last two days of an account.

NIL PAID: A new share offer, usually a rights issue, on which no payment has been made.

NOMINAL: A price is nominal when a market maker quotes it but is not prepared to deal. It is thus merely an indication of a possible dealing price.

NOMINAL VALUE: The face value as opposed to the market value.

NOMINEE NAME: Name in which securities are registered which does not disclose the name of the beneficial owner.

NO PAR VALUE (NPV): Shares, mostly American and Canadian, without a face, a nominal or par value.

NOT TO PRESS (NTP): When a transaction is dealt in NTP it means that the buyer agrees with the market maker that he will not put in motion the Stock Exchange buying-in machinery for obtaining delivery if this is delayed beyond a normal period.

●

OFFERED: When a price is so much 'offered' it generally means that there are more sellers than buyers, or it is the price at which a market maker will sell.

OFFERED NOT BID: The price at which potential sellers are offering to sell but at which potential buyers are not prepared to buy.

OFFICIAL LIST: *The Stock Exchange Daily Official List* which covers all listed securities and which gives particulars of latest dividends, ex-dividend dates and dates of payment and official quotations. Market prices are usually much closer than the official quotations. The 'List' is used for probate and similar valuations. It includes data for the Unlisted Securities Market stocks and shares.

ONE, TWO, THREE ... : Stock Exchange abbreviations for one thousand, two thousand, three thousand and so on.

ONE-WAY PRICE: When a market maker says he is 'one-way only' it means that he cannot deal both ways but can only bid for or offer stock.

OPENING PRICES: Prices ruling at the official opening of the Stock Exchange each day.

OPTION: The right on payment of a consideration to buy or not to buy (call option) a particular security at a stated price, or to sell or not to sell (put option) a particular security also at a stated price over a given period of, say, one, two or three months. A double option gives the right to buy or sell. See also 'traded option'.

OVER-SUBSCRIBED: An offer of securities is over-subscribed when applications exceed the amount offered. Popular offerings can be subscribed many times over and applications are scaled-down or rejected.

●

PAR: The nominal value of a security, which is generally £100 for stock and 10p, 25p, 50p, £1 or some other amount for shares.

PARI PASSU: Equal in all respects and usually used to describe new issues of securities which have the same rights as similar issues already in existence.

PARTLY-PAID: Securities on which the full nominal value has not been paid and a liability to pay the balance exists. The balance is usually payable in one or more instalments, though there can be instances where the balance is only callable at the discretion of the directors or in specified circumstances. Australian exploration companies are widespread users of the part-paid method of calling up further amounts as money is needed for further work or expansion.

PITCH: The podium on the floor of the House where a market maker was to be found in pre – Big Bang days.

PORTFOLIO: A list of securities owned.

POSITION: A market maker has a position where he holds stock (is a bull) or is short of stock (is a bear).

PREFERENTIAL FORMS: Usually called 'pink forms' because of their colour, preferential forms, when used, give priority treatment to application for new share issues to people closely associated with the companies concerned, such as employees and existing shareholders. Allotments are usually limited to a specific number of shares, a percentage of the issue or a maximum number per applicant.

PREMIUM: A security stands at a premium when the price is more than its paid-up or par value. For example, a 25p paid-up share priced at 30p stands at a premium of 5p.

PRICE/EARNINGS RATIO (P/E): This is the number of times the market price of an equity share is related to the latest earnings per share. For instance, if earnings are 5p a share and the price is 50p the P/E is 10. Put another way, the P/E equals the number of years it would take for the latest annual earnings to equal the share price.

PRIOR CHARGES: Debentures, loan stocks and preference shares the interest and dividends on which must be paid before any dividend can be paid on the ordinary capital. In a liquidation or winding-up such capital ranks for repayment before the equity capital.

PRIORITY PERCENTAGES: The proportion of annual profits needed to service the different classes of capital, and shown in order of priority as a percentage of the amount available.

PROBATE PRICE: The price at which securities are valued for Inheritance Tax and other taxation purposes. It is a quarter up on the difference between the two prices in the Official List, e.g., 100–4 means a price of 101.

PROVISIONAL ALLOTMENT LETTER: A notification sent to shareholders in companies making rights issues offering to allot new shares in a fixed proportion of those already held at a fixed price. Rights can usually be sold. But if they are not taken up the opportunity is lost and the provisional allotment becomes void.

PROXY CARD: A form provided by a company for a shareholder to empower someone else to vote for him/her at a meetimg. It must be delivered at least forty-eight hours before the meeting to be valid.

PUT and CALL OPTION: The right either to buy or to sell shares under an option.

PUT OPTION: The option to sell a stated amount of securities at a specified price during a specified limited period.

PUT-THROUGH: The sale of securities to a market maker simultaneously with their repurchase by the same broker.

●

QUOTATION: The price made by jobbers and market makers. Also refers to the grant by the Stock Exchange Council of a listing in new securities.

●

REDEMPTION DATE: The date, or dates, when gilt-edged, debentures and loan stocks are repayable, also redeemable preference shares with 'dates'.

REDEMPTION YIELD: The flat yield plus an annualised proportion of the profit which will accrue on the purchase of a fixed interest stock at a price below its redemption price. Alternatively, if the market price is more than the redemption price, the flat yield *less* the annualised loss on repayment.

REGISTERED STOCKS/SHARES: Securities the ownership of which is recorded in stock or share registers, and which change ownership by deed of transfer as opposed to bearer stocks which are transferred hand to hand.

RENUNCIATION: New issues of shares are usually made by means of allotment letters or renounceable certificates. During a period of renunciation, holders may dispose of their allotment to a new owner.

REVERSE YIELD GAP: See Yield Gap.

RIGHTS ISSUE: The issue of new shares to existing shareholders in a fixed ratio to those already held at a price which is generally below the market price of the old shares.

RIGHTS LETTER: The document offering shares under a rights issue.

ROUND AMOUNTS: Amounts of stock or numbers of shares in which market makers are ready to deal on a normal price basis as opposed to 'odd lot' amounts or numbers. Examples are £100 nominal of stock and 50 or 100 shares.

●

SCRIP: Specifically, a provisional document such as an allotment letter, but, more widely, any form of security.

SCRIP ISSUE: See capitalisation issue.

SEAQ: The Stock Exchange Automated Quotation system, a continuously updated computer database containing quotations for trade reports on UK securities.

SEAQ INTERNATIONAL: The electronic screen system for non-UK equities displaying quotes from competing market makers.

SECONDARY OFFER: The offer of a block of existing quoted shares by a holder, or holders, wishing to reduce their interest for one reason or another. The Government's sale of some of its British Petroleum shares is an outstanding example of such an operation.

SELLERS ONLY: Added to his quotation this means that a market maker will sell but not buy.

SEPON: Stock Exchange Pool Nominees, the Stock Exchange nominee company into which all sold stock is registered during the course of settlement.

SETTLEMENT: Payment for securities can be for cash, which means the day after purchase or sale, or for the account, which means ten days after the close of the fortnightly or three-weekly account.

SETTLEMENT/ACCOUNT DAY: The day on which dealings during a Stock Exchange account are settled. This is usually a Monday ten days after the end of each account.

SHOP: Term used to describe the merchant bank, finance house and/or stock-brokers who have sponsored capital issues and who continue to act for the companies or bodies concerned.

SHORT: Anyone who has sold securities he does not own.

SHORTS: Gilt-edged and similar stocks due for repayment within five years.

SIZE OF MARKET: The amount in which a market maker is making his price.

SMALL: An indication by a market maker that the price made is for less than a normal market quantity.

SPREAD: The difference between a market maker's buying and selling price. Also called a turn.

STAG: A speculator who applies for new issues not as a permanent investor but in the hope that an allotment can be sold at a profit when dealings commence.

STAMP DUTIES: The *ad valorem* duty payable on the consideration money on the transfer of securities to a buyer. Government stocks, some overseas stocks not on a UK register and certain other securities are transferable 'free of stamp'.

STOCK: Specifically, the description of a security denominated in multiples of £100. Loosely, a general term for any kind of Stock Exchange security. In North America, it is the name given to shares.

STOCK EXCHANGE DAILY OFFICIAL LIST: See 'Official List'.

●

TAKER/TAKER-IN: A seller of shares previously paid for who is prepared to 'take-in' the shares and receive a rate under a contango instead of delivering in the normal way and receiving payment. Also a speculator who has sold short and is not able to cover his position by the end of the Stock Exchange account by making delivery, and who is ready to take a contango rate from a 'giver'. A taker is likewise a seller of an option (q.v.).

TALISMAN: Transfer Accounting Lodgement for Investors, Stock MANagement for Jobbers is the simplified transfer system for most UK-listed company securities. Also available for North American and Australian stocks.

TAP: A term for a security, a supply of which is freely available, such as

Government stocks which have not been fully subscribed on issue and which are made available at stated prices by the 'Departments' holding them. Also applies to a large line of shares coming on offer.

TAP STOCK: A Government stock on offer as above.

TENDER: Issues, such as Government, water and other company stocks, offered for subscription at minimum prices which are allotted to the highest bidders or at the minimum prices if undersubscribed.

THIRD MARKET: The market for small and 'greenfields' companies, not qualifying for the Listed and USM markets.

TO OPEN: A declaration that an order is to buy or to sell, or to get another party to 'open'.

TOPIC: The Exchange's Videotex network for dissemination of prices and other information.

TOUCH: The closest price quoted between market makers, or the highest price bid by one and the lowest price offered by another market maker.

TRADED OPTION: An option to buy ('call') or sell ('put') a share; the option itself can be bought and sold in the traded options market.

TRANSFER DEED: The document transferring securities from seller to buyer, which is normally signed only by the seller (transferor).

TRUSTEE INVESTMENTS: Securities in which trustees are permitted to invest trust funds under the terms of a trust deed or under the Trustee Investments Act 1961. The latter allows considerable latitude and extends the 'spread' beyond gilt-edged and similar fixed interest stocks to equities.

●

UNASSENTED BONDS: Bonds in respect of which the original contract terms have been varied and the variation has not been accepted by holders. Bonds whose holders have accepted the variation are called 'assented bonds'. There can, therefore, be a market in both assented and unassented, naturally with a difference in their respective prices.

UNCALLED CAPITAL: The part of a company's capital which has not been called-up. For instance, a £1 ordinary share may be paid-up to the extent of only 50p, thus leaving 50p a share uncalled. Once a feature of bank share finance, few UK companies today have uncalled shares in issue.

UNDATED: Government and similar stocks which have no fixed dates for repayment. Alternatively described as 'irredeemables'.

UNDERSUBSCRIBED: An issue is undersubscribed when applications total less than the amount offered for sale or subscription. If the issue is underwritten, the underwriters have to take up the amount not subscribed *pro rata* to their commitments. In such cases it is not unusual for dealings in the security to begin at a discount on the issue price.

UNDERWRITER: An insurer who, in return for an underwriting commission, undertakes to apply for, or to find, other applicants for all or part of an issue or offer which is not taken up by the public. An underwriter usually passes on part or all of his commitment to *sub-underwriters* such as stockbrokers, market makers, pension funds, insurance offices, merchant banks, investment trusts, finance houses and individuals who share in the commission.

UNFRANKED INCOME: Interest and dividends received by a company from securities which have not suffered UK corporation tax.

UNQUOTED SECURITIES: Stocks and shares not officially listed on the Stock

Exchange or on any other recognised stock exchange. Such securities may be dealt-in under rule 535 of the Stock Exchange, or 'over-the-counter'.

UNSECURED LOAN STOCK: A stock which is not secured on any or all of the assets of a company and which therefore ranks as an ordinary creditor in a winding-up.

●

WARRANT: An option to subscribe for shares or other securities at a future date or dates at a specified price(s) and usually dealt-in on its own.

WIDE PRICE: A more than normal difference (spread) between bid and offered prices, such as 60p–72$\frac{1}{2}$p.

WITHHOLDING TAX: Tax deducted from dividend payments to non-residents by companies in the USA, Canada, South Africa, Australia, Holland and other countries.

●

YANKEES: A market term to describe American securities.

YIELD: The return on an investment which may be current, flat or running, or redemption (q.v.). Also applies to *earnings yield*, which is the amount earned per share in relation to the market price.

YIELD GAP: The difference between the average yield on gilt-edged stocks and equity shares. For many years prior to the 1960s the gilt-edged was generally lower than the yield on the riskier ordinary shares. But for some years now there has been a *reverse yield gap* with gilts generally yielding more than equities, often substantially more.

# Index